Apache Hive Cookbook

Easy, hands-on recipes to help you understand Hive and its integration with frameworks that are used widely in today's big data world

Hanish Bansal

Saurabh Chauhan

Shrey Mehrotra

[PACKT] open source*

PUBLISHING   community experience distilled

BIRMINGHAM - MUMBAI

Apache Hive Cookbook

First published: April 2016

Production reference: 1260416

Published by Packt Publishing Ltd.

Livery Place
35 Livery Street
Birmingham B3 2PB, UK.
ISBN 978-1-78216-108-0

www.packtpub.com

Credits

Authors

Hanish Bansal

Saurabh Chauhan

Shrey Mehrotra

Reviewer

Aristides Villarreal Bravo

Commissioning Editor

Wilson D'souza

Acquisition Editor

Tushar Gupta

Content Development Editor

Anish Dhurat

Technical Editor

Vishal K. Mewada

Copy Editor

Dipti Mankame

Project Coordinator

Bijal Patel

Proofreader

Safis Editing

Indexer

Priya Sane

Graphics

Kirk D'Penha

Production Coordinator

Shantanu N. Zagade

Cover Work

Shantanu N. Zagade

About the Authors

Hanish Bansal is a software engineer with over 4 years of experience in developing big data applications. He loves to study emerging solutions and applications mainly related to big data processing, NoSQL, natural language processing, and neural networks. He has worked on various technologies such as Spring Framework, Hibernate, Hadoop, Hive, Flume, Kafka, Storm, and NoSQL databases, which include HBase, Cassandra, MongoDB, and search engines such as Elasticsearch.

In 2012, he completed his graduation in Information Technology stream from Jaipur Engineering College and Research Center, Jaipur, India. He was also the technical reviewer of the book *Apache Zookeeper Essentials*. In his spare time, he loves to travel and listen to music.

You can read his blog at `http://hanishblogger.blogspot.in/` and follow him on Twitter at `https://twitter.com/hanishbansal786`.

I would like to thank my parents for their love, support, encouragement and the amazing chances they've given me over the years.

Saurabh Chauhan is a module lead with close to 8 years of experience in data warehousing and big data applications. He has worked on multiple Extract, Transform and Load tools, such as Oracle Data Integrator and Informatica as well as on big data technologies such as Hadoop, Hive, Pig, Sqoop, and Flume.

He completed his bachelor of technology in 2007 from Vishveshwarya Institute of Engineering and Technology. In his spare time, he loves to travel and discover new places. He also has a keen interest in sports.

I would like to thank everyone who has supported me throughout my life.

Shrey Mehrotra has 6 years of IT experience and, since the past 4 years, in designing and architecting cloud and big data solutions for the governmental and financial domains.

Having worked with big data R&D Labs and Global Data and Analytical Capabilities, he has gained insights into Hadoop, focusing on HDFS, MapReduce, and YARN. His technical strengths also include Hive, Pig, Spark, Elasticsearch, Sqoop, Flume, Kafka, and Java.

He likes spending time performing R&D on different big data technologies. He is the co-author of the book *Learning YARN*, a certified Hadoop developer, and has also written various technical papers. In his free time, he listens to music, watches movies, and spending time with friends.

I would like to thank my mom and dad for giving me support to accomplish anything I wanted. Also, I would like to thank my friends, who bear with me while I am busy writing.

About the Reviewer

Aristides Villarreal Bravo is a Java developers, a member of the NetBeans Dream Team, and a Java User Groups leader.

He has organized and participated in various conferences and seminars related to Java, JavaEE, NetBeans, NetBeans Platform, free software, and mobile devices, nationally and internationally.

He has written tutorials and blogs about Java, NetBeans, and web development. He has participated in several interviews on sites such as NetBeans, NetBeans Dzone, and JavaHispano. He has developed plugins for NetBeans. He has been a technical reviewer for the book *PrimeFaces Blueprints*.

Aristides is the CEO of Javscaz Software Developers. He lives in Panamá

To my mother, father, and all family and friends.

---

www.PacktPub.com

eBooks, discount offers, and more

Did you know that Packt offers eBook versions of every book published, with PDF and ePub files available? You can upgrade to the eBook version at `www.PacktPub.com` and as a print book customer, you are entitled to a discount on the eBook copy. Get in touch with us at `customercare@packtpub.com` for more details.

At `www.PacktPub.com`, you can also read a collection of free technical articles, sign up for a range of free newsletters and receive exclusive discounts and offers on Packt books and eBooks.

https://www2.packtpub.com/books/subscription/packtlib

Do you need instant solutions to your IT questions? PacktLib is Packt's online digital book library. Here, you can search, access, and read Packt's entire library of books.

Why Subscribe?

- ► Fully searchable across every book published by Packt
- ► Copy and paste, print, and bookmark content
- ► On demand and accessible via a web browser

Table of Contents

Preface

Hive is an open source big data framework in the Hadoop ecosystem. It provides an SQL-like interface to query data stored in HDFS. Underlying it runs MapReduce programs corresponding to the SQL query. Hive was initially developed by Facebook and later added to the Hadoop ecosystem.

Hive is currently the most preferred framework to query data in Hadoop. Because most of the historical data is stored in RDBMS data stores, including Oracle and Teradata. It is convenient for the developers to run similar SQL statements in Hive to query data.

Along with simple SQL statements, Hive supports wide variety of windowing and analytical functions, including rank, row num, dense rank, lead, and lag.

Hive is considered as de facto big data warehouse solution. It provides a number of techniques to optimize storage and processing of terabytes or petabytes of data in a cost-effective way.

Hive could be easily integrated with a majority of other frameworks, including Spark and HBase. Hive allows developers or analysts to execute SQL on it. Hive also supports querying data stored in different formats such as JSON.

What this book covers

Chapter 1, Developing Hive, helps you out in configuring Hive on a Hadoop platform. This chapter explains a different mode of Hive installations. It also provides pointers for debugging Hive and brief information about compiling Hive source code and different modules in the Hive source code.

Chapter 2, Services in Hive, gives a detailed description about the configurations and usage of different services provided by Hive such as HiveServer2. This chapter also explains about different clients of Hive, including Hive CLI and Beeline.

Chapter 3, Understanding the Hive Data Model, takes you through the details of different data types provided by Hive in order to be helpful in data modeling.

Chapter 4, Hive Data Definition Language, helps you understand the syntax and semantics of creating, altering, and dropping different objects in Hive, including databases, tables, functions, views, indexes, and roles.

Chapter 5, Hive Data Manipulation Language, gives you complete understanding of Hive interfaces for data manipulation. This chapter also includes some of the latest features in Hive related to CRUD operations in Hive. It explains insert, update, and delete at the row level in Hive available in Hive 0.14 and later versions.

Chapter 6, Hive Extensibility Features, covers a majority of advance concepts in Hive. This chapter explain some concepts such as SerDes, Partitions, Bucketing, Windowing and Analytics, and File Formats in Hive with the detailed examples.

Chapter 7, Joins and Join Optimization, gives you a detailed explanation of types of Join supported by Hive. It also provides detailed information about different types of Join optimizations available in Hive.

Chapter 8, Statistics in Hive, allows you to capture and analyze tables, partitions, and column-level statistics. This chapter covers the configurations and commands use to capture these statistics.

Chapter 9, Functions in Hive, gives you the detailed overview of the extensive set of inbuilt functions supported by Hive, which can be used directly in queries. This chapter also covers how to create a custom User-Defined Function and register in Hive.

Chapter 10, Hive Tuning, helps you out in optimizing the complex queries to reduce the throughput time. It covers different optimization techniques using predicate pushdown, by reducing number of maps, and by sampling.

Chapter 11, Hive Security, covers concepts to secure the data from any unauthorized access. It explains the different mechanisms of authentication and authorization that can be implement in Hive for security purposes. In case of critical or sensitive data, security is the first thing that needs to be considered.

Chapter 12, Hive Integration with Other Frameworks, takes you through the integration mechanism of Hive with some other popular frameworks such as Spark, HBase, Accumulo, and Google Drill.

What you need for this book

To practice in parallel with reading the book, you need a machine or set of machines on which Hadoop is installed in either pseudo distributed or clustered mode.

To have a better understanding of metastore concept, you should have configured Hive with local or remote metastore using MySQL at the backend.

You also need a sample dataset to practice different windowing and analytical functions available in Hive and to optimize queries using concepts such as partitions and bucketing.

Who this book is for

This book has covered almost all concepts of Hive. So, if you are a beginner in the big data Hadoop domain, you can start with installing Hive, understanding Hive services and clients, and using Hive data modeling concepts to design your data model. If you have basic knowledge of Hive, you can deep dive into some of the advance concepts covered in the book such as partitions, bucketing, file formats, security, and windowing and analytics.

In a nutshell, this book is helpful for both a Hadoop developer and a Hadoop analyst who want to explore Hive.

Sections

In this book, you will find several headings that appear frequently (Getting ready, How to do it, How it works, There's more, and See also).

To give clear instructions on how to complete a recipe, we use these sections as follows:

Getting ready

This section tells you what to expect in the recipe, and describes how to set up any software or any preliminary settings required for the recipe.

How to do it...

This section contains the steps required to follow the recipe.

How it works...

This section usually consists of a detailed explanation of what happened in the previous section.

There's more...

This section consists of additional information about the recipe in order to make the reader more knowledgeable about the recipe.

See also

This section provides helpful links to other useful information for the recipe.

Conventions

In this book, you will find a number of text styles that distinguish between different kinds of information. Here are some examples of these styles and an explanation of their meaning.

Code words in text, database table names, folder names, filenames, file extensions, pathnames, dummy URLs, user input, and Twitter handles are shown as follows: By default, this location is set to the `/metastore_dbinconf/hive-default.xml` file.

A block of code is set as follows:

```
<property>
    <name>hive.metastore.warehouse.dir</name>
    <value>/user/Hive/warehouse </value>
    <description>The directory relative to fs.default.name where
managed tables are stored.
    </description>
</property>
```

Any command-line input or output is written as follows:

```
hive --service metastore &
```

New terms and **important** words are shown in bold. Words that you see on the screen, for example, in menus or dialog boxes, appear in the text like this: Create a **Maven** project in **Eclipse** by going to **File** | **New** | **Project**.

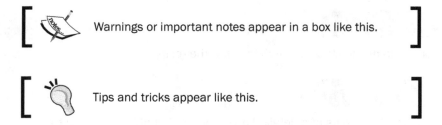

Warnings or important notes appear in a box like this.

Tips and tricks appear like this.

Reader feedback

Feedback from our readers is always welcome. Let us know what you think about this book—what you liked or disliked. Reader feedback is important for us as it helps us develop titles that you will really get the most out of.

To send us general feedback, simply e-mail `feedback@packtpub.com`, and mention the book's title in the subject of your message.

If there is a topic that you have expertise in and you are interested in either writing or contributing to a book, see our author guide at `www.packtpub.com/authors`.

Customer support

Now that you are the proud owner of a Packt book, we have a number of things to help you to get the most from your purchase.

Downloading the example code

You can download the example code files for this book from your account at `http://www.packtpub.com`. If you purchased this book elsewhere, you can visit `http://www.packtpub.com/support` and register to have the files e-mailed directly to you.

You can download the code files by following these steps:

1. Log in or register to our website using your e-mail address and password.
2. Hover the mouse pointer on the **SUPPORT** tab at the top.
3. Click on **Code Downloads & Errata**.
4. Enter the name of the book in the **Search** box.
5. Select the book for which you're looking to download the code files.
6. Choose from the drop-down menu where you purchased this book from.
7. Click on **Code Download**.

You can also download the code files by clicking on the **Code Files** button on the book's webpage at the Packt Publishing website. This page can be accessed by entering the book's name in the **Search** box. Please note that you need to be logged in to your Packt account.

Once the file is downloaded, please make sure that you unzip or extract the folder using the latest version of:

- WinRAR / 7-Zip for Windows
- Zipeg / iZip / UnRarX for Mac
- 7-Zip / PeaZip for Linux

Downloading the color images of this book

We also provide you with a PDF file that has color images of the screenshots/diagrams used in this book. The color images will help you better understand the changes in the output. You can download this file from `http://www.packtpub.com/sites/default/files/downloads/ApacheHiveCookbook_ColorImages.pdf`.

Errata

Although we have taken every care to ensure the accuracy of our content, mistakes do happen. If you find a mistake in one of our books—maybe a mistake in the text or the code—we would be grateful if you could report this to us. By doing so, you can save other readers from frustration and help us improve subsequent versions of this book. If you find any errata, please report them by visiting `http://www.packtpub.com/submit-errata`, selecting your book, clicking on the **Errata Submission Form** link, and entering the details of your errata. Once your errata are verified, your submission will be accepted and the errata will be uploaded to our website or added to any list of existing errata under the Errata section of that title.

To view the previously submitted errata, go to `https://www.packtpub.com/books/content/support` and enter the name of the book in the search field. The required information will appear under the **Errata** section.

Piracy

Piracy of copyrighted material on the Internet is an ongoing problem across all media. At Packt, we take the protection of our copyright and licenses very seriously. If you come across any illegal copies of our works in any form on the Internet, please provide us with the location address or website name immediately so that we can pursue a remedy.

Please contact us at `copyright@packtpub.com` with a link to the suspected pirated material.

We appreciate your help in protecting our authors and our ability to bring you valuable content.

Questions

If you have a problem with any aspect of this book, you can contact us at `questions@packtpub.com`, and we will do our best to address the problem.

1
Developing Hive

In this chapter, we will cover the following recipes:

- ▸ Deploying Hive on a Hadoop cluster
- ▸ Deploying Hive Metastore
- ▸ Installing Hive
- ▸ Configuring HCatalog
- ▸ Understanding different components of Hive
- ▸ Compiling Hive from source
- ▸ Hive packages
- ▸ Debugging Hive
- ▸ Running Hive
- ▸ Changing configurations at runtime

Introduction

Hive, an Apache Hadoop ecosystem component is developed by Facebook to query the data stored in **Hadoop Distributed File System** (**HDFS**). Here, HDFS is the data storage layer of Hadoop that at very high level divides the data into small blocks (default 128 MB) and stores these blocks on different nodes.

Hive provides a SQL-like query model named **Hive Query Language** (**HQL**) to access and analyze big data. It is also termed **Data Warehousing framework of Hadoop** and provides various analytical features, such as **windowing** and **partitioning**.

Deploying Hive on a Hadoop cluster

Hive is supported by a wide variety of platforms. GNU/Linux and Windows are commonly used as the production environment, whereas Mac OS X is commonly used as the development environment.

Getting ready

In this book, we will assume a GNU/Linux-based installation of Apache Hive for installation and other instructions.

Before installing Hive, the first step is to make sure that a Java SE environment is installed properly. Hive requires version 6 or later, which can be downloaded from `http://www.oracle.com/technetwork/java/javase/downloads/index.html`.

How to do it...

To install Hive, just download it from `http://Hive.apache.org/downloads.html` and unpack it. Choose the latest stable version.

 At the time of writing this book, Hive 1.2.1 was the latest stable version available.

How it works...

By default, Hive is configured to use an embedded Derby database whose disk storage location is determined by the Hive configuration variable named `javax.jdo.option.ConnectionURL`. By default, this location is set to the `/metastore_dbinconf/hive-default.xml` file. Hive with Derby as metastore in embedded mode allows at most one user at a time.

The other modes of installation are **Hive with local metastore** and **Hive with remote metastore**, which will be discussed later.

Deploying Hive Metastore

Apache Hive is a client-side library that provides a table-like abstraction on top of the data in HDFS for data processing. Hive jobs are converted into a map reduce plan, which is then submitted to the Hadoop cluster. Hadoop cluster is the set of nodes or machines with HDFS, MapReduce, and YARN deployed on these machines. MapReduce works on the distributed data stored in HDFS and processes a large datasets in parallel, as compared with traditional processing engines that process whole task on a single machine and wait for hours or days for a single query. **Yet Another Resource Negotiator (YARN)** is used to manage RAM the and CPU cores of the whole cluster, which are critical for running any process on a node.

The Hive table and database definitions and mapping to the data in HDFS is stored in a metastore. A metastore is a central repository for Hive metadata. A metastore consists of two main components, which are really important for working on Hive. Let's take a look at these components:

▸ Services to which the client connects and queries the metastore

▸ A backing database to store the metadata

Getting ready

In this book, we will assume a GNU/Linux-based installation of Apache Hive for installation and other instructions.

Before installing Hive, the first step is to make sure that a Java SE environment is installed properly. Hive requires version 6 or later, which can be downloaded from `http://www.oracle.com/technetwork/java/javase/downloads/index.html`.

How to do it...

In Hive, a metastore (service and RDBMS database) could be configured in one of the following ways:

▸ An embedded metastore

▸ A local metastore

▸ A remote metastore

When we install Hive on the preinstalled Hadoop cluster, Hive, by default, gets the embedded database. This means that we need not configure any database as a Hive metastore. Let's check out what these configurations are and why we call them the embedded and remote metastore.

By default, the metastore service and the Hive service run in the same JVM. Hive needs a database to store metadata. In default mode, it uses an embedded Derby database stored on the local file system. The embedded mode of Hive has the limitation that only one session can be opened at a time from the same location on a machine as only one embedded Derby database can get lock and access the database files on disk:

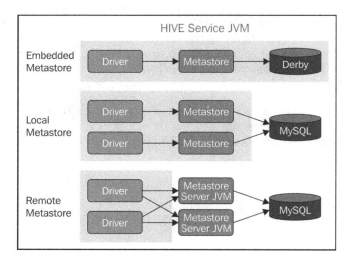

An **Embedded Metastore** has a single service and a single JVM that cannot work with multiple nodes at a time.

To solve this limitation, a separate RDBMS database runs on same node. The metastore service and Hive service still run in the same JVM. This configuration mode is named **local metastore**. Here, local means the same environment of the JVM machine as well as the service in the same node.

There is one more configuration where one or more metastore servers run in a separate JVM process to the Hive service connecting to a database on a remote machine. This configuration is named **remote metastore**.

The Hive service is configured to use a remote metastore by setting `hive.metastore.uris` to metastore server URIs, separated by commas. The Hive metastore could be configured using properties specified in the following sections.

In the following diagram, the pictorial representation of the metastore and driver is given:

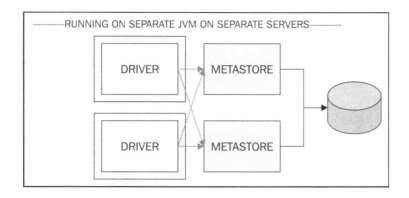

```
<property>
    <name>hive.metastore.warehouse.dir</name>
    <value>/user/Hive/warehouse </value>
    <description>The directory relative to fs.default.name where
managed tables are stored.
    </description>
</property>

<property>
    <name> hive.metastore.uris</name>
    <value></value>
    <description> The URIs specifying the remote metastore servers to
connect to. If there are multiple remote servers, clients connect in a
round-robin fashion
    </description>
</property>

<property>
    <name>javax.jdo.option. ConnectionURL</name>
    <value>jdbc:derby:;databaseName=hivemetastore;
create=true</value>
    <description> The JDBC URL of database.
    </description>
</property>

<property>
    <name> javax.jdo.option.ConnectionDriverName </name>
    <value> org.apache.derby.jdbc.EmbeddedDriver </value>
    <description> The JDBC driver classname.
    </description>
</property>
```

```
<property>
    <name>javax.jdo.option.ConnectionUserName</name>
    <value>username</value>
    <description>metastore username to connect with
    </description>
</property>

<property>
    <name> javax.jdo.option.ConnectionPassword </name>
    <value>password</value>
    <description>metastore password to connect with
    </description>
</property>
```

Installing Hive

We will now take a look at installing Hive along with all the prerequisites.

Getting ready

Let's download the stable version from one of the mirrors:

```
$ wget http://a.mbbsindia.com/hive/hive-1.2.1/apache-hive-1.2.1-bin.tar.
gz
```

How to do it...

This can be achieved in three ways.

Hive with an embedded metastore

Once you have downloaded the Hive `tar-ball` file, installing and setting up a Hive is pretty simple and straightforward. Extract the compressed tar:

```
$tar -xzvf apache-hive-1.2.1-bin.tar.gz
```

Export the location where Hive is extracted as the environment variable HIVE_HOME:

```
$ cd  apache-hive-1.2.1-bin
$ export HIVE_HOME={{pwd}}
```

Hive has all its installation scripts in the $HIVE_HOME/bin directory. Export this location to the PATH environment variable so that you can run all scripts from any location directly from a command-line:

```
$ export PATH=$HIVE_HOME/bin:$PATH
```

Alternatively, if you want to set the Hive path permanently for the user, then make the entry of Hive environment variables in the .bashrc or .bash_profile files available or could be created in the user's home folder:

1. Add the following to ~/.bash_profile:

   ```
   export HIVE_HOME=/home/hduser/apache-hive-1.2.1-bin
   export PATH=$PATH:$HIVE_HOME/bin
   ```

2. Here, hduser is the name of user with which you have logged in and Hive-1.2.1 is the Hive directory extracted from the tar file. Run Hive from a terminal:

   ```
   hive
   ```

3. Make sure that the Hive node has a connection to Hadoop cluster, which means Hive would be installed on any of the Hadoop nodes, or Hadoop configurations are available in the node's class path.

4. This installation uses the embedded Derby database and stores the data on the local filesystem. Only one Hive session can be open on the node.

5. If different users try to run the Hive shell, the second would get the Failed to start database 'metastore_db' error.

6. Run Hive queries for the datastore to test the installation:

   ```
   hive> SHOW TABLES;

   hive> CREATE TABLE sales(id INT, product String, age INT) ROW
   FORMAT DELIMITED FIELDS TERMINATED BY '\t';
   ```

7. Logs are generated per user bases in the /tmp/<usrename> folder.

Hive with a local metastore

Follow these steps to configure Hive with the local metastore. Here, we are using the MySQL database as a metastore:

1. Add following to ~/.bash_profile:

   ```
   export HIVE_HOME=/home/hduser/apache-hive-1.2.1-bin
   export PATH=$PATH:$HIVE_HOME/bin
   ```

Here, `hduser` is the user name, and `apache-hive-1.2.1-bin` is the `Hive` directory extracted from the `tar` file.

2. Install a SQL database such as MySQL on the same machine where you want to run Hive.

3. For the Ubuntu, MySQL could be installed by running the following command on the node's terminal:

   ```
   sudo apt-get install mysql-server
   ```

4. In case of MySql, Hive needs the `mysql-connector` jar. Download the latest mysql-connector jar from `http://dev.mysql.com/get/Downloads/Connector-J/mysql-connector-java-5.1.35.tar.gz` and copy it to the `lib` folder of your Hive `home` directory.

5. Create a file, `hive-site.xml`, in the `conf` folder of Hive and add the following entries to it:

   ```
   <configuration>
   <property>
   <name>javax.jdo.option.ConnectionURL</name>
   <value>jdbc:mysql://localhost:3306/metastore_db?createDatabaseIfNo
   tExist=true</value>
   <description>metadata is stored in a MySQL server</description>
   </property>
   <property>
   <name>javax.jdo.option.ConnectionDriverName</name>
   <value>com.mysql.jdbc.Driver</value>
   <description>MySQL JDBC driver class</description>
   </property>
   <property>
   <name>javax.jdo.option.ConnectionUserName</name>
   <value>hduser</value>
   <description>user name for connecting to mysql server
   </description>
   </property>
   <property>
   <name>javax.jdo.option.ConnectionPassword</name>
   <value>passwd</value>
   <description>password for connecting to mysql server</description>
   </property>
   </configuration>
   ```

6. Run Hive from the terminal:

   ```
   hive
   ```

There is a known "JLine" jar conflict issue with Hadoop 2.6.0 and Hive 1.2.1. If you are getting the error "unable to load class jline.terminal," you need to remove the older version of the jline jar from the yarn lib folder using the following command:

```
sudo rm -r $HADOOP_PREFIX/share/hadoop/yarn/lib/
jline-0.9.94.jar
```

Hive with a remote metastore

Follow these steps to configure Hive with a remote metastore.

1. Download the latest version of Hive from http://a.mbbsindia.com/hive/hive-1.2.1/apache-hive-1.2.1-bin.tar.gz.

2. Extract the package:

   ```
   tar -xzvf apache-hive-1.2.1-bin.tar.gz
   ```

3. Add the following to ~/.bash_profile:

   ```
   sudo nano ~/.bash_profile
   export HIVE_HOME=/home/hduser/apache-hive-1.2.1-bin
   export PATH=$PATH:$HIVE_HOME/bin
   ```

   Here, hduser is the user name and apache-hive-1.2.1-bin is the Hive directory extracted from the tar file.

4. Install a SQL database such as MySQL on a remote machine to be used for the metastore.

5. For Ubuntu, MySQL can be installed with the following command:

   ```
   sudo apt-get install mysql-server
   ```

6. In the case of MySQL, Hive needs the mysql-connector jar file. Download the latest mysql-connector jar from http://dev.mysql.com/get/Downloads/Connector-J/mysql-connector-java-5.1.35.tar.gz and copy it to the lib folder of your Hive home directory.

7. Add the following entries to hive-site.xml:

   ```
   <configuration>
   <property>
   <name>javax.jdo.option.ConnectionURL</name>
   <value>jdbc:mysql://<ip_of_remote_host>:3306/metastore_db?createDatabaseIfNotExist=true</value>
   <description>metadata is stored in a MySQL server</description>
   </property>
   <property>
   <name>javax.jdo.option.ConnectionDriverName</name>
   ```

```
<value>com.mysql.jdbc.Driver</value>
<description>MySQL JDBC driver class</description>
</property>
<property>
<name>javax.jdo.option.ConnectionUserName</name>
<value>hduser</value>
<description>user name for connecting to mysql server
</description>
</property>
<property>
<name>javax.jdo.option.ConnectionPassword</name>
<value>passwd</value>
<description>password for connecting to mysql server</description>
</property>
</configuration>
```

8. Start the Hive metastore interface:

   ```
   bin/hive --service metastore &
   ```

9. Run Hive from the terminal:

   ```
   hive
   ```

10. The Hive metastore interface by default listens at port `9083`:

    ```
    netstat -an | grep 9083
    ```

11. Start the Hive shell and make sure that the **Hive Data Definition Language** and **Data Manipulation Language** (**DDL** or **DML**) operations are working by creating tables in Hive.

> There is a known "JLine" jar conflict issue with Hadoop 2.6.0 and Hive 1.2.1. If you are getting the error "unable to load class jline.terminal," you need to remove the older version of jline jar from the yarn lib folder using the following command:
>
> ```
> sudo rm -r $HADOOP_PREFIX/share/hadoop/yarn/lib/
> jline-0.9.94.jar
> ```

Configuring HCatalog

Assuming that Hive has been configured in the remote metastore, let's look into how to install and configure HCatalog.

Getting ready

The HCatalog CLI supports these command-line options:

Option	Usage	Description
-g	`hcat -g mygrp`	The HCatalog table, which needs to be created, must have the group "`mygrp`".
-p	`hcat -p rwxrwxr-x`	The HCatalog table, which needs to be created, must have permissions "`rwxrwxr-x`".
-f	`hcat -f myscript.hcat`	Tells HCatalog that `myscript.hcat` is a file containing DDL commands to execute.
-e	`hcat -e 'create table mytable(a int);'`	Treat the following string as a DDL command and execute it.
-D	`hcat -Dkey=value`	Pass the key-value pair to HCatalog as a **Java System Property**.
	`Hcat`	Prints a usage message.

How to do it...

Hive 0.11.0 HCatalog is packaged with Hive binaries. Because we have already configured Hive, we could access the HCatalog command-line `hcat` command on shell. The script is available at the `hcatalog/bin` directory.

Understanding different components of Hive

Besides the Hive metastore, Hive components could be broadly classified as Hive clients and Hive servers. Hive servers provide interfaces to make the metastore available to external applications and check for user's authorization and authentication, and Hive clients are various applications used to access and execute Hive queries on the Hadoop cluster.

HiveServer

Let's take a look at its various components.

Hive metastore

Hive metastore URIs start a metastore service on the specified port. Metastore provides APIs to query the database, tables, schema, and other entities stored in the RDBMS datastore.

How to do it...

The metastore service starts as a Java process in the backend. You can start the Hive metastore service with the following command:

```
hive --service metastore &
```

HiveServer2

HiveServer2 is an interface that allows clients to execute Hive queries and get the result. It is based on Thrift RPC and supports multiple clients a against single client in HiveServer. It also provisioned for the authentication and authorization of the user.

How to do it...

The HiveServer2 service also starts as a Java process in the backend. You can start HiveServer2 with the following command:

```
hive --service hiveserver2 &
```

Hive clients

The following are the different clients available in Hive to query metastore data or to submit Hive queries to Hive servers.

Hive CLI

The following are the various sections included in Hive CLI.

Getting ready

Hive **Command-line Interface** (**CLI**) can be used to run Hive queries in either interactive or batch mode.

How to do it...

To run Hive CLI, use the following command:

```
$ HIVE_HOME/bin/hive
```

Queries are submitted by username of the user logged in to the UNIX system.

Beeline

The following are the various sections included in Beeline.

Getting ready

If you have configured HiveServer2, then a Beeline client can be used to interact with Hive.

How to do it...

To run Beeline, use the following command:

```
$ HIVE_HOME/bin/beeline
```

Using beeline, a connection could be made to any HiveServer2 instance with any username and password.

Compiling Hive from source

In this recipe, we will see how to compile Hive from source.

Getting ready

Apache Hive is an open source framework available for compilation and modification by any user. Hive source code is a maven project. The source has intermittent scripts executed on a UNIX platform during compilation.

The following prerequisites need to be installed:

- ▶ **UNIX OS**: UNIX is preferable for Hive source compilation. Although the source could also be compiled on Windows, you need to comment out the intermittent scripts execution.

- ▶ **Maven**: The following are the steps to configure maven:

    1. Download the Apache maven binaries for Linux (.tar.gz) from https://maven.apache.org/download.cgi.

       ```
       wget http://mirror.olnevhost.net/pub/apache/maven/
       maven-3/3.3.3/binaries/apache-maven-3.3.3-bin.tar.gz
       ```

    2. Extract the tar file:

       ```
       tar -xzvf apache-maven-3.3.3-bin.tar.gz
       ```

3. Create a folder and move maven binaries to that folder:

   ```
   sudo mkdir -p /usr/lib/maven
   mv apache-maven-3.3.3-bin/usr/lib/maven/
   ```

4. Open /etc/environment:

   ```
   sudo nano /etc/profile
   ```

5. Add the following variable for the environment PATH:

   ```
   export M2_HOME=/usr/lib/maven/apache-maven-3.3.3-bin
   export M2=$M2_HOME/bin
   export PATH=$M2:$PATH
   ```

6. Use the command source /etc/environment to add variables to PATH without restart:

   ```
   source /etc/environment
   ```

7. Check whether maven is properly installed or not:

   ```
   mvn -version
   ```

How to do it...

Follow these steps to compile Hive on a Unix OS:

1. Download the latest version of the Hive source tar file:

   ```
   sudo wget http://a.mbbsindia.com/hive/hive-1.2.1/apache-hive-1.2.1-src.tar.gz
   ```

2. Extract the source folder:

   ```
   tar -xzvf apache-hive-1.2.1-src.tar.gz
   ```

3. Move to the Hive directory:

   ```
   cd apache-hive-1.2.1-src
   ```

4. To import Hive packages in eclipse, run the following command:

   ```
   mvn eclipse:eclipse
   ```

5. To compile Hive with Hadoop 2 binaries, run the following command:

   ```
   mvn clean install -Phadoop-2,dist
   ```

6. In case you want to skip tests execution, run the earlier command with the following switch:

   ```
   mvn clean install -DskipTests -Phadoop-2,dist
   ```

7. To generate a tarball file from the source code, run the following command:

```
mvn clean package -DskipTests -Phadoop-2 -Pdist
```

Hive packages

The following are the various sections included in Hive packages.

Getting ready

Hive source consists of different modules categorized by the features they provide or as a submodule of some other module.

How to do it...

The following is the list of Hive modules and their usage in Hive:

- `accumulo-handler`: Apache `accumulo` is a distributed key-value datastore based on Google Big Table. This package includes the components responsible for mapping the Hive table to the `accumulo` table. `AccumuloStorageHandler` and `AccumuloPredicateHandler` are the main classes responsible for mapping tables. For more information, refer to the official integration documentation available at `https://cwiki.apache.org/confluence/display/Hive/AccumuloIntegration`.

- `ant`: This tool is used to build earlier versions of Hive source. Ant is also needed to configure the **Hive Web Interface** server.

- `beeline`: A Hive client used to connect with HiveServer2 and run Hive queries.

- `bin`: This package includes scripts to start Hive clients and services.

- `cli`: This is a Hive **Command-line Interface** implementation.

- `common`: These are utility classes used by other modules.

- `conf`: This contains default configurations and uses defined configuration objects.

- `contrib`: This contains `Serdes`, generic `UDF`, and `fileformat` contributed by third parties to Hive.

- `hbase-handler`: This module allows Hive SQL statements to access HBase tables for `SELECT` and `INSERT` commands. It also provides interfaces to access HBase and Hive tables for `join` and `union` in a single query. More information is available at `https://cwiki.apache.org/confluence/display/Hive/HBaseIntegration`.

- `hcatalog`: This is a table management framework that helps other frameworks such as Pig or MapReduce to access the Hive metastore and table schema.

- ▶ `hwi`: This module provides an implementation of a web interface to run Hive queries. Also, the `WebHCat` APIs provide `REST` APIs to access the Hive metastore.

- ▶ `Jdbc`: This is a connector that accepts JDBC connections and calls to execute Hive queries on the cluster.

- ▶ `Metastore`: This is the API that provides access to metastore entities including database, table, schema, and serdes.

- ▶ `odbc`: This module implements the **Open Database Connectivity (ODBC)** API, enabling ODBC applications to connect and execute queries over Hive.

- ▶ `ql`: This module provides an interface to clients that checks for query semantics and provides an implementation for driver, parser, and query planner.

- ▶ `Serde`: This module has an implementation of serializer and deserializer used by Hive to read and write data. It helps in validating and parsing record and field types.

- ▶ `shims`: This is the module that transparently intercepts and modifies calls to the Hive API, usually for compatibility purposes.

- ▶ `spark-client`: This module provides an interface to execute Hive SQLs on a Spark framework.

Debugging Hive

Here, we will take a quick look at the command-line debugging option in Hive.

Getting ready

Hive code could be debugged by assigning a port to Hive and adding socket details to Hive JVM. To add debugging configuration to Hive, execute the following properties on an OS terminal or add it to `bash_profile` of the user:

```
export HIVE_DEBUG_PORT=8000

export HIVE_DEBUG="-Xdebug -Xrunjdwp:transport=dt_socket,address=${HIVE_DEBUG_PORT},server=y,suspend=y"
```

How to do it...

Once a debug port is attached to Hive and Hive server suspension is enabled at startup, the following steps will help you debug Hive queries:

1. After defining previously mentioned properties, run the Hive CLI in debug mode:

   ```
   hive --debug
   ```

2. If you have written up your own `Test` class and want to execute unit test cases written in that class, then you need to execute the following command specifying the class name you want to execute:

```
mvn test -Dtest=ClassName
```

Running Hive

Let's see how to run Hive from the command-line.

Getting ready

Once you have the binaries of Hive either compiled or downloaded, you need to configure a metastore for Hive where it keeps information about different entities. Once that is configured, start Hive metastore and HiveServer2 to access the entities from different clients.

How to do it...

Follow these steps to start different components of Hive on a node:

1. Run Hive CLI:

   ```
   $HIVE_HOME/bin/hive
   ```

2. Run HiveServer2 and Beeline:

   ```
   $HIVE_HOME/bin/hiveserver2
   $HIVE_HOME/bin/beeline -u jdbc:Hive2://$HiveServer2_
   HOST:$HiveServer2_PORT
   ```

3. Run HCatalog and start up the HCatalog server:

   ```
   $HIVE_HOME/hcatalog/sbin/hcat_server.sh
   ```

4. Run the HCatalog CLI:

   ```
   $HIVE_HOME/hcatalog/bin/hcat
   ```

5. Run WebHCat:

   ```
   $HIVE_HOME/hcatalog/sbin/webhcat_server.sh
   ```

Changing configurations at runtime

Let's see how we can change various configuration settings at runtime.

How to do it...

Follow these steps to change any of the Hive configuration properties at runtime for a particular session or query:

1. Configuration for Hive and underlying MapReduce could be changed at runtime through beeline or the CLI. The general syntax to set a property is as follows:

   ```
   SET key=value;
   ```

2. The configuration set is only applicable for that session. If you want to set it permanently, then you need to set it in Hive-site.xml. The examples are as follows:

   ```
   beeline> SET mapred.job.tracker=example.host.com:50030;

   Hive> SET Hive.exec.mode.local.auto=false;
   ```

2
Services in Hive

In the previous chapter, you learned how we could install Hive with different metastore configurations. We also have gone through Hive clients and Hive services in brief.

In this chapter, we will cover the following recipes in detail:

- Introducing HiveServer2
- Understanding HiveServer2 properties
- Configuring HiveServer2 high availability
- Using HiveServer2 clients
- Introducing the Hive metastore service
- Configuring high availability of metastore service
- Introducing Hue

Introducing HiveServer2

HiveServer2 is an enhancement of HiveServer provided in earlier versions of Hive. The major limitations of HiveServer related to concurrency and authentication is resolved in HiveServer2. HiveServer2 is based on **Thrift RPC**. It supports multiple types of clients, including JDBC and ODBC.

How to do it...

Assuming that you have installed Hive on your machine, as explained in *Chapter 1, Developing Hive*. Before starting HiveServer2, you need to add the following property to `hive-site.xml`:

```
<property>
    <name>hive.server2.thrift.port</name>
    <value>10000</value>
    <description>TCP port number to listen on, default 10000
    </description>
</property>
```

Starting HiveServer2 is easy. All you need to do is run the following command on the terminal of your machine, as shown in the following screenshots:

```
# hive --service hiveserver2 &
```

```
[root@localhost ~]# hive --service hiveserver2 &
[1] 3713
[root@localhost ~]#
```

```
[root@localhost ~]#
[root@localhost ~]# jps
3066 NodeManager
2642 DataNode
3713 RunJar
2970 ResourceManager
2549 NameNode
2826 SecondaryNameNode
3806 Jps
[root@localhost ~]#
```

How it works...

Let's look into the series of actions that starts with HiveServer2:

 ► A Java service is started on default port `10000`
 ► Minimum worker threads are initialized with `5`
 ► Maximum worker threads are set to `500`
 ► The background operation thread pool size is initialized with `100`
 ► The background operation thread wait queue size is initialized with `100`
 ► The background operation thread keep alive time is set to `10` seconds

For more information about HiveServer2 configuration, refer to the next recipe, *Understanding HiveServer2 properties.*

Understanding HiveServer2 properties

By default, HiveServer2 is started with `default` configurations. The configurations are mainly related to the port and host on which the server is going to start and number of threads that could be configured for client and background operations.

How to do it...

You can change the default properties for HiveServer2 by overriding the value in `hive-site.xml` in the `conf` folder of Hive package.

Property	Default Value	Description
`hive.server2.thrift.port`	`10000`	HiveServer2 thrift interface
`hive.server2.thrift.bind.host`	`localhost`	HiveServer2 bind host
`hive.server2.thrift.min.worker.threads`	`5`	Minimum thrift worker threads
`hive.server2.thrift.max.worker.threads`	`500`	Maximum thrift worker threads
`hive.server2.authentication`	`None`	None/LDAP/KERBEROS/PAM/NOSASL
`hive.server2.authentication.kerberos.keytab`	`""`	A keytab file for kerberos principal
`hive.server2.authentication.kerberos.principal`	`""`	The Kerberos principal
`hive.server2.enable.doAs`	`true`	Execute Hive operations as the user making the calls
`hive.server2.authentication.ldap.url`	`""`	LDAP connection URLs
`hive.server2.authentication.ldap.baseDN`	`""`	LDAP DN
`hive.server2.authentication.ldap.Domain`	`""`	The LDAP domain
`hive.server2.thrift.http.port`	`10001`	Port number in HTTP mode

How it works...

When you override the configurations in `hive-site.xml` and restart HiveServer2, then it reads the updated properties. For example, you can define HiveServer2 to start on a port other than the default `10000` by defining the following property:

```
<property>
    <name>hive.server2.thrift.port</name>
     <value>11111</value>
</property>
```

When you restart HiveServer2, it starts listening on the new port `11111`.

See also

For more configurations about HiveServer2 configuration, you can refer to Hive online documentation available at `https://cwiki.apache.org/confluence/display/Hive/Configuration+Properties#ConfigurationProperties-HiveServer2`.

Configuring HiveServer2 high availability

HiveServer2 for a cluster of thousands of nodes could be a single point of failure if HiveServer2 is not configured with a high availability concept. If HiveServer2 service goes down, none of the clients would be able to access metastore or submit Hive queries to cluster. To solve this limitation, high availability of HiveServer2 is configured. It needs a **ZooKeeper** quorum running on a set of nodes.

ZooKeeper is an open source centralized service for providing coordination between distributed applications. It is also used to store some common configuration and metadata to provide distributed synchronization. Hive uses ZooKeeper to store configuration information to provide high availability of HiveServer2.

Getting ready

For configuring high availability of HiveServer2, you will need a ZooKeeper quorum running.

The installation of ZooKeeper is not in the scope of this book. You can refer to the following links for the installation of ZooKeeper.

- ▸ Refer to the following for ZooKeeper's installation in the standalone mode: `http://www.protechskills.com/big-data/hadoop-ecosystem/zookeeper/zookeeper-standalone-installation`.

- ▸ Refer to the following for ZooKeeper's installation in the distributed mode: `http://www.protechskills.com/big-data/hadoop-ecosystem/zookeeper/zookeeper-clustered-mode-installation`.

How to do it...

For enabling HiveServer2 High Availability with ZooKeeper, you need to set the following properties in `hive-site.xml`:

```
<property>
    <name>hive.zookeeper.quorum</name>
    <value>Zookeeper client's session timeout in milliseconds  </value>
</property>
<property>
    <name>hive.zookeeper.session.timeout</name>
    <value>Comma separated list of zookeeper quorum</value>
</property>
<property>
    <name>hive.server2.support.dynamic.service.discovery</name>
    <value>true</value>
</property>
<property>
    <name>hive.server2.zookeeper.namespace</name>
    <value>hiveserver2</value>
</property>
```

How it works...

If more than one HiveServer2 instance is registered with ZooKeeper and all instances fail except one, ZooKeeper passes the link to the instance that is running so that client can connect successfully with running HiveServer2.

ZooKeeper doesn't control autostart of services of failed instances, so if any HiveServer2 instance goes down, then it must be restarted manually.

See also

To read more about HiveServer2 High Availability, you can refer to Hortonwork's blog at `http://docs.hortonworks.com/HDPDocuments/HDP2/HDP-2.3.2/bk_hadoop-ha/content/ha-hs2-service-discovery.html`.

Using HiveServer2 clients

Once we started HiveServer2, we could connect to the server with different clients as per our requirements and run **Hive Query Language** (**HiveQL**). The different client includes beeline, JDBC, ODBC, and so on. We will be going through each client in detail.

Getting ready

This recipe requires Hive installed as described in the *Installing Hive* recipe of *Chapter 1, Developing Hive*. For connecting with HiveServer2 using a client, you must run HiveServer2, as described in the *Introducing HiveServer2 recipe* in this chapter.

How to do it...

There are multiple ways of connecting with HiveServer2, as described in the following sections.

Beeline

Beeline is a shell client that could be executed from the terminal by running the following command:

```
beeline
```

Once you enter the `beeline` shell, you can make a connection to the HiveServer2 service as a user using the following command:

```
!connect jdbc:hive2://localhost:10000 scott tiger org.apache.hive.jdbc.HiveDriver
```

If the connection is successful, then further SQL queries could be executed in the same way as on Hive shell, as shown in the following screenshot:

```
[root@localhost ~]# beeline
Beeline version 1.2.1 by Apache Hive
beeline> !connect jdbc:hive2://localhost:10000 scott tiger org.apache.hive.jdbc.Hive
Driver
Connecting to jdbc:hive2://localhost:10000
Connected to: Apache Hive (version 1.2.1)
Driver: Hive JDBC (version 1.2.1)
Transaction isolation: TRANSACTION_REPEATABLE_READ
0: jdbc:hive2://localhost:10000>
```

The following is the set of common commands you can execute from beeline:

Command	Description
`Reset`	This changes all settings to default values
`set <key>=<value>`	This sets a value for a particular key
`Set`	This displays the list of all overridden settings
`set -v`	This displays all Hive and Hadoop configurations

`add FILE[S] <filepath>`
`<filepath>*`
`add JAR[S] <filepath>`
`<filepath>*`
`add ARCHIVE[S] <filepath>`
`<filepath>*`
	This adds files or jars in the distributed cache of Hadoop

`list FILE[S]`
`list JAR[S]`
`list ARCHIVE[S]`
	This lists files or jars available in the distributed cache

`delete FILE[S] <filepath>*`
`delete JAR[S] <filepath>*`
`delete ARCHIVE[S] <filepath>*`
	This deletes files or jars from the distributed cache

`dfs <dfs command>`	This runs HDFS commands from beeline
`<query string>`	This runs Hive queries

Beeline command options

While running the beeline command, there are different options available that you use directly with the beeline CLI:

Command	Description
`-u <database URL>`	JDBC URL. For example, `jdbc:mysql://localhost:3306/mydb`
`-n <username>`	Username
`-p <password>`	User password
`-d <driver class>`	The driver class
`-e <query>`	The query to be in double quotes
`-f <file>`	The script file to be executed
`--showHeader=[true/false]`	Whether to show columns in the result
`--delimiterForDSV=DELIMITER`	The delimiter for queries output stream; default is `'|'`.

These are the commonly used options. For more options, type `beeline --help` on your terminal.

The following is the example of beeline command option:

1. Running Hive queries:

```
beeline -u 'jdbc:hive2://localhost:10000/default' -n root -p xxx
-d org.apache.hive.jdbc.HiveDriver -e "select * from sales;"
```

```
[root@localhost ~]# beeline -u 'jdbc:hive2://localhost:10000/default' -n root -p ▆▆▆▆▆ -d org.apache.hive.jdbc.HiveDrive
r -e "select * from sales;"
SLF4J: Class path contains multiple SLF4J bindings.
SLF4J: Found binding in [jar:file:/opt/spark-1.6.0-bin-hadoop2.6/lib/spark-assembly-1.6.0-hadoop2.6.0.jar!/org/slf4j/impl/
StaticLoggerBinder.class]
SLF4J: Found binding in [jar:file:/opt/hadoop-2.6.0/share/hadoop/common/lib/slf4j-log4j12-1.7.5.jar!/org/slf4j/impl/Static
LoggerBinder.class]
Connecting to jdbc:hive2://localhost:10000/default
Connected to: Apache Hive (version 1.2.1)
Driver: Hive JDBC (version 1.2.1)
Transaction isolation: TRANSACTION_REPEATABLE_READ
OK
+-----------+-------------+--------------+-----------+-----------------+------------+
| sales.id  | sales.fname | sales.state  | sales.zip |    sales.ip     | sales.pid  |
+-----------+-------------+--------------+-----------+-----------------+------------+
| 0         | Zena        | Tennessee    | 21550     | 192.168.56.101  | PI_09      |
| 1         | Elaine      | Alaska       | 06429     | 192.168.56.101  | PI_03      |
| 2         | Sage        | Nevada       | 08899     | 192.168.56.102  | PI_03      |
| 3         | Cade        | Missouri     | 11233     | 192.168.56.103  | PI_06      |
| 4         | Abra        | New Jersey   | 21550     | 192.168.56.101  | PI_09      |
| 5         | Stone       | Nebraska     | 03560     | 192.168.56.104  | PI_08      |
| 6         | Regina      | Tennessee    | 21550     | 192.168.56.105  | PI_10      |
| 7         | Donovan     | New York     | 95234     | 192.168.56.106  | PI_05      |
| 8         | Aileen      | Illinois     | 68284     | 192.168.56.106  | PI_02      |
| 9         | Mariam      | Hawaii       | 95234     | 192.168.56.107  | PI_07      |
+-----------+-------------+--------------+-----------+-----------------+------------+
```

Here, "`default`" is the database name; also replace `localhost` with the IP of your HiveServer2 node.

2. Running Hive scripts:

```
beeline -u 'jdbc:hive2://localhost:10000/default' -n root -p xxx
-d org.apache.hive.jdbc.HiveDriver -f  /opt/hivescript
```

```
[root@localhost ~]# beeline -u 'jdbc:hive2://localhost:10000/default' -n root -p xxx -d org.apache.hive.jdbc.HiveDriver -f
 /opt/hivescript
SLF4J: Class path contains multiple SLF4J bindings.
SLF4J: Found binding in [jar:file:/opt/spark-1.6.0-bin-hadoop2.6/lib/spark-assembly-1.6.0-hadoop2.6.0.jar!/org/slf4j/impl/
StaticLoggerBinder.class]
SLF4J: Found binding in [jar:file:/opt/hadoop-2.6.0/share/hadoop/common/lib/slf4j-log4j12-1.7.5.jar!/org/slf4j/impl/Static
LoggerBinder.class]
0: jdbc:hive2://localhost:10000/default> select fname from sales;
OK
+---------+
|  fname  |
+---------+
| Zena    |
| Elaine  |
| Sage    |
| Cade    |
| Abra    |
| Stone   |
| Regina  |
| Donovan |
| Aileen  |
| Mariam  |
+---------+
10 rows selected (0.332 seconds)
0: jdbc:hive2://localhost:10000/default>
```

JDBC

A JDBC client allows connection to HiveServer2 from Java code. The JDBC connection could be made in Remote, Embedded, or HTTP mode. The following are the configurations for the modes:

- The connection URL for Remote or Embedded mode:
  - For a Remote server, the URL format is `jdbc:hive2://<host>:<port>/<database>` (default port for HiveServer2 service is `10000`)
  - For an Embedded server, the URL format is `jdbc:hive2://` (no host or port)

- The connection URL when HiveServer2 is running in HTTP mode.
  - The JDBC connection URL is:

    `jdbc:hive2://<host>:<port>/<db>?hive.server2.transport.mode=http;hive.server2.thrift.http.path=<http_endpoint>,`

    The following are description of the JDBC connection URL:

    - `<http_endpoint>` is the corresponding HTTP endpoint configured in `https://cwiki.apache.org/confluence/display/Hive/AdminManual+Configuration#AdminManualConfiguration-ConfiguringHive`. The default value is `cliservice`.
    - The default port for HTTP transport mode is `10001`.

Once the connection mode is set, the JDBC connection in Java code could be made with the following steps:

1. Load the JDBC `drivers` class:

   ```
   Class.forName("org.apache.hive.jdbc.HiveDriver");
   ```

2. Connect to the database by creating a `Connection` object with the JDBC driver:

   ```
   Connection conn = DriverManager.getConnection
   ("jdbc:hive2://<host>:<port>", "<user>", "<password>");
   ```

   Here, the default port is `10000` and the password is ignored if HiveServer2 is running in a nonsecure mode.

3. Execute your query as follows:

   ```
   Statement stmt = conn.createStatement();
   ResultSet rset = stmt.executeQuery("SELECT fname FROM sales");
   ```

4. Process the result as returned in `ResultSet`.

JDBC client sample code using Eclipse

The following are the steps to create and execute the Hive JDBC client in **Eclipse**:

1. Create a **Maven** project in **Eclipse** by going to **File** | **New** | **Project**.

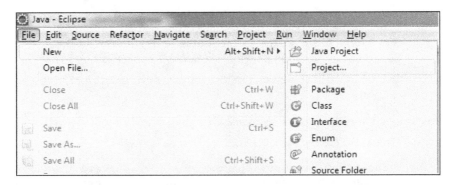

2. Now search for the **Maven** project by typing `maven` in the search box, as shown in the following screenshot, and click on the **Maven Project**. Now click on the **Next** button to continue:

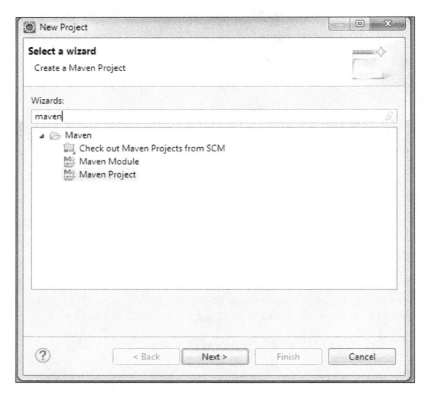

3. Provide **Group Id** and **Artifact Id** for your project, then select **0.0.1 SNAPSHOT** as the **Version**, as shown in the following screenshot:

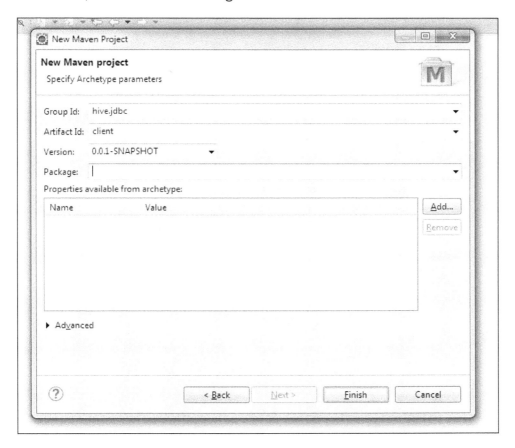

4. Add the following dependencies in `pom.xml`, as shown in the following screenshot:

```xml
<dependency>
    <groupId>org.apache.hive</groupId>
    <artifactId>hive-jdbc</artifactId>
    <version>1.2.1</version>
</dependency>
<dependency>
    <groupId>org.apache.hadoop</groupId>
    <artifactId>hadoop-common</artifactId>
    <version>2.6.0</version>
</dependency>
```

```
M  client/pom.xml ⌗
 1  <project xmlns="http://maven.apache.org/POM/4.0.0" xmlns
 2      xsi:schemaLocation="http://maven.apache.org/POM/4.0.0
 3      <modelVersion>4.0.0</modelVersion>
 4
 5      <groupId>hive.jdbc</groupId>
 6      <artifactId>client</artifactId>
 7      <version>0.0.1-SNAPSHOT</version>
 8      <packaging>jar</packaging>
 9  |
10      <dependencies>
11        <dependency>
12            <groupId>org.apache.hive</groupId>
13            <artifactId>hive-jdbc</artifactId>
14            <version>1.2.1</version>
15        </dependency>
16        <dependency>
17            <groupId>org.apache.hadoop</groupId>
18            <artifactId>hadoop-common</artifactId>
19            <version>2.6.0</version>
20        </dependency>
21        <dependency>
22            <groupId>junit</groupId>
23            <artifactId>junit</artifactId>
24            <version>3.8.1</version>
25            <scope>test</scope>
26        </dependency>
27      </dependencies>
```

5. Create the class `HiveClient` by following these steps:

1. Right-click on **src/main/java** and then navigate to **New** | **Class** to create a new class named `HiveClient` in your maven project:

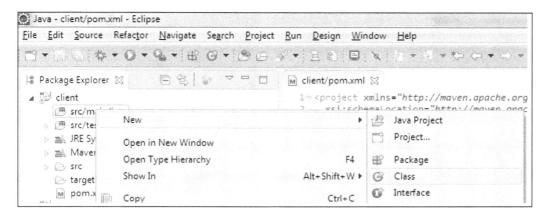

2. In the **Name** section, type `HiveClient` and click on **Finish**:

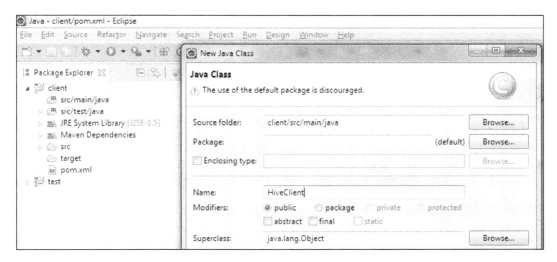

3. Add the following code to the class `HiveClient`:

```java
import java.sql.Connection;
import java.sql.DriverManager;
import java.sql.ResultSet;
import java.sql.SQLException;
import java.sql.Statement;

public class HiveClient {

    private static String driverName = "org.apache.hive.
jdbc.HiveDriver";

    public static void main(String[] args) {
        try {
        Class.forName(driverName);
        } catch (ClassNotFoundException e) {
        e.printStackTrace();
        System.exit(1);
        }
        //replace "root" here with the name of the user the
queries should run as
        Connection conn;
        try {
        conn = DriverManager.getConnection("jdbc:hi
ve2://192.168.56.101:10000/default", "root", "");

        Statement stmt = conn.createStatement();
        String table_name = "testtable";
        stmt.execute("drop table if exists " + table_name);
        stmt.execute("create table " + table_name + " (id
int, fname string,age int)");

        // 1. show tables
        String sqlQuery = "show tables";
        System.out.println("Running query: " + sqlQuery);
        ResultSet rst = stmt.executeQuery(sqlQuery);
        if (rst.next()) {
          System.out.println(rst.getString(1));
        }

        // 2. describe table
        sqlQuery = "describe " + table_name;
        System.out.println("Executing query: " + sqlQuery);
        rst = stmt.executeQuery(sqlQuery);
```

```
        while (rst.next()) {
            System.out.println(rst.getString(1) + "\t" + rst.
getString(2));
        }

        // 3. load data into table
        /** filepath is local to Hive server
        NOTE: /opt/sample_10000.txt is a '\t' separated
file with ID and First Name values. */
        String filepath = "/opt/sample_10000.txt";
        sqlQuery = "load data local inpath '" + filepath +
"' into table " + table_name;
        System.out.println("Executing query: " + sqlQuery);
        stmt.execute(sqlQuery);

        // 4. select * query
        sqlQuery = "select * from " + table_name;
        System.out.println("Executing query: " + sqlQuery);
        rst = stmt.executeQuery(sqlQuery);
        while (rst.next()) {
            System.out.println(String.valueOf(rst.getInt(1)) +
"\t" + rst.getString(2));
        }

        // 5. regular Hive query
        sqlQuery = "select count(*) from " + table_name;
        System.out.println("Running: " + sqlQuery);
        rst = stmt.executeQuery(sqlQuery);
        while (rst.next()) {
            System.out.println(rst.getString(1));
        }

    } catch (SQLException e) {
        e.printStackTrace();
    }
    }


}
```

Running the JDBC sample code from the command-line

To execute the client on a Hadoop/Hive cluster, you need to run the following command:

```
java -cp $CLASSPATH HiveClient
```

Here, $CLASSPATH is the path to the Hadoop and Hive `home` directories.

JDBC datatypes

The following table lists the data types implemented for HiveServer2 JDBC:

Hive Type	Java Type	Specification
TINYINT	byte	A signed or unsigned 1-byte integer
SMALLINT	short	A signed 2-byte integer
INT	int	A signed 4-byte integer
BIGINT	long	A signed 8-byte integer
FLOAT	double	A single-precision number
DOUBLE	double	A double-precision number
DECIMAL	`java.math.BigDecimal`	A fixed-precision decimal value
BOOLEAN	boolean	A single bit (0 or 1)
STRING	String	A character string
TIMESTAMP	`java.sql.Timestamp`	The date and time value
BINARY	String	Binary data
ARRAY	String – json encoded	Values of one data type
MAP	String – json encoded	Key-value pairs
STRUCT	String – json encoded	Structured values

Other clients

Languages such as Python or Ruby could also connect to HiveServer2 using the client APIs:

- ▶ Python: A Python client driver is available on GitHub at `https://github.com/BradRuderman/pyhs2`.

- ▶ Ruby Client: A Ruby client driver is available on GitHub at `https://github.com/forward3d/rbhive`.

Introducing the Hive metastore service

In Hive, the data is stored in HDFS and the table, database, schema, and other HQL definitions are stored in a metastore. The metastore could be any RDBMS database, such as MySQL or Oracle. Hive creates a database and a set of tables in metastore to store HiveQL definitions.

There are three modes of configuring a metastore:

- ▶ Embedded
- ▶ Local
- ▶ Remote

The detailed description and configuration steps of different modes are available in *Chapter 1, Developing Hive.*

How to do it...

The Hive metastore could be made available as a service. All you need to do is run the following command on the terminal of your machine:

```
hive --service metastore
```

```
[root@localhost ~]# hive --service metastore &
[2] 3929
[root@localhost ~]#
```

How it works...

In the case of a remote metastore configuration, all clients connect to the metastore service to query the underlying datastore (MySQL, Oracle, and so on). The communication is done through the `Thrift` protocol. At the client's side, a user needs to add the following configurations to make the client connect to a metastore service:

Command	Description
hive.metastore.uris	It is used to specify the URI of a metastore server
hive.metastore.warehouse.dir	It is used to specify the data location in HDFS. The default value is /user/hive/warehouse

If MySQL is used as a metastore, then the user needs to add `mysql connector jar` to the `lib` folder of Hive. Also if you want to change the metastore port, you need to start the metastore with the following command:

```
hive --service metastore -p <port_num>
```

If you want to run the metastore as a backend service, append `&` at the end of service:

```
hive --service metastore -p <port_num> &
```

You can verify whether the metastore service is running or not using the `jps` command. It will run as the `RunJar` service, as shown in the following screenshot:

```
[root@localhost ~]#
[root@localhost ~]# jps
3066 NodeManager
3929 RunJar
2642 DataNode
3713 RunJar
2970 ResourceManager
2549 NameNode
2826 SecondaryNameNode
4024 Jps
[root@localhost ~]#
```

Configuring high availability of metastore service

The Hive metastore service is a single point of communication between different clients and metastore data. If the metastore service is down or unavailable, then clients would not be able to run any HiveQL as metastore data is not accessible.

How to do it...

The High Availability solution is designed to provide the failover control of the Hive metastore service. To configure metastore in the High Availability mode, you need to concurrently start the metastore service on multiple machines. Every client will read the `hive.metastore.uris` property from the configuration file. The property could have a comma-separated list of machines on which metastore services are running:

```
<property>
    <name>hive.metastore.uris</name>
    <value>thrift://$Hive_Metastore_Server_Host_Machine_FQDN
    </value>
    <description> A comma separated list of metastore uris on which
metastore service is running.
    </description>
</property>
```

Here, `$Hive_Metastore_Server_Host_Machine_FQDN` is the comma-separated, fully qualified domain name of machines on which the Hive metastores are running.

Introducing Hue

Hadoop User Experience (**Hue**) is an open source web interface for analyzing data with Hadoop and its ecosystem components.

Hue brings together the most common Apache Hadoop components into a single web interface. Its main goal is to allow the users to use Hadoop without worrying about underlying complexity or using a command-line interface.

Getting ready

The following are the major features of Hue:

- ► The file browser for HDFS
- ► The job browser for MapReduce or YARN
- ► Query editors for Apache Hive
- ► Query editors for Apache Pig
- ► The Apache Sqoop2 editor
- ► The Apache ZooKeeper browser
- ► The Apache HBase browser

We will focus on the **Query** editors for Apache Hive.

How to do it...

To run Hue, there are various steps that need to be followed. The installation of Hue might seem a little complex, but once Hue is set up, it will ease up the running Hive queries through the web interface without using terminal screens.

Prepare dependencies

If you are installing Hue on Ubuntu, you need to install the following libraries:

```
sudo apt-get install -y ant
sudo apt-get install -y gcc g++
sudo apt-get install -y libkrb5-dev libmysqlclient-dev
sudo apt-get install -y libssl-dev libsasl2-dev libsasl2-modules-gssapi-mit
sudo apt-get install -y libsqlite3-dev
sudo apt-get install -y libtidy-0.99-0 libxml2-dev libxslt-dev
sudo apt-get install -y maven
sudo apt-get install -y libldap2-dev
sudo apt-get install -y python-dev python-simplejson python-setuptools python-ldap
sudo apt-get install  libgmp3-dev
```

If you are installing Hue on CentOS, you need to install and configure the following libraries:

```
sudo yum install -y ant
sudo yum install -y gcc g++
sudo yum  install python-devel.x86_64
sudo yum groupinstall "Development Tools"
sudo yum install krb5-devel
sudo yum install libxslt-devel libxml2-devel
sudo yum install mysql-devel.x86_64
sudo yum install ncurses-devel zlib-devel texinfo gtk+-devel gtk2-devel
qt-devel tcl-devel tk-devel kernel-headers kernel-devel
sudo yum install gmp-devel.x86_64
sudo yum intall sqlite-devel.x86_64
sudo yum install cyrus-sasl.x86_64
sudo yum install postfix system-switch-mail cyrus-imapd cyrus-plain
cyrus-md5 cyrus-utils
sudo yum install libevent libevent-devel
sudo yum install memcached-devel.x86_64
sudo yum install postfix
sudo yum install cyrus-sasl
sudo yum install cyrus-imapd
sudo yum install openldap-devel
```

 Installing the latest version of Maven is necessary.

Downloading and installing Hue

1. Downloading the latest version of Hue is important (which at the time of writing was 3.9). Run the following command on the machine on which Hue is to be installed:

   ```
   wget https://dl.dropboxusercontent.com/u/730827/hue/
   releases/3.9.0/hue-3.9.0.tgz
   ```

2. Extract the Hue packages using the following command:

   ```
   tar -xzvf hue-3.9.0.tgz
   ```

3. Installing Hue via the following command:

   ```
   sudo make install
   ```

By default, Hue installs to `/usr/local/hue` in your node's local filesystem. Running the previous command will give logs, as shown in the following screenshot:

```
Post-processed 'zookeeper/js/base64.js' as 'zookeeper/js/base64.ce5e02af31e5.js'
Post-processed 'zookeeper/help/index.html' as 'zookeeper/help/index.7570dbb625f3
1'
907 static files copied to '/usr/local/hue/build/static', 907 post-processed.
make[1]: Leaving directory `/usr/local/hue/apps'
--- Setting up Desktop database
make -C /usr/local/hue/desktop syncdb
make[1]: Entering directory `/usr/local/hue/desktop'
make[1]: Nothing to be done for `syncdb'.
make[1]: Leaving directory `/usr/local/hue/desktop'
```

 Check carefully at last of logs that there is no error message.

The default ownership of Hue files and folders is set to the `root` user.

Let's change Hue permissions so that it can run without `root` permissions:

sudo chown -R hadoop:hadoop /usr/local/hue

Here, `hadoop` is the user name and group name too.

Configuring Hive with Hue

Hue contains a configuration file named `hue.ini` located at `/usr/local/hue/desktop/conf/hue.ini`:

```
[beeswax]
# Host where HiveServer2 is running at: hive_server_host=localhost
```

 Replace `localhost` by the hostname to point to Hive running on the other machine.

Starting Hue

We start the Hue server using the `supervisor` command in Hue's `bin`:

cd /usr/local/hue/build/env/bin

./supervisor

Use the `-d` switch to start the Hue supervisor in the **daemon** mode (as background process):

```
./supervisor -d
```

Accessing Hive with Hue

To access Hive via Hue, the URL format will be `http:<HOST_NAME>:8888`. Here, `HOST_NAME` will be the IP address or URL of Hive; for example, `http://192.168.56.111:8888`.

This would prompt for a username and a password. You can give any username and password of your choice. Remember the username and password for future reference. For example, you can use the username `admin` and the password `admin` for the first time.

After successful login into the Hue web interface, it will describe the configuration of various supported components. For accessing Hive through the Hue web interface, HiveServer2 must be running.

As shown in the following screenshot, to access the Hive editor on Hue, click on **Hive** under the **Query Editors** tab:

The left-hand side panel will show the list of databases and all tables of the selected database in the dropdown icon. In the right-hand side panel, you can execute any Hive query and retrieve the result.

There is one table named `sales` in the `default` database. Now let's execute a query on Hue to retrieve the result.

For demonstration purposes, let's retrieve the first and last names of 10 users from the `sales` table:

```
SELECT fname, lname FROM sales LIMIT 10;
```

After clicking on the **Execute** button, get the 10 users' names from the `sales` table, as shown in the following screenshot:

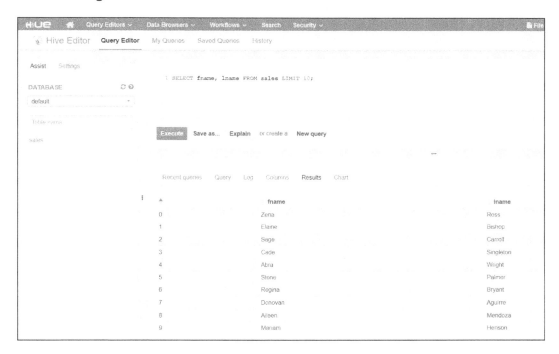

As shown in the previous screenshot, after executing the query, it will show the result on the same page. Similarly, you can execute any Hive query through this web interface without using terminal screens.

You can also check the history of recently executed queries through Hue:

As shown in the preceding screenshot, in the right panel, there is a **Recent queries** tab where you can see all commands that have recently been executed. You can also check the results of particular query by clicking on **See results**.

3
Understanding the Hive Data Model

In this chapter, we will cover the following recipes:

- ► Using numeric data types
- ► Using string data types
- ► Using Date/Time data types
- ► Using miscellaneous data types
- ► Using complex data types
- ► Using operators
- ► Partitioning
- ► Partitioning a managed table
- ► Partitioning an external table
- ► Bucketing

Introduction

In previous chapters, you learned the installation of different Hive components such as Hive metastore, HiveServer2, and working with different services in Hive.

In this chapter, we will cover the following sub topics:

- ▶ Using data types
- ▶ Using operators
- ▶ Partitioning
- ▶ Bucketing

Introducing data types

Hive supports various data types that are primarily divided into two parts:

- ▶ Primitive data types
- ▶ Complex data types

Hive supports many primitive data types that are similar to relational databases, such as `INT`, `SMALLINT`, `TINYINT`, `BIGINT`, `BOOLEAN`, `FLOAT`, and `DOUBLE`. In addition to primitive data type, Hive also supports few complex data types, such as `ARRAY`, `MAP`, `STRUCT`, and `UNION`.

Primitive data types

Hive supports large number of primitive data types, which are divided into the four following different categories:

- ▶ Numeric data types
- ▶ String data types
- ▶ Date/Time data type
- ▶ Miscellaneous data types

All these primitive data types are similar to RDBMS primitive data types.

Complex data types

The following are the three complex data types supported by Hive:

- ▶ STRUCT
- ▶ MAP
- ▶ ARRAY

Using numeric data types

Hive supports a set of data types that can be used for table columns, expression values, and function arguments, and return values.

In the following table, primitive numeric data types are listed with sizes and examples:

Data Type	Size	Example
TINYINT	1-byte signed integer	50
SMALLINT	2-byte signed integer	20,000
INT	4-byte signed integer	1,000
BIGINT	8-byte signed integer	50,000
FLOAT	4-byte single-precision floating point	400.50
DOUBLE	8-byte double-precision floating point	20,000.50
DECIMAL	17-byte precision up to 38 digits	DECIMAL(20,2)

By default, all integral literals are treated as the INT values until they cross the range of INT values. If some integral literal crosses the range of the INT value, then it is treated as the BIGINT value. There is a mechanism of postfix, which is used to specify an integral literal as TINYINT, SMALLINT, and BIGINT.

To specify an integral literal as TINYINT, the postfix Y is used. For example, you can specify 50 as 50Y.

To specify an integral literal as SMALLINT, the postfix S is used. For example, you can specify 50 as 50S.

To specify an integral literal as BIGINT, the postfix L is used. For example, you can specify 50 as 50L.

The DECIMAL data type is defined using the fixed precision and scale value. It is very useful for financial and other arithmetic use cases where Float and Double don't meet all requirements. The DECIMAL data type is defined using a DECIMAL(precision, scale) syntax. The Default value of scale is 0, which means no fractional digits, and the default value of precision is 10, which means 10 digits. Therefore, the default DECIMAL with no precision or scale values is equivalent to DECIMAL(10,0). The precision value must be between 1 and 38. For example, to represent integer values up to 9999 and floating point values up to 99.99, both require a precision of 4. The maximum integral value for decimal is represented by DECIMAL(38,0), that is, 999 with 9 repeated 38 times.

How to do it...

The following are the few examples for using primitive data types in Hive.

The following statement creates a table named `customer` with `id` as the `BIGINT` data type and `age` as the `TINYINT` data type:

```
CREATE TABLE customer (id BIGINT, age TINYINT);
```

The following statement creates a table `customer_order` table with `id` as the `BIGINT` data type and `price` as the `DECIMAL` data type:

```
CREATE TABLE customer_order (id BIGINT, price DECIMAL(10,2));
```

Using string data types

Hive supports three types of String data type, `STRING`, `VARCHAR`, and `CHAR`:

- ▶ **STRING**: It is a sequence of characters that can be expressed using single quotes (`'`) as well as double quotes (`"`).
- ▶ **VARCHAR**: It is variable-length character type. It is defined using a length specifier, which specifies the maximum number of characters allowed in the character string. Its syntax is `VARCHAR(max_length)`. The value of the `varchar` data type gets *truncated* during processing if necessary to fit within the specified length. While converting the string value to the `varchar` value, if a string value exceeds the length specifier, then the string gets silently truncated. The maximum length of `varchar` type is `65355`.
- ▶ **CHAR**: It is fixed-length character type. It is defined in the same way as the `varchar` type. If the value is shorter as compared with the specified length, then the value is padded with trailing spaces to achieve the specified length. The maximum length of the `char` type is 255.

 The `varchar` and `char` data type cannot be used in a nongeneric **User-Defined Function** (**UDF**) or **User-Defined Aggregate** (**UDA**) function.

How to do it...

The following is an example of using `String` data types in Hive:

```
CREATE TABLE customer (id BIGINT, name String, sex CHAR(6), role
VARCHAR(64));
```

The preceding statement creates a table, `customer`, with `id` as the `BIGINT` data type, `name` as the `String` data type, `sex` as the `CHAR` data type, and `role` as the `VARCHAR` data type.

How it works...

If you declare a field of the `CHAR (12)` data type, then it will always take 12 bytes irrespective of size of data you store. For example, whether you store the 1 character or the 12 character in the `CHAR(12)` field, it will take 12 bytes in both the cases. Also, because the field is declared as the `CHAR(12)` data type, we can store a maximum of 12 characters in this column.

On the other hand, `VARCHAR` is a variable-length data type. It takes storage equal to the actual size of the field. For example, if you declare a field of the `VARCHAR (12)` data type, it will take the number of bytes equal to the number of characters stored in this column. For example, if you store only one character in this column, then it will take only 1 byte and if you store 10 characters, then it will take 10 bytes. Also if a field is declared as the `VARCHAR(n)` data type, then a maximum of n characters can be stored in this column.

Using Date/Time data types

Hive supports two data types for Date/Time-related fields—`Timestamp` and `Date`:

The `Timestamp` data type is used to represent a particular time with the date and time value. It supports variable-length encoding of the traditional UNIX timestamp with an optional nanosecond precision.

It supports different conversions. The `timestamp` value provided as an integer numeric type is interpreted as a UNIX timestamp in seconds; a timestamp value provided as a floating point numeric type is interpreted as a UNIX timestamp in seconds with decimal precision; the timestamp value provided as string is interpreted as the `java.sql.Timestamp` format `YYYY-MM-DD HH:MM:SS.fffffffff`.

If the timestamp value is in another format than `yyyy-mm-dd hh:mm:ss[.f...]`, then `UDF` can be used to convert them to the timestamp format. The `Date` type is used to represent only the date part of timestamp, that is, `YYYY-MM-DD`. This type doesn't represent the time of day component. The `Date` ranges allowed are `0000-01-01` to `9999-12-31`.

The `Date` types can be casted in the `Date`, `Timestamp`, or `String` types and vice versa.

How to do it...

The following is an example of using the `Date` and `Timestamp` data types in Hive:

```
CREATE TABLE timestamp_example (id int, created_at DATE, updated_at
TIMESTAMP);
```

Using miscellaneous data types

Hive supports two miscellaneous data types: `Boolean` and `Binary`:

`Boolean` accepts `true` or `false` values.

`Binary` is a sequence of bytes. It is similar to the `VARBINARY` data type found in many relational databases. If a field is declared as the `binary` type, then it is stored within a record, not separately like `BLOB`s. The `binary` data type is used when a record has hundreds of columns, and the user is just interested in a few columns and doesn't bother about an exact type information of other columns. In such cases, a user can define the type of those columns as `binary`, so Hive will not try to interpret those columns. It is used to include the `arbitrary` types in record, and Hive doesn't attempt to parse them as numbers, strings, and so on.

How to do it...

The following is the example in order to use the `Boolean` data types in Hive:

```
CREATE TABLE example (id INT, status BOOLEAN, description STRING);
```

The preceding statement creates a table, `example`, with the status as the `Boolean` data type.

Using complex data types

In addition to primitive data types, Hive also supports a few complex data types: `Struct`, `MAP`, and `Array`. Complex data types are also known as **collection** data types. Most relational databases don't support such data types.

Complex data types can be built from primitive data types:

> ▸ `STRUCT`: The struct data type in Hive is analogous to the `STRUCT` in C programming language. It is a record type that holds a set of named fields that can be of any primitive data types. Fields in the `STRUCT` type are accessed using the DOT (`.`) notation.
>
> Syntax: `STRUCT<col_name : data_type [COMMENT col_comment], ...>`

For example, if a column `address` is of the type `STRUCT {city STRING; state STRING}`, then the city field can be referenced using `address.city`.

▶ `MAP`: The map data type contains key-value pairs. In Map, elements are accessed using the keys. For example, if a column `name` is of type Map: `'firstname' -> 'john'` and `'lastname' -> 'roy'`, then the last name can be accessed using the name `['lastname']`.

▶ `ARRAY`: This is an ordered sequence of similar elements. It maintains an index in order to access the elements; for example, an array `day`, containing a list of elements `['Sunday', 'Monday', 'Tuesday', 'Wednesday']`. In this, the first element `Sunday` can be accessed using `day[0]`, and similarly, the third element can be accessed using `day[2]`.

▶ `UNIONTYPE`: This data type enables you to store different data types in the same memory location. It is an efficient way of using the same memory location for multipurpose. It is similar to `Unions` in the C programming language. You can define a `union` type with many data types, but at a time, only one data type can be hold by it.

Syntax: `UNIONTYPE<data_type, data_type, ...>`

How to do it...

The following are some different examples of how to use complex data types:

1. To create a `customer` table with `name` as the `struct` data type, the following command can be used:

   ```
   CREATE TABLE customer(id INT, name STRUCT<firstname:STRING,
   lastname:STRING>);
   ```

   Here, the column `name` is of the type `STRUCT` with two fields—`firstname` and lastname—then the `firstname` field can be referenced using `name.firstname`. Similarly, the `lastname` field can be referenced using `name.lastname`.

2. Let's create a table `test` with the usage of different data types, such as `int`, `double`, `array`, and `struct` as `uniontype`.

   ```
   CREATE TABLE test(column1 UNIONTYPE<int, double, array<string>, st
   ruct<age:int,country:string>>);
   ```

3. When we retrieve the data, it will return the result with `index` of data type and value. The first part will give the information about which part of `union` is being used. In the following example, `index 0` means the first `data_type` from the definition, which is an `int`, and `index 1` means the second data type, which is `double`, and so on:

   ```
   SELECT column1 FROM test;
   ```

```
{1:6.0}                               // For second data type DOUBLE
{0:5}                                 // For first data type INT
{2:["sunday","monday"]}               // For third data type ARRAY
{3:{"age":28,"country":"INDIA"}}      // For fourth data type STRUCT
{2:["tuesday","wednesday"]}           // For third data type ARRAY
{3:{"age":21,"country":"US"}}         // For fourth data type STRUCT
{0:3}                                 // For first data type INT
{1:6.5}                               // For second data type DOUBLE
```

Using operators

Hive supports various built-in operators. There are four types of operator in Hive:

- ► Relational operators
- ► Arithmetic operators
- ► Logical operators
- ► Complex operators

Using relational operators

Relational operators are used to compare two operands. The output of comparison produces TRUE or FALSE depending on the comparison of operands.

The following table describes relational operators available in Hive:

Operator	Operand Type	Description
A = B	All primitive data types	This returns True if primitives are equal, otherwise False.
A != B	All primitive data types	This returns True if primitive A is not equal to B, False otherwise. It would return Null if A or B is NULL.
A <=> B	All primitive data types	This returns the same result as the EQUAL operator for non-null primitives. It would return TRUE if both A and B are NULL, FALSE if one of the primitives among A and B is NULL.
A <> B	All primitive data types	This returns the same result as the NOT EQUAL (!=) operator.

Operator	Operand Type	Description
A < B	All primitive data types	This returns NULL if either primitive A or B is NULL. It would return TRUE if the expression A is less than B. Otherwise, it would return FALSE.
A <= B	All primitive data types	This returns NULL if any of primitive A or B is NULL. It would return TRUE if the expression A is less than or equal to the expression B, otherwise FALSE.
A > B	All primitive data types	This returns TRUE if the expression A is greater than the expression B, otherwise FALSE. It would return NULL if primitive A or B is NULL.
A >= B	All primitive data types	This returns TRUE if the expression A is greater than or equal to the expression B, otherwise FALSE. It would return NULL if primitive A or B is NULL.
A BETWEEN B AND C	All primitive data types	This returns TRUE if the value of A lies within B and C, otherwise FALSE. It would return NULL if primitive A, B, or C is NULL.
A NOT BETWEEN B AND C	All primitive data types	This returns TRUE if A doesn't lie between B and C, otherwise FALSE. It would return NULL if primitive A, B, or C is NULL.
A IS NULL	All primitive data types	It will return TRUE if the expression A evaluates to NULL; otherwise; it would return FALSE.
A IS NOT NULL	All primitive data types	It will return FALSE if the expression A evaluates to NULL; otherwise, it would return TRUE.

Operator	Operand Type	Description
A LIKE B	String	This returns TRUE if the string A matches the SQL regular expression B; otherwise, it would return FALSE. It would return NULL if primitive A or B is NULL.
A NOT LIKE B	String	This returns TRUE if string A does not match the SQL regular expression B, otherwise FALSE. It would return NULL if primitive A or B is NULL.
A RLIKE B	String	This returns TRUE if any substring (possibly empty) of A matches the specified Java regular expression B, otherwise FALSE. It would return NULL if primitive A or B is NULL. For example, `'hivefunction' RLIKE 'hive'` will return TRUE.
A REGEXP B	String	It is the same as RLIKE.

How to do it...

Let's assume that the `customer` table is composed of fields named `id`, `name`, `gender`, and `age`, as shown in the following table. Generate a query to retrieve the customer details whose age is 41:

id	name	gender	Age
1	Kate	Male	35
2	John	Male	41
3	Mike	Male	50
4	Dave	Male	32

The following statement will get the job done:

```
hive> SELECT * FROM customer WHERE age = 41 AND gender = 'Male';
```

On the successful execution of a query, you will get the following response:

Id	name	gender	age
2	John	Male	41

In the following SQL statement, we are trying to get the details of those customers whose age is between 30 and 40:

```
hive> SELECT * FROM customer WHERE age BETWEEN 30 AND 40;
```

On the successful execution of a query, you will get the following response:

id	name	gender	age
1	Kate	Male	35
4	Dave	Male	32

The following statement will return the details of those customers, whose names start with `k`:

```
hive> SELECT * FROM customer WHERE name LIKE 'k%';
```

On the successful execution of a query, you will get the following response:

id	name	gender	age
1	Kate	Male	35

Using arithmetic operators

Arithmetic operators are used to perform arithmetic operations on operands such as addition, subtraction, multiplication, division, and so on. All these types of operators return numbers.

If any operand is NULL while performing arithmetic operations, then result will also be NULL.

The following table describes arithmetic operators available in Hive:

Operator	Operand Type	Description
A + B	Numeric data types	It gives the sum (addition) of A and B
A - B	Numeric data types	It gives the difference between (subtraction) B and A
A * B	Numeric data types	It gives the multiplication of A and B
A / B	Numeric data types	It gives the division of A by B
A % B	Numeric data types	It gives the remainder value resulting from the division of A by B

Operator	Operand Type	Description
A & B	Numeric data types	It gives the result of a bitwise AND operation of the operands A and B
A | B	Numeric data types	It gives the result of a bitwise OR operation of the operands A and B
A ^ B	Numeric data types	It gives the result of a bitwise XOR operation of the operands A and B
~A	Numeric data types	It gives the result of a bitwise NOT operation of the operand A

How to do it...

The following are a few simple examples to use arithmetic operators in Hive:

1. To add two numbers, execute the following command:

   ```
   hive> SELECT 10+10 ADD FROM test;
   ```

   After executing this query, you will get the result 20. Similarly, you can give two or more column names to get the sum of their values.

2. To multiply two numbers, we will use the following command:

   ```
   hive> SELECT 10*10 MULTIPLE FROM test;
   ```

   After executing this query, you will get the result 100. Similarly, you can give two or more column names to multiply their values.

 This is just an example, To get output of this command table must have at least one row. Valid use cases for arithmetic operator are in where clauses or doing some complex operations.

Using logical operators

Logical operators are used for logical operations AND, OR, and so on. All these types of operators return TRUE or FALSE.

If any operand is NULL while performing logical operations, then result will also be NULL.

The following table describes the logical operators available in Hive:

Operator	Operand Type	Description
A AND B	Boolean	It will return TRUE in case of both A and B is TRUE, otherwise FALSE.

Operator	Operand Type	Description
`A && B`	Boolean	Same as `A AND B`
`A OR B`	Boolean	It will return `TRUE` if either `A` or `B` are `TRUE` or both are `TRUE`, otherwise `FALSE`
`A || B`	Boolean	Same as `A OR B`
`NOT A`	Boolean	It will return `TRUE` if `A` is `FALSE`. It will return `NULL` if `A` is `NULL`, otherwise `FALSE`.
`! A`	Boolean	Same as `NOT A`
`A IN (value1, value2, …)`	Boolean	It will return `TRUE` if the value of `A` is equal to any of the given values.
`A IN (subquery)`	Boolean	It will return `TRUE` if `A` is equal to any of the values returned by subquery.
`A NOT IN (value1, value2, …)`	Boolean	It will return `TRUE` if the value of `A` is not equal to any of the given values.
`A NOT IN (subquery)`	Boolean	It will return `TRUE` if the value of `A` is not equal to any of the values returned by subquery.
`EXISTS (subquery)`	Boolean	It will return `TRUE` if the the subquery returns at least one record.
`NOT EXISTS (subquery)`	Boolean	It will return `TRUE` if the subquery returns no record.

How to do it...

Let's assume that the `customer` table is composed of fields named `id`, `name`, `gender`, and `age`.

The following are some examples of using logical operators:

▶ Select all customers of age 21, 41, and 60:

```
hive> SELECT * FROM customer where age IN (21,41,60);
```

On the successful execution of query, you will get the following response:

Id	Name	Gender	Age
2	John	Male	41

▶ Select all the male customers of age more than 40:

```
hive> SELECT * FROM customer WHERE gender = 'Male' AND age > 40;
```

On the successful execution of a query, you will get the following response:

Id	name	gender	age
2	John	Male	41
3	Mike	Male	50

Using complex operators

Complex operators are used to access the elements of complex type.

The following table describes complex operators available in Hive:

Operator	Operand type	Description
A[i]	A is an array object, and i is the index of an element in the array.	It will return the element at the i index of array.
M[key]	M is the map object, that is, **key-value** pair.	It will return the value corresponding to the specified key in the map.
S.a	S is the Struct object.	Returns the a field of S.

How to do it...

Let's first create a table, person, with different complex types:

```
CREATE TABLE person (
    id INT,
    phones ARRAY<INT>,
    otherDetails MAP<STRING, STRING>,
    address STRUCT<street:STRING, city:STRING, state:STRING>
);
```

Now to access the different values of complex type attribute, different complex operators can be used.

To access an alternative phone number of a user, execute the following command:

```
hive> SELECT phones[1] FROM person;
```

Let's assume that the person has some other details such as `hometown='HG'` and `preference="homepage"`, then we can access each element using the particular key of the `otherDetails` field:

```
hive> SELECT otherDetails[' hometown'] FROM person;
```

To access `city` of a person from the `address` attribute, execute the following command:

```
hive> SELECT address.city FROM person;
```

Partitioning

Partitioning in Hive is used to increase query performance. Hive is very good tool to perform queries on large datasets, especially datasets that require a scan of an entire table. Generally, users are aware of their data domain, and in most of cases they want to search for a particular type of data. For such cases, a simple query takes large time to return the result because it requires the scan of the entire dataset. The concept of partitioning can be used to reduce the cost of querying the data. Partitions are like horizontal slices of data that allows the large sets of data as more manageable chunks.

Table partitioning means dividing the table data into some parts based on the unique values of particular columns (for example, city and country) and segregating the input data records into different files or directories.

Getting ready

This recipe requires Hive installed as described in the *Installing Hive* recipe of *Chapter 1, Developing Hive*. You will also need Hive CLI or the Beeline client to run the commands.

How to do it...

Partitioning in Hive is done using the `PARTITIONED BY` clause in the `create table` statement of table. Table can have one or more partitions. A table can be partitioned on the basis of one or more columns. The columns on which partitioning is done cannot be included in the data of table. For example, you have the four fields `id`, `name`, `age`, and `city`, and you want to partition the data on the basis of the `city` field, then the `city` field will not be included in the columns of create table statement and will only be used in the `PARTITIONED BY` clause. You can still query the data in a normal way using `where city=xyz`. The result will be retrieved from the respective partition because data is stored in a different directory with the city name for each city.

If you try to repeat the table column in partitioning columns, then Hive will throw the error, `FAILED: Error in semantic analysis: Column repeated in partitioning columns`:

```
CREATE [EXTERNAL] TABLE [IF NOT EXISTS] [database_name.]table_name
  [(column_name data_type [COMMENT column_comment], ...)]
  [PARTITIONED BY (column_name data_type [COMMENT column_comment], ...)];
```

There are two main types of table in Hive—**Managed** tables and **External** tables. Both tables support partitioning mechanism.

Partitioning a managed table

Managed tables can be partitioned using the `PARTITIONED BY` clause. In a managed table, if you delete a table, then the data of that table will also get deleted. Similarly, if you delete a partition, then the data of that partition will also get deleted.

How to do it...

Let's take an example of the `customer` table data and imagine that we have the data of different customers of different country. Now if we don't enable any partitioning, then by default, all data will go into one directory. Let's assume that data size is around 1 TB. Now if we query for customers belonging to India, then this query will be executed on entire data of 1 TB size and this query will take more time. By enabling partitioning this query, execution can be much faster. If we want to split the data on the country basis, then the following command can be used to create a table with the partitioned column `country`:

```
CREATE TABLE customer(id STRING, name STRING, gender STRING, state
STRING) PARTITIONED BY (country STRING);
```

The partitioning of tables changes the structure of storing the data. A root-level directory structure remains the same as a normal table; for example, if we create this `customer` table in the `xyz` database, there will be a root-level directory, as shown here:

```
hdfs://hadoop_namenode_server/user/hive/warehouse/xyz.db/customer
```

However, Hive will now create subdirectories reflecting the partitioning structure, for example:

```
.../customer/country=OI
.../customer/country=UK
.../customer/country=IN
...
```

These subdirectories have the data of respective countries. Now if a query is executed for a particular country, then only a selected partition will be used to return the query result.

One more interesting thing is that partitioning can also be done on the basis of multiple parameters. In the preceding example, we have a field, `state`, in a customer record. Now if we want to keep the data of each state in different file for each `country`, then we can partition the data on the `country` as well as `state` attributes. The following command can be used for this purpose:

```
CREATE TABLE customer(id STRING, name STRING, gender STRING) PARTITIONED
BY (country STRING, state STRING);
```

We have not included the `country` and `state` columns in the schema of table as these columns are defined as the `partition` keys. If we try to include these columns in `schema` as well, then we will get the following error: `FAILED: SemanticException [Error 10035]: Column repeated in partitioning columns.`

Hive will now create subdirectories for `state` as well. Consider the following example:

```
.../customer/country=OI/state=AB
.../customer/country=OI/state=DC
.../customer/country=UK/state=JR
.../customer/country=IN/state=UP
.../customer/country=IN/state=DL
.../customer/country=IN/state=RJ
...
```

The following query selects all the customers in the state of Delhi from the country India:

```
SELECT * FROM customer WHERE country = 'IN' AND state = 'DL';
```

This query will return the result only from a particular partition.

Data partitioning is mainly done for the fast execution of queries. In the case of very large datasets, a partitioning mechanism can improve query performance very effectively.

Predicates added to the `WHERE` clauses that filter on partition values are named **partition filters**.

When you have large data with high number of partitions, executing query without any partition filters might trigger an enormous MapReduce job. To avoid such cases, there is the `map-reduce` mode configuration `hive.mapred.mode`, which prevents running risky queries on Hive. The default value of `hive.mapred.mode` is set to `nonstrict`. This mode specifies how Hive operations are being performed. By setting the value of `hive.mapred.mode` to strict, it will prevent running risky queries. For example, in `strict` mode, you cannot run a full table scan query:

```
hive> set hive.mapred.mode=strict;


hive> SELECT * FROM customer c;
FAILED: Error in semantic analysis: No partition predicate found for
Alias "c" Table "customer"


hive> set hive.mapred.mode=nonstrict;


hive> SELECT * FROM customer c;
21 john m RJ IN

...
```

Listing partitions' information of a `table`: SHOW PARTITIONS command can be used to list all partitions of a table:

```
hive> SHOW PARTITIONS customer

country=US/state=AB
country=US/state=DC
country=UK/state=JR
country=IN/state=UP
country=IN/state=DL
country=IN/state=RJ

...
```

When you have a lot of partitions and you want to filter out the partitions with a specific key or you want to check whether partitions have been created for a specific partition key then you can further restrict the command with an optional PARTITION clause that specifies one or more partitions with specific values:

```
hive> SHOW PARTITIONS customer PARTITION(country = 'US')
```

```
country=US/state=AB

country=US/state=DC

...


hive> SHOW PARTITIONS customer PARTITION(country = 'US', state='DC')


country=US/state=DC
```

 If the table is not a partitioned table, then the SHOW PARTITIONS command will throw the error FAILED: Execution Error, return code 1 from org.apache.hadoop.hive.ql.exec. DDLTask. The table sales is not a partitioned table.

To check which columns are defined as partitioning columns, the DESCRIBE <table-name> command can be used:

```
hive> DESCRIBE customer;
OK
id          string
name        string
gender      string
country     string
state       string
# Partition Information
# col_name      data_type
country     string
state       string
```

Adding new partitions

The following command can be used to add new partitions to a table:

```
ALTER TABLE table_name ADD [IF NOT EXISTS] PARTITION partition_spec
    [LOCATION 'loc1'] partition_spec [LOCATION 'loc2'] ...;


partition_spec:
    : (partition_column = partition_column_value, partition_column =
partition_column_value, ...)
```

You can add multiple partitions to a table using the preceding command.

Renaming partitions

The following command can be used to rename a partition:

```
ALTER TABLE table_name PARTITION partition_spec RENAME TO PARTITION
partition_spec;
```

Exchanging partitions

You can also exchange partitions from one table to another table:

```
ALTER TABLE table_name_1 EXCHANGE PARTITION (partition_spec) WITH TABLE
table_name_2;
```

Using the preceding statement, the data is moved from the target table to the source table. Both tables should have the same schema. The source table should not have existed partition specified in the preceding statement:

```
ALTER TABLE table1 EXCHANGE PARTITION (ct='1') WITH TABLE table2;
```

This command moves the data from `table2` to `table1@ct=1`. If `table@ct=1` is already exists or the schema of `table1` and `table2` is different, then this operation will be failed.

Dropping the partitions

You can drop the partitions using the following command:

```
ALTER TABLE table_name DROP [IF EXISTS] PARTITION partition_spec [,
PARTITION partition_spec, ...] [IGNORE PROTECTION] [PURGE];
```

The preceding statement deletes the actual data and metadata of the specified partition. If trash is configured, then data will be moved to the `.Trash/Current` directory. If the `PURGE` option is specified in the preceding command, then the partition data will not go to the `.Trash/Current` directory. This means that data cannot be retrieved in the event of a mistaken drop.

Loading data in a managed partitioned table

There are two ways of creating partitions in a table:

▶ **Static Partitioning**: While creating static partitions, we specify for which value a partition is to be created:

The `LOAD` command can be used to insert the data from a file to a Hive table in specified partitions. If there are more than one partition columns in table, then you will have to specify values for all partitioning columns.

Consider the following syntax:

```
LOAD DATA [LOCAL] INPATH 'filepath' [OVERWRITE] INTO TABLE
tablename [PARTITION (partcolumn1=value1, partcolumn2=value2 ...)]
```

Here, `filepath` can refer to a single file or directory `path` with multiple files. The `INSERT` command can be used to insert the data from a query result of an other Hive table:

```
INSERT OVERWRITE TABLE tablename1 [PARTITION (partcolumn1=value1,
partcolumn2=value2 ...)] select_statement1 FROM from_statement;


INSERT INTO TABLE tablename1 [PARTITION (partcolumn1=value1,
partcolumn2=value2 ...)] select_statement1 FROM from_statement;
```

When we use the `INSERT OVERWRITE` statement to insert the data into a partition, it will overwrite the existing data of that partition. If we use the `INSERT INTO` statement to insert the data into a partition, then it will not delete any existing data of that partition and will append the new data to that partition.

- ▶ **Dynamic partitioning**: In dynamic partitioning, we don't have to specify values for partition columns in the `PARTITION` clause while inserting the data. We just specify the name of partition columns in the `PARTITION` clause, and the partitions are created on the basis of unique values of that partition column. If a partition column value is given, it is named static partition.

To insert the data, the dynamic partition columns must be specified in last among the columns in the `SELECT` statement and in the same order in which they appear in the `PARTITION()` clause.

Dynamic partitioning is disabled by default. The minimal configuration to enable dynamic partitioning is as follows:

```
SET hive.exec.dynamic.partition = true;
```

```
SET hive.exec.dynamic.partition.mode = nonstrict;
```

You can set this configuration at a session level using Hive `shell` or at the global level using the Hive configuration file `hive-site.xml`. After setting up these two properties, you can create dynamic partitions.

The syntax is as follows:

```
INSERT OVERWRITE TABLE tablename PARTITION (partcol1[=val1],
partcol2[=val2] ...) select_statement FROM from_statement;


INSERT INTO TABLE tablename PARTITION (partcol1[=val1],
partcol2[=val2] ...) select_statement FROM from_statement;
```

There are some other important configurations used for dynamic partition inserts:

Property	Default Value	Description
`hive.exec.dynamic.partition`	`false`	Needs to be set to `true` to enable dynamic partition inserts.
`hive.exec.dynamic.partition.mode`	`strict`	In the `strict` mode, the user must specify at least one static partition in case the user accidentally overwrites all partitions. In the `nonstrict` mode, all partitions are allowed to be dynamic.
`hive.exec.max.dynamic.partitions.pernode`	100	Maximum number of dynamic partitions allowed to be created in the each `mapper/reducer` node.
`hive.exec.max.dynamic.partitions`	1000	Maximum number of dynamic partitions allowed to be created in total.
`hive.exec.max.created.files`	100000	Maximum number of HDFS files created by all `mappers/reducers` in a MapReduce job.
`hive.error.on.empty.partition`	`false`	Whether to throw an exception if a dynamic partition insert generates empty results.

Partitioning an external table

Partitioning external tables works in the same way as in managed tables. Except this in the external table, when you delete a partition, the data file doesn't get deleted.

How to do it...

First create an EXTERNAL table for the customer data using the following command:

```
CREATE EXTERNAL TABLE customer_external(id STRING, name STRING, gender
STRING, state STRING) PARTITIONED BY (country STRING);
```

Now a partition can be added to the EXTERNAL table, using the ALTER TABLE ADD PARTITION command:

```
ALTER TABLE customer_external ADD PARTITION(country='UK') LOCATION '/
user/hive/warehouse/customer/country=UK'
```

Bucketing

Bucketing is a technique that allows you to decompose your data into more manageable parts, that is, fix the number of buckets. Usually, partitioning provides a way of segregating the data of a Hive table into multiple files or directories. Partitioning is used to increase the performance of queries, but the partitioning technique is efficient only if there is a limited number of partitions. Partitioning doesn't perform well if there is a large number of partitions; for example, we are doing partitioning on a column that has large number of unique values, then there will be a large number of partitions.

To overcome the problem of partitioning, Hive provides the concept of bucketing. In bucketing, we specify the fixed number of buckets in which entire data is to be decomposed. Bucketing concept is based on the hashing principle, where same type of keys are always sent to the same bucket.

In bucketing, records with the same bucketed columns will always go to the same bucket. When data is inserted into a bucketed table, the following formula is used to derive the bucket into which record should be inserted:

```
Bucket number = hash_function(bucketing_column) mod num_buckets
```

The bucket number calculated using the formula depends on bucketing columns. The hash function for integer columns gives the same value, which means hash_int(i) == i. For example, if a bucketing column is of the data type INT and there were 10 buckets, we would expect all records of which bucketing column end in 0 to be in bucket 1, all records of which bucketing column end in 1 to be in bucket 2, and so on. For another data types, the hash function behaves differently. If the bucketing column is of the data type BIGINT, then the value of hash of that column will be different from the actual value. If the bucketing column is of the data type STRING or any other complex data type, then the value of hash of that column will be some number that is derived from the value.

Generally, in bucketing, data is evenly distributed among all buckets based on the hashing principle.

> If bucketing column data type is different during the insert and read operations, then tables may not be populated properly.

Getting ready

In Hive, by default, bucketing is disabled. You will have to set the value of property hive.enforce.bucketing to true for enabling bucketing:

```
set hive.enforce.bucketing=true;
```

The preceding command can be used to enable bucketing for a particular session.

You can also define this property in the Hive configuration file hive-site.xml to enable bucketing permanently.

How to do it...

Once bucketing is enabled, you can create a bucketed table using the following command:

```
CREATE [EXTERNAL] TABLE [db_name.]table_name
    [(col_name data_type [COMMENT col_comment], ...)]
    CLUSTERED BY (col_name data_type [COMMENT col_comment], ...)
INTO N BUCKETS;
```

The preceding command will create a bucketed table based on the columns provided in the CLUSTERED BY clause. The number of buckets will be as specified in the CREATE TABLE statement.

The following is the example of bucketing the sales data of the `sales_bucketed` table:

```
CREATE TABLE sales_bucketed (id INT, fname STRING, lname STRING, address
STRING,city STRING,state STRING, zip STRING, IP STRING, prod_id STRING,
date1 STRING) CLUSTERED BY (id) INTO 10 BUCKETS;
```

You can use the simple `INSERT` statement to insert the data into a bucketed table.

Let's put the data from another table `sales` into our bucketed table `sales_bucketed`:

```
INSERT INTO sales_bucketed SELECT * from sales;
```

You can see the bucketing structure of this table in the HDFS web browser:

How it works...

In this example, we have defined the `id` attribute as a bucketing column and the number of buckets is equal to `10`. As shown in the preceding screenshot, all the data is distributed into `10` buckets based on the hashing of the `id` attribute. Data is evenly distributed between all buckets based on the hashing principle.

Now when a query is executed to fetch a record for a particular `id`, a framework will use the hashing algorithm to identify the bucket number for that record and will return the result. For example:

```
SELECT * FROM sales_bucketed where id = 1000;
```

Rather than scanning the entire table, the preceding command will be executed on a particular bucket, the ID of which is equal to 1000.

In bucketing the following two bullet points need to be considered:

> ▶ In partitioning, a column defined as a partitioned column is not included in a schema columns of a Hive table. But in bucketing, a column defined as a bucketed column is included in the schema columns of the Hive table.

> ▶ We cannot use the LOAD DATA statement to load the data into the bucketed table as we do in partitioned table. Rather, we have to use the INSERT statements to insert data by selecting data from some other table.

4

Hive Data Definition Language

In this chapter, you will learn:

- ▶ Creating a database schema
- ▶ Dropping a database schema
- ▶ Altering a database schema
- ▶ Using a database schema
- ▶ Showing database schemas
- ▶ Describing a database schema
- ▶ Creating tables
- ▶ Dropping tables
- ▶ Truncating tables
- ▶ Renaming tables
- ▶ Altering table properties
- ▶ Creating views
- ▶ Dropping views
- ▶ Altering the view properties
- ▶ Altering the view as select
- ▶ Showing tables
- ▶ Showing partitions
- ▶ Show the table properties
- ▶ Showing create table
- ▶ HCatalog
- ▶ WebHCat

Introduction

For your overall understanding of the Hive language, it is necessary to learn about the **Data Definition Language** (**DDL**) commands for the creation of a database, table, view, and so on. This chapter provides you with a detailed description of all the DDLs with examples. There are two types of DDLs in Hive: database level and table level.

Creating a database schema

In this recipe, you will learn how to create a database in Hive.

Getting ready

The `Create Database` statement is used to create a database in Hive. By default, there is a database in Hive named `default`.

The general format of creating a database is as follows:

```
CREATE (DATABASE|SCHEMA) [IF NOT EXISTS] database_name
  [COMMENT database_comment]
  [LOCATION hdfs_path]
  [WITH DBPROPERTIES (property_name=property_value, ...)];
```

Where:

- `DATABASE|SCHEMA`: These are the same thing. These words can be used interchangeably.

- `[IF NOT EXISTS]`: This is an optional clause. If not used, an error is thrown when there is an attempt to create a database that already exists.

- `[COMMENT]`: This is an optional clause. This is used to place a comment for the database. This comment clause can be used to add a description about the database. The comment must be in single quotes.

- `[LOCATION]`: This is an optional clause. This is used to override the default location with the preferred one.

- `[WITH DBPROPERTIES]`: This is an optional clause. This clause is used to set properties for the database. These properties are key-value pairs that can be associated with the database to attach additional information with the database.

How to do it...

Follow these steps to create a database in Hive:

1. The following statement will create a database called `Hive_learning`:

   ```
   Create database Hive_learning;
   ```

2. The preceding statement creates a database with the name `Hive_learning`. There is no comment or HDFS path used here:

   ```
   Create database if not exists Hive_learning;
   ```

3. If there is an attempt to create a database that is already present in Hive, an error is thrown as follows:

   ```
   FAILED: Execution Error, return code 1 from org.apache.hadoop.
   hive.ql.exec.DDLTask. Database <Database_name > already exists.
   ```

4. To avoid this error, place the `If Not Exists` clause in the statement:

   ```
   Create database if not exists Hive_learning
        Comment 'This is my first DB';
   ```

5. The preceding statement creates the database `Hive_learning` with the comment:

   ```
        Create database if not exists Hive_learning
   Comment 'This is my first DB'
   Location '/my/directory';
   ```

6. Hive creates a `default` directory for each database. All the tables in that database will be stored in the subdirectories under that database directory. The location clause in the `create database` statement is used to override the default location with the preferred one. The location of the database can be seen with the help of the `DESCRIBE` statement, which is discussed later in this chapter:

   ```
        Create database if not exists Hive_learning
   Comment 'This is my first DB'
   Location '/my/directory'
   With dbproperties ('Created by' = 'User',
   'Created on' = '1-Jan-2015');
   ```

7. The preceding statement creates a database with the dbproperties `'Created by'` and `'Created on'`. These two dbproperties are only adding extra information to the database.

Dropping a database schema

In this recipe, you will learn how to drop a database in Hive.

Getting ready

`Drop Database` statements drop the database and the objects inside that database. When a database is dropped, its directory is also deleted. The general format of dropping a database is as follows:

```
DROP (DATABASE|SCHEMA) [IF EXISTS] database_name [RESTRICT|CASCADE];
```

Where:

- ▶ `DATABASE | SCHEMA`: These are the same thing. These words can be used interchangeably.
- ▶ `[IF EXISTS]`: This is an optional clause. If not used, an error is thrown when there is an attempt to drop a database that does not exist.
- ▶ `[RESTRICT|CASCADE]`: This is an optional clause. `RESTRICT` is used to restrict the database from getting dropped if there are one or more tables present in the database. `RESTRICT` is the default behavior of the database. `CASCADE` is used to drop all the tables present in the database before dropping the database.

How to do it...

Follow these steps to drop a database in Hive:

1. The following statement drops the database from Hive. The database needs to be empty (without any object), otherwise an error is thrown:

    ```
    Drop database Hive_learning;
    ```

2. If there is an attempt to drop a database (without the `IF EXISTS` clause) that does not exist, an error is thrown as follows:

    ```
    FAILED: SemanticException [Error 10072]: Database does not exist:
    <database_name>
    ```

3. To avoid the preceding error, place the `If Exists` clause in the statement.

    ```
    Drop database if exists Hive_learning;
    ```

4. If you want to restrict the database from getting dropped if there is one or more tables present in the database, then the `restrict` clause is used:

    ```
    Drop database if exists Hive_learning restrict;
    ```

5. If there is an attempt to drop a database (without the `cascade` clause, which is equivalent to the `restrict` clause) that contains tables, an error is thrown, as follows next:

```
FAILED: Execution Error, return code 1 from org.apache.hadoop.
hive.ql.exec.DDLTask. InvalidOperationException(message:Database
<databasme_name> is not empty. One or more tables exist.)
```

6. To avoid the preceding error, use the `cascade` clause to drop all the tables present in the database before dropping the database:

```
Drop database if exists Hive_learning cascade;
```

Altering a database schema

In this recipe, you will learn how to alter a database in Hive.

Getting ready

The `ALTER DATABASE` command in Hive is used to alter `dbproperties` or set the `dbproperties` of a database. Using the `ALTER DATABASE` command, we can only alter `dbproperties` and nothing else (not even the name and directory location of a database can be altered). No other metadata about the database can be changed. The general format for altering a database is as follows:

```
ALTER (DATABASE|SCHEMA) database_name SET DBPROPERTIES (property_
name=property_value, ...);
```

Where:

DATABASE|SCHEMA: These are the same thing. These words can be used interchangeably:

```
SET DBPROPERTIES (property_name=property_value, ...)
```

This clause is used to set the properties for a database. These properties are key-value pairs that can be associated with the database to attach additional information about the database.

How to do it...

Follow these steps to alter a database in Hive:

The preceding statement alters the `dbproperties` `'Created by'` as well as `'Created on'` of the `Hive_learning` database in Hive:

```
Alter database Hive_learning set dbproperties ('Created by' = 'User1',
'Created on' = '15-Jan-2015');
```

Using a database schema

In this recipe, you will learn how to use a database in Hive.

Getting ready

The `USE DATABASE` command is used to switch to the database, or it sets the database as the working database. It is analogous to the one used in the other RDBMS. The general format of using a database is as follows:

```
USE (DATABASE|SCHEMA) database_name;
```

Where:

`DATABASE | SCHEMA`: These are the same thing. These words can be used interchangeably.

How to do it...

The following command sets the database as the working database:

```
Use database Hive_learning;
```

Showing database schemas

In this recipe, you will learn how to show databases in Hive.

Getting ready

The `SHOW DATABASE` command is used to list all the databases in the Hive metastore. The general format of using the `SHOW DATABASE` command is as follows:

```
SHOW (DATABASES|SCHEMAS) [LIKE identifier_with_wildcards];
```

Where:

▶ `DATABASE | SCHEMA`: These are the same thing. These words can be used interchangeably.

▶ `[LIKE]`: Is an optional clause. This clause is used to filter the databases with the help of a regular expression. There can only be two wildcards in the regular expression, which are * for any character(s) or | for a choice.

How to do it...

Follow these steps to show a database in Hive:

- ▶ The following command lists all the databases in Hive:

  `Show databases;`

- ▶ This command lists the `Hive_learning` database, which is used in our previous examples:

  `Show database like 'Hive*';`

Describing a database schema

In this recipe, you will learn how to describe databases in Hive.

Getting ready

The `DESCRIBE DATABASE` command is used to get information about the database, such as the name of the database, its comment (if attached during the creation of the database), its location on the filesystem, and its `dbproperties`. The general format of using the `DESCRIBE DATABASE` command is as follows:

`DESCRIBE DATABASE [EXTENDED] db_name;`

`DESCRIBE SCHEMA [EXTENDED] db_name;`

Where:

- ▶ `DATABASE | SCHEMA`: These are the same thing. These words can be used interchangeably.
- ▶ `[EXTENDED]`: This is an optional clause. This clause will list all the `dbproperties` attached to a particular database in Hive.

How to do it...

Follow these steps to describe a database in Hive:

- ▶ The following example lists the name of the database, the comment on the database, and the directory location on the filesystem:

  `Describe database Hive_learning;`

- ▶ The following example gives the same result as previous one:

  `Describe schema Hive_learning;`

▶ This example shows extra information (dbproperties) that is attached to the database:

```
Describe database extended Hive_learning;
```

Creating tables

In this recipe, you will learn how to create tables in Hive.

How to do it...

The CREATE TABLE statement creates metadata in the database. The table in Hive is the way to read data from files present in HDFS in the table or a structural format. The general format of using the CREATE TABLE command is as follows:

```
CREATE [TEMPORARY] [EXTERNAL] TABLE [IF NOT EXISTS]
    [db_name.] table_name
    [(col_name data_type [COMMENT col_comment], ...)]
    [COMMENT table_comment]
    [PARTITIONED BY (col_name data_type
    [COMMENT col_comment], ...)]
    [CLUSTERED BY (col_name, col_name, ...) [SORTED BY
    (col_name [ASC|DESC], ...)] INTO num_buckets BUCKETS]
    [SKEWED BY (col_name, col_name, ...)
    ON ((col_value, col_value, ...),
    (col_value, col_value, ...), ...)
    [STORED AS DIRECTORIES]
    [
    [ROW FORMAT row_format]
    [STORED AS file_format]
    | STORED BY 'storage.handler.class.name'
    [WITH SERDEPROPERTIES (...)]
    ]
    [LOCATION hdfs_path]
    [TBLPROPERTIES (property_name=property_value, ...)]
    [AS select_statement];
```

Create table LIKE

The LIKE clause in a create table command creates a copy of an existing table with a different name and without the data. It just creates a structure like that of an existing table without copying its data.

How it works

Let us take a look at all the parameters involved:

- [TEMPORARY]: This is an optional clause. This clause is used to create temporary tables. These tables once created are only present in the database until the session is active. Once the session comes to an end, all the temporary tables are deleted. Once a temporary table is created, you cannot access the permanent table in that session so you need to either drop or rename the temporary table to access the original one. You cannot create a partition or index on temporary tables.

- [EXTERNAL]: This is an optional clause. This clause is used to create external tables the same as in the case of RDBMS. The external table works as a window for the data present in the file format in HDFS. For an external table, the data or file need not be present in the default location but can be kept anywhere in the filesystem and can be referred to from that location. Once the external table is dropped, data is not lost from that location.

- [IF NOT EXISTS]: This is an optional clause. If there is an attempt to create a table that is already present in the database, an error is thrown. To avoid such an error, the IF NOT EXISTS clause is used. When this clause is used, Hive ignores the statement if the table already exists.

- [db_name]: This is an optional clause. This clause is used to create tables in the specified database.

- [COMMENT col_comment]: This is an optional clause. This is used to attach comments to a particular column. This comment clause can be used to add a description about the column. The comment must be in single quotes.

- [COMMENT table_comment]: This is an optional clause. This is used to attach comments to a table. This comment clause can be used to add a description about the table. The comment must be in single quotes.

- [PARTITIONED BY]: This is an optional clause. This clause is used to create partitioned tables. There can be more than one partition columns in a table. Partitions in Hive work in the same way as in any RDBMS. They speed up the query performance by keeping the data in specific partitions.

- [CLUSTERED BY]: This is an optional clause. This clause is used for bucketing purposes. The table or partitions can be bucketed using CLUSTERED BY columns. The CLUSTERED BY creation command doesn't have any impact on how data is inserted into a table; it impacts only during read operations. Users must be careful to insert data correctly by specifying the number of reducers to be equal to the number of buckets, and using CLUSTER BY and SORT BY commands in their query.

- ▶ [SKEWED BY]: This option is used to improve performance for tables where one or more columns have skewed values. Tables created with this option are known as skewed tables. When this option is specified, the values that appear very often (heavy skew) are split into separate files and the rest of the values go to some other file.

- ▶ [LOCATION hdfs_path]: This option is used while creating external tables. This is the location where files are placed, which is referred to by the external table for the data.

- ▶ [TBLPROPERTIES]: This is an optional clause. This clause allows you to attach more information about the table in the form of a key-value pair.

- ▶ [AS select_statement]: **Create Table As Select**, popularly known as **CTAS**, is used to create a table based on the output of the other table or existing table.

Dropping tables

In this recipe, you will learn how to drop a table in Hive.

Getting ready

DROP TABLE command removes the table from the database, including the data from the table. This is equivalent to the SQL DROP command, but the only difference is that the data is moved to the Trash folder in the home directory (if Trash is configured). If Trash is not configured, data is removed from the filesystem as well and is lost forever.

> In the case of an external table, data remains in the filesystem even if the table is dropped from the database.

The general format of using the DROP TABLE command is as follows:

```
DROP TABLE [IF EXISTS] table_name [PURGE];
```

Where:

- ▶ [IF EXISTS]: Is an optional clause. If not used, an error is thrown when there is an attempt to drop a table that does not exist in the database.

- ▶ [PURGE]: Is an optional clause. If specified, the data is not saved in the Trash folder under the home directory and is lost forever.

How to do it...

Follow these steps to drop a table in Hive:

- ▶ The following command drops the table `Hive_Test_Table1` from the database and the data is saved into the `Trash` folder:

  Drop table if exists Hive_Test_table1;

- ▶ The following command drops the table `Hive_Test_Table1` from the database and the data is not saved into the `Trash` folder; that is, the data is lost forever:

  Drop table if exists Hive_Test_table1 purge;

Truncating tables

In this recipe, you will learn how to truncate a table in Hive.

Getting ready

The `TRUNCATE` command removes all rows from the table as well as from the partition, but keeps the table structure as it is. Truncating a table in Hive is indirectly removing the files from the HDFS as a table in Hive is just a way of reading the data from the HDFS in the table or structural format. The general format of using the Truncate table command is as follows:

`TRUNCATE TABLE table_name [PARTITION partition_spec];`

Where:

`partition_spec:`

`(partition_column = partition_col_value, partition_column = partition_col_value, ...)`

How to do it...

Follow these steps to truncate a table in Hive:

The preceding command truncates the table named `Sales`:

Truncate table Sales;

Renaming tables

In this recipe, you will learn how to rename a table in Hive.

Getting ready

The renaming command renames the old table name with a new table name. The general format of using the RENAME table command is as follows:

```
ALTER TABLE table_name RENAME TO new_table_name;
```

How to do it...

Use this command to rename a table in Hive:

```
Alter Table Hive_Test_table1 RENAME TO Hive_Test_table;
```

Altering table properties

In this recipe, you will learn how to alter table properties in Hive.

Getting ready

The ALTER TABLE properties command alters the table properties. The general format of using the ALTER TABLE command is as follows:

```
ALTER TABLE table_name SET TBLPROPERTIES table_properties;
```

How to do it...

Follow these steps to alter a table in Hive. The following statement changes the old comment to a new one:

```
Alter Table Hive_Test_table SET TBLPROPERTIES ('comment' = 'This is a new comment');
```

Creating views

In this recipe, you will learn how to create a `view` in Hive.

Getting ready

A `view` is a virtual table that acts as a window to the data for the underlying table commonly known as the `base` table. It consists of rows and columns but no physical data. So when a `view` is accessed, the underlying `base` table is queried for the output.

 A `base` table can also be a `view` that will have a `base` table of its own. So if the first `view` is accessed, then the `base` table of the second `view` gives the output for the query.

The general syntax of creating a `view` is as follows:

```
CREATE VIEW [IF NOT EXISTS] view_name [(column_name [COMMENT column_
comment], ...)]
    [COMMENT view_comment]
    [TBLPROPERTIES (property_name = property_value, ...)]
    AS SELECT ...;
```

Where:

- ► `[IF NOT EXISTS]`: Is an optional clause. If there is an attempt to create a `view` that is already present in the database, then an error is thrown. In such cases, the `IF NOT EXISTS` clause is used, which will ignore the entire statement and no error is thrown.

- ► `[COMMENT col_comment]`: Is an optional clause. This is used to attach comments to a particular column. This comment clause can be used to add a description about the column. The comment must be in single quotes.

- ► `[COMMENT table_comment]`: Is an optional clause. This is used to attach comments to a `view`. This comment clause can be used to add a description about the `view`. The comment must be in single quotes.

- ► `[TBLPROPERTIES (property_name = property_value, ...)]`: Is an optional clause. This clause allows you to attach more information about the table in the form of a key-value pair.

How to do it...

Follow these steps to create a view in Hive:

▶ The following command creates a view named `Hive_view` in the database. The use of the * symbol indicates that all the columns from the table are present in the view:

```
Create view Hive_view
As select * from Hive_learning;
```

▶ The following command creates a view with only two columns (`id` and `firstname`). Also, you can specify the ORDER BY as well as the LIMIT clause while creating a view:

```
Create view if not exists Hive_view_2
As select id, firstname from Hive_learningWhere firstname =
'John';
```

Dropping views

In this recipe, you will learn how to drop a view in Hive.

Getting ready

The DROP VIEW command removes the view from the database. It removes the metadata, but the base table remains intact. If a base table is a view that is dropped, then the dependent view remains in an invalid state, which is either dropped or recreated. The general syntax for dropping a view is as follows:

```
DROP VIEW [IF EXISTS] view_name;
```

Where:

[IF EXISTS]: Is an optional clause. If there is an attempt to drop a view that does not exist, an error is thrown. To prevent this error, the IF EXISTS clause is specified.

How to do it...

The following statement drops a `view` in Hive:

```
Drop view Hive_view;
```

Altering the view properties

In this recipe, you will learn how to alter the view properties in Hive.

Getting ready

This command is used to alter the view properties, the same as in the case of tables. The general syntax for altering a view is as follows:

```
ALTER VIEW view_name SET TBLPROPERTIES table_properties;
```

Where:

`table_properties` is defined as : `(property_name = property_value, property_name = property_value, ...)`

How to do it...

Follow these steps to alter the view properties in Hive. The following statement changes the old comment to a new one:

```
Alter View Hive_view SET TBLPROPERTIES ('comment' = 'This is a new comment');
```

Altering the view as select

In this recipe, you will learn how to alter the view as select in Hive.

Getting ready

This command is used to change the `SELECT` query for the view. The general syntax for altering a view is as follows:

```
ALTER VIEW view_name AS select_statement;
```

Where:

`select_statement`: This is the new `SELECT` statement for the existing view.

How to do it...

Follow these steps to alter the view as select in Hive. The following SELECT statement is the new statement for the existing view, `Hive_view`:

```
alter view hive_view as select id, firstname from sales;
```

Showing tables

In this recipe, you will learn how to list tables in Hive.

Getting ready

This command lists all the tables and views in a database. We can also use wildcards for listing specific tables. The general syntax for showing tables is as follows:

```
SHOW TABLES [IN database_name] ['identifier_with_wildcards'];
```

Where:

- ▶ `[IN database_name]`: Is an optional clause. This clause is used to list all the tables and views from a different database that is currently not in use.
- ▶ `['identifier_with_wildcards']`: Is an optional clause. There can only be two wildcards used in this command: * for any character(s) or | for a choice.

How to do it...

Use the following commands to show a table in Hive:

- ▶ The following command will list all the tables and views present in the current database:

  ```
  Show tables;
  ```

- ▶ The following command will list all the tables and views from the `Hive_learning` database:

  ```
  Show tables in Hive_learning;
  ```

- ▶ The following command will list all the tables and views starting with `Hive`:

  ```
  Show tables 'Hive*';
  ```

Showing partitions

In this recipe, you will learn how to list all the partitions in Hive.

Getting ready

This command lists all the partitions for a table. The general syntax for showing partitions is as follows:

```
SHOW PARTITIONS [db_name.]table_name [PARTITION(partition_spec)];
```

Where:

▶ [db_name.]: Is an optional clause. This is used to list partitions of the table from a given database.

▶ [PARTITION(partition_spec)]: Is an optional clause. This is used to list a specific partition of a table.

How to do it...

Use the following commands to show partitions in Hive:

▶ The following command will list all the partitions present in the Sales table:

```
Show partitions Sales;
```

▶ The following command will list a specific partition of the Sales table:

```
Show partitions Sales partition(dop='2015-01-01');
```

▶ The following command will list a specific partition of the Sales table from the Hive_learning database:

```
Show partitions Hive_learning. Sales partition(dop='2015-01-01');
```

Show the table properties

In this recipe, you will learn how to list all the properties of a table in Hive.

Getting ready

This command lists the properties of a table. The general syntax for showing table properties is as follows:

```
SHOW TBLPROPERTIES tblname;
```

How to do it...

Use these commands to show table properties in Hive:

- ► This command will list all the properties for the `Sales` table:

  ```
  Show tblproperties Sales;
  ```

- ► The preceding command will list only the property for `numFiles` in the `Sales` table:

  ```
  Show partitions Sales ('numFiles');
  ```

Showing create table

In this recipe, you will learn how to see the create statement of a table in Hive.

Getting ready

This command shows the `CREATE TABLE` statement of a table. The general syntax for showing the `CREATE TABLE` statement is as follows:

```
SHOW CREATE TABLE ([db_name.]table_name|view_name);
```

Where:

`[db_name.]`: Is an optional clause. This is used when you want to see the `CREATE TABLE` statement of a table from a different database.

How to do it...

Use the following commands to show `CREATE TABLE` in Hive:

- ► This command will show the `CREATE TABLE` statement for the `Sales` table:

  ```
  Show create table Sales;
  ```

- ► This command will show the `CREATE TABLE` statement for the `Sales` table under the `Hive_learning` database:

  ```
  Show create table Hive_learning.Sales;
  ```

HCatalog

In this recipe, you will learn how you can define tables in HCatalog.

Getting ready

HCatalog is a storage management tool that enables frameworks other than Hive to leverage a data model to read and write data. HCatalog tables provide an abstraction on the data format in HDFS and allow frameworks such as `PIG` and `MapReduce` to use the data without being concerned about the data format, such as `RC`, `ORC`, and text files.

`HCatInputFormat` and `HCatOutputFormat`, which are the implementations of Hadoop `InputFormat` and `OutputFormat`, are the interfaces provided to `PIG` and `MapReduce`.

How to do it...

Data is defined using the HCatalog CLI. Data is modeled as tables and tables are stored in databases. The table could be partitioned based on keys.

HCatalog DMLs

The following are the metrics of DMLs supported by HCatalog:

Command	Support	Description
CREATE TABLE	Yes	Same as Hive, but if created with the CLUSTERED BY clause then write to table with PIG and MapReduce is not available
DROP TABLE	Yes	Same as Hive
ALTER TABLE	Yes	Same as Hive, except REBUILD and CONCATENATE options
CREATE VIEW	Yes	Same as Hive
DROP VIEW	Yes	Same as Hive
ALTER VIEW	Yes	Same as Hive
SHOW TABLES	Yes	Same as Hive
SHOW PARTITIONS	No	
SHOW FUNCTIONS	Yes	Same as Hive
DESCRIBE	Yes	Same as Hive
Create Index	Yes	Same as Hive
Drop Index	Yes	Same as Hive

Command	Support	Description
Create Function	Yes	Same as Hive
Drop Function	Yes	Same as Hive
"dfs" Command	Yes	Same as Hive
"set" Command	Yes	Same as Hive

WebHCat

In this recipe, you will learn how you can define tables using WebHCat APIs.

Getting ready

WebHCat, formerly called **Templeton**, allows access to the HCatalog service using REST APIs. Unlike HCatalog, which executed the command directly, WebHCat keeps the Hive, PIG, and MapReduce jobs in queues. The jobs can then be monitored and stopped as needed. The client needs to specify a HDFS location where the output of the job is stored.

How to do it...

HCatlog resources can be accessed by REST APIs using the following URI format:

http://www.myserver.com/templeton/v1/resource.

In the preceding URL, www.myserver.com is the URL where your WebHCat is running and the resource is the HCatalog resource name.

The following is a CURL command to get all databases in Hive:

```
curl -s 'http://localhost:50111/templeton/v1/ddl/database?user.
name=shrey'
```

See also...

Refer to the following URL for more information on WebHCat APIs:

https://cwiki.apache.org/confluence/display/Hive/WebHCat+Reference.

5
Hive Data Manipulation Language

In this chapter, you will learn about the following recipes:

- ▶ Loading files into tables
- ▶ Inserting data into Hive tables from queries
- ▶ Inserting data into dynamic partitions
- ▶ Writing data into files from queries
- ▶ Enabling transactions in Hive
- ▶ Inserting values into tables from SQL
- ▶ Updating data
- ▶ Deleting data

Introduction

As we finished with the **Data Definition Language** in *Chapter 4*, *Hive Data Definition Language*, let's discuss the **Data Manipulation Language** (commonly known as **DML**) commands in Hive. This chapter gives a detailed description of DML in Hive with examples.

Loading files into tables

Loading data into a Hive table is one of the variants of inserting data into a Hive table. In this method, the entire file is copied/moved to a directory that corresponds to Hive tables. If the table is partitioned, then data is loaded into partitions one at a time. The general syntax of loading the data into a table is as follows:

```
LOAD DATA [LOCAL] INPATH 'filepath' [OVERWRITE] INTO TABLE tablename
[PARTITION (partcol1=val1, partcol2=val2 ...)]
```

Where:

- ▶ [LOCAL]: This is an optional clause. If this clause is specified, the preceding command will look for the file in the local filesystem. The command will follow the file path in the local filesystem.

- ▶ FILEPATH: This is the path where files reside either in the local filesystem or HDFS.

- ▶ [OVERWRITE]: Is an optional clause. If this clause is specified, the data in the table or partition is deleted and new data is loaded based on the file path in the statement.

- ▶ tablename: This is the name of the table.

- ▶ [PARTITION (partcol1=val1, partcol2=val2 ...)]: This is an optional clause for partitioned tables.

Getting ready

This recipe requires having Hive installed, as described in the *Installing Hive* recipe of *Chapter 1*, *Developing Hive*. You will also need the Hive CLI or Beeline client to run the commands.

How to do it...

Follow these steps to insert data into a table in Hive:

```
LOAD DATA LOCAL INPATH '/tmp/sales.txt' INTO TABLE sales;

LOAD DATA INPATH '/sales.txt' INTO TABLE sales;

LOAD DATA INPATH ' /sales.txt' OVERWRITE INTO TABLE sales;
```

How it works...

The LOAD DATA command is used to load data from files to Hive tables. Files may reside either in the local filesystem or the **Hadoop Distributed File System** (**HDFS**) that you can specify in a command using the LOCAL keyword. You can use the PARTITION clause if the table is partitioned and data needs to be inserted in the partitioned table based on a partitioned key one at a time.

For this, we have truncated the sales table, the output of which is shown next:

```
hive> select * from sales;
OK
Time taken: 0.146 seconds
```

The first command listed in the previous section, LOAD DATA LOCAL INPATH '/tmp/sales.txt' INTO TABLE sales;, loads the data from the sales.txt file into the sales table in Hive. Since the LOCAL keyword is specified here, the file will be picked from the local filesystem. The files will be copied from the local filesystem to the Hive warehouse or Hive filesystem:

```
hive> LOAD DATA LOCAL INPATH '/tmp/sales.txt' INTO TABLE sales;
Loading data to table default.sales
Table default.sales stats: [numFiles=1, numRows=0, totalSize=1014721, rawDataSize=0]
OK
Time taken: 0.805 seconds
```

Now, once the first statement is executed, the data is loaded into the sales table as shown in the following figure:

```
hive> select count(*) from sales;
OK
10000
Time taken: 19.353 seconds, Fetched: 1 row(s)
```

For the second statement, we have truncated the sales table, the output of which is shown next:

```
hive> select * from sales;
OK
Time taken: 0.146 seconds
```

The second command, `LOAD DATA INPATH '/sales.txt' INTO TABLE sales;`, loads the data from the `sales.txt` file into the `sales` table in Hive. Since the `LOCAL` keyword is omitted here, the file will be picked from the HDFS. The files will be moved from the HDFS to the Hive warehouse or Hive filesystem:

```
hive> LOAD DATA INPATH '/sales.txt' INTO TABLE sales;
Loading data to table default.sales
Table default.sales stats: [numFiles=1, numRows=0, totalSize=1014721, rawDataSize=0]
OK
Time taken: 1.682 seconds
```

Now, once the first statement is executed, the data is loaded into the `sales` table as shown in the following figure:

```
hive> select count(*) from sales;
OK
10000
Time taken: 19.353 seconds, Fetched: 1 row(s)
```

The third statement, `LOAD DATA INPATH '/sales.txt' OVERWRITE INTO TABLE sales;`, will overwrite the data present in the `sales` table. If there is data present in the table, then first the data will be deleted and new data will be inserted as per the file path. If data is not present in the table, then data will be inserted like a normal insert statement:

```
hive> LOAD DATA INPATH '/sales.txt' OVERWRITE INTO TABLE sales ;
Loading data to table default.sales
Table default.sales stats: [numFiles=1, numRows=0, totalSize=1014721, rawDataSize=0]
OK
Time taken: 1.29 seconds
```

Now, once the first statement is executed, the data is loaded into the `sales` table as shown in the following figure:

```
hive> select count(*) from sales;
OK
10000
Time taken: 22.67 seconds, Fetched: 1 row(s)
```

Inserting data into Hive tables from queries

In this recipe, you will learn how to insert data through queries into a table in Hive.

This is another variant of inserting data into a Hive table. Data can be appended into a Hive table that already contains data. Data can also be overwritten in the Hive table. Data can also be inserted into multiple tables through a single statement only. The general format of inserting data into a table from queries is as follows:

```
INSERT OVERWRITE TABLE tablename [PARTITION (partcol1=val1, partcol2=val2
...) [IF NOT EXISTS]] select select_statement FROM from_statement;
```

Where:

- `tablename`: This is the name of the table
- `OVERWRITE`: This is used to overwrite existing data in the table
- `[PARTITION (partcol1=val1]`: This option is used when data needs to be inserted into a partitioned table
- `[IF NOT EXISTS]`: This is an optional clause

The second syntax of inserting the data into a Hive table is as follows:

```
INSERT INTO TABLE tablename [PARTITION (partcol1=val1, partcol2=val2
...)] select select_statement FROM from_statement;
```

Where:

- `tablename`: This is the name of the table.
- `INTO`: This is used to insert data into the Hive table. If the data is already present, new data will be appended.
- `[PARTITION (partcol1=val1]`: This option is used when data needs to be inserted into a partitioned table.

The third syntax of inserting the data into a Hive table is as follows:

```
FROM from_statement
INSERT OVERWRITE TABLE tablename1 [PARTITION (partcol1=val1,
partcol2=val2 ...) [IF NOT EXISTS]] select select_statement1
[INSERT OVERWRITE TABLE tablename2 [PARTITION ... [IF NOT EXISTS]] select
select_statement2]
[INSERT INTO TABLE tablename2 [PARTITION ...] select select_statement2]
...;
```

In the preceding statement, only the first `INSERT OVERWRITE` statement is mandatory and the rest are optional. The first statement overwrites the data present in the table or partition. If there is another statement that inserts data into the same table, then the data will be appended into the table:

```
FROM from_statement
INSERT INTO TABLE tablename1 [PARTITION (partcol1=val1, partcol2=val2
...)] select select_statement1
[INSERT INTO TABLE tablename2 [PARTITION ...] select select_statement2]
[INSERT OVERWRITE TABLE tablename2 [PARTITION ... [IF NOT EXISTS]] select
select_statement2] ...;
```

In the preceding statement, only the first `INSERT INTO` statement is mandatory and the rest are optional. The first statement overwrites the data present in the table or partition. If there is another statement that overwrites data from the same table, then the data will be overwritten from the table.

Getting ready

This recipe requires the `sales_rgn` table to be created first before proceeding with data insertion into the `sales` table.

How to do it...

Follow these steps to insert data into tables in Hive:

```
INSERT INTO sales SELECT * FROM sales_rgn;
INSERT INTO sales SELECT * FROM sales_rgn WHERE state = 'Maryland';
INSERT OVERWRITE TABLE sales SELECT * FROM sales_rgn;
INSERT OVERWRITE TABLE sales SELECT * FROM sales_rgn WHERE id = 1;
```

How it works...

The `INSERT INTO` statement is used to append the data into a Hive table or partition. It keeps the existing data as it is and adds new data into one or more new data files. The `INSERT OVERWRITE` statement is used to overwrite existing data with the new data source.

The initial count of the `sales` tables is 2 as shown next:

```
hive> select count(*) from sales;
OK
2
Time taken: 20.086 seconds, Fetched: 1 row(s)
```

The total values present in `sales_rgn` is `5000` as shown next:

```
hive> select count(*) from sales_rgn;
OK
5000
Time taken: 20.086 seconds, Fetched: 1 row(s)
```

The preceding first command listed, `INSERT INTO sales SELECT * FROM sales_rgn;`, inserts the data into the `sales` table from `sales_rgn`. It will append the entire data of the `sales_rgn` table to the `sales` table:

```
hive> select count(*) from sales;
OK
5002
Time taken: 19.925 seconds, Fetched: 1 row(s)
```

The second statement, `INSERT INTO sales SELECT * FROM sales_rgn WHERE state = 'Maryland';`, is the same as the first statement. The only difference is that an extra `WHERE` clause is inserted into the statement showing that we can also insert filtered records into the table:

```
hive> select count(*) from sales;
OK
103
Time taken: 19.703 seconds, Fetched: 1 row(s)
```

The third statement, `INSERT OVERWRITE TABLE sales SELECT * FROM sales_rgn;`, overwrites the existing data into the `sales` table from the data present in `sales_rgn`. Once the statement is executed, the total count is `5000`, as shown in the following screenshot:

```
hive> select count(*) from sales;
OK
5000
Time taken: 21.019 seconds, Fetched: 1 row(s)
```

The fourth statement, `INSERT OVERWRITE TABLE sales SELECT * FROM sales_rgn WHERE id = 1;`, will overwrite the data present in the `sales` table with the filtered data as the output of the `WHERE` clause of the `SELECT` statement. If there is only one record found after the `WHERE` clause, then the `sales` table will have only one record after the execution of the statement:

```
hive> select count(*) from sales;
OK
1
Time taken: 21.019 seconds, Fetched: 1 row(s)
```

Inserting data into dynamic partitions

Until now, we have learned how to insert data into partitions in a table one at a time. For that, it was important for us to know in which partition we need to insert data. Further, only one partition can be inserted using one `INSERT` statement. Now, we will learn how to insert data into multiple partitions through a single statement. The general syntax of inserting data into multiple partitions is as follows:

```
FROM tablename
INSERT OVERWRITE TABLE tablename1 PARTITION(root_partition_
name='value',child_partition_name)
SELECT select_statment;
```

Where:

- ▸ `tablename`: This is the name of the table from which the value is to be taken by the select statement
- ▸ `tablename1`: This is the name of the table in which the data will be inserted
- ▸ `root_partition_name`: This is the static partition column
- ▸ `child_partition_name`: This is the dynamic partition column

Getting ready

This recipe requires having Hive installed as described in the *Installing Hive* recipe of *Chapter 1, Developing Hive*. You will also need the Hive CLI or Beeline client to run the commands.

Dynamic partitioning is disabled by default. The minimum configuration to enable dynamic partitioning is as follows:

```
SET hive.exec.dynamic.partition = true;
SET hive.exec.dynamic.partition.mode = nonstrict;
```

You can set this configuration at the session level using the Hive shell or at the global level using the Hive configuration file `/opt/hive-1.1.0/conf/hive-site.xml`. After setting up these two properties, you can create dynamic partitions.

How to do it...

Execute the following command for dynamic partitioning of the `sales` table:

```
FROM sales_region slr
INSERT OVERWRITE TABLE sales PARTITION(dop='2015-10-20', city) SELECT
slr.id, slr.firstname, slr.lastname, slr.city;
```

How it works...

The preceding statement will insert/overwrite data into the `sales` table from `sales_region`. Here, `dop` is the root partition and `city` is the child partition. The child partition has to be the last column in the `PARTITION` clause to maintain the hierarchical order. Also, the `city` column is added to the `SELECT` statement as the last column. There can be more than one dynamic partition column in the `PARTITION` clause, but the same order has to be maintained in the `SELECT` statement as well. If the dynamic partition column is not supplied in the `SELECT` statement, the value is picked from the column that is present as the last column. That means if the names do not match, then the value will be picked from the last column/s in the `SELECT` clause, indicating that values are, not picked on the basis of the column names but the values.

There is no need to specify the static partition column in the table as its value is already specified in the `PARTITION` clause.

The value of a static partition must always be provided in the `PARTITION` clause. In the preceding example, we cannot specify (`dop, city = 'UK'`).

There's more...

Apart from the basic configuration of dynamic inserts, there are some other parameters that can be tuned:

Configuration property	Default
hive.error.on.empty.partition	false
hive.exec.dynamic.partition	false
hive.exec.dynamic.partition.mode	strict
hive.exec.max.created.files	100000
hive.exec.max.dynamic.partitions	1000
hive.exec.max.dynamic.partitions.pernode	100

The following are the configuration properties:

▶ `hive.exec.max.dynamic.partitions.pernode` (default value = 100): This property tells us the maximum number of dynamic partitions that can be created per node by a mapper or reducer, beyond which an error will be thrown.

▶ `hive.exec.max.dynamic.partitions` (default value = 1000): This property corresponds to the maximum number of partitions that can be created irrespective of the maximum number of dynamic partitions per node does not exceed the limit mentioned in the preceding property.

- `hive.exec.max.created.files` (default value = 100000): This property tells us what will be the maximum number of files that will be created including all the nodes.
- `hive.exec.dynamic.partition`: This property must be set to `true` for a dynamic partitions insert. The default value is `false`.
- `hive.exec.dynamic.partition.mode`: This property by default is `strict`, which means that there has to be at least one static partition.

Writing data into files from queries

In this recipe, you will learn how to write data into a file from a query in Hive.

This part helps you insert data into a file with the help of a query; that is, the output of a query to be saved into a file. The general format of inserting data into a file is as follows:

Standard syntax:

```
INSERT OVERWRITE [LOCAL] DIRECTORY directory1 [ROW FORMAT row_format]
[STORED AS file_format]SELECT select_statment FROM from_statment.
```

Hive extension (multiple inserts):

```
FROM from_statement

INSERT OVERWRITE [LOCAL] DIRECTORY directory1 select_statement1

[INSERT OVERWRITE [LOCAL] DIRECTORY directory2 select_statement2] ...
```

Where:

- `[LOCAL]`: Is an optional clause. If this clause is specified, the preceding command will look for the file in the local filesystem. The command will follow the file path in the local filesystem.
- `[ROW FORMAT row_format]`: Is an optional clause. With the help of this, we can specify the row format; that is, the delimiters or the fields terminated by any character.
- `[STORED AS file_format]`: Is an optional clause. With the help of this clause, we can specify the file format in which we want to save the data.
- `Select_statment`: This is the column in the clause will be inserted into the file.
- `from_statment`: This part contains the table name along with the filter condition, if any.

Getting ready

This recipe requires the `sales` directory to be present in the local filesystem.

How to do it...

Use these commands to insert data into a file in Hive:

```
INSERT OVERWRITE LOCAL DIRECTORY '/sales'
SELECT sle.id, sle.fname, sle.lname, sle.address
FROM sales sle;
```

The preceding statement will load data in the specified directory in the local filesystem.

Enabling transactions in Hive

In this recipe, you will learn how to configure the Hive metastore to enable **Atomicity, Consistency, Isolation, Durability** (**ACID**) properties for a Hive table. Insert, Update and Delete are not possible in Hive until the ACID properties are not enabled. Also table must to be Bucketed in Hive if Insert, Update and Delete feature are to be used.

Transactions including inserts, updates, and deletes are available from Hive 1.0.0 and above.

Getting ready

To allow the user to execute transactional commands, the user needs to configure the metastore with transactional tables. The user needs to set the following properties in `hive-site.xml`:

```
<configuration>
    <property>
        <name>javax.jdo.option.ConnectionURL</name>
        <value>jdbc:mysql://localhost:3306/hivedb</value>
        <description>metadata is stored in a MySQL server</
description>
    </property>
    <property>
        <name>javax.jdo.option.ConnectionDriverName</name>
        <value>com.mysql.jdbc.Driver</value>
        <description>MySQL JDBC driver class</description>
    </property>
    <property>
```

```
        <name>javax.jdo.option.ConnectionUserName</name>
        <value>root</value>
        <description>user name for connecting to mysql server</
description>
    </property>
    <property>
        <name>javax.jdo.option.ConnectionPassword</name>
        <value>root</value>
        <description>password for connecting to mysql server</
description>
    </property>
 <property>
        <name>hive.support.concurrency</name>
        <value>true</value>
    </property>
 <property>
        <name>hive.enforce.bucketing</name>
        <value>true</value>
    </property>
 <property>
        <name>hive.exec.dynamic.partition.mode</name>
        <value>nonstrict</value>
    </property>
 <property>
        <name>hive.txn.manager</name>
        <value>org.apache.hadoop.hive.ql.lockmgr.DbTxnManager</
value>
    </property>
 <property>
        <name>hive.compactor.initiator.on</name>
        <value>true</value>
    </property>
 <property>
        <name>hive.compactor.worker.threads</name>
        <value>1</value>
    </property>
</configuration>
```

How to do it...

Once the properties are configured in `hive-site.xml`, the user needs to run the following command to create metastore tables in RDBMS:

```
$HIVE_HOME/bin/schematool -dbType mysql -initSchema
```

This command will create the transactional tables in the `hivedb` metastore, along with other schema tables.

 Create an empty database, `hivedb`, in RDMS before executing this command.

`Change-dbType` with the name of your RDBMS metastore.

Inserting values into tables from SQL

In this recipe, you will learn how to insert data from SQL into a table in Hive.

Inserting data into a Hive table through a SQL statement is the third variant of inserting data. This is the traditional way of inserting data into a table in any RDBMS. Inserting in a table through SQL statements can only be performed if the table supports ACID. The general format of inserting data into a table is as follows:

```
INSERT INTO TABLE table_name [PARTITION (partcol1[=val1], partcol2[=val2]
...)] VALUES values_row [, values_row ...]
```

Where:

- `tablename`: This is the name of the table
- `values_row`: This is the value that is to be inserted into the table

Getting ready

This recipe requires having Hive installed as described in the *Installing Hive* recipe of *Chapter 1, Developing Hive*. You will also need the Hive CLI or Beeline client to run the commands.

This recipe requires transactions to be enabled, so refer to *Enabling transactions in Hive* for that (`https://cwiki.apache.org/confluence/display/Hive/Hive+Transactions`).

How to do it...

Follow these steps to insert data into a table in Hive:

```
INSERT INTO sales VALUES (1, 'John', 'Terry', 'H-43 Sector-23', 'Delhi',
'India', '10.10.10.10', 'P_1', '15-11-1985');
```

```
INSERT INTO sales VALUES (2, 'Terry', 'John', 'H-43 Sector-23', 'Delhi',
'India', '10.10.10.10', '', '');
```

```
INSERT INTO sales VALUES (2, 'Terry', 'John', 'H-43 Sector-23', 'Delhi',
'India', '10.10.10.10');
```

```
Create table employees (name string, age int, job string) clustered by
(age) into 2 buckets stored as orc;
```

```
Insert into employees values ('John', 30, 'IT'), ('Jerry', 35, 'Sales');
```

```
Create table department (name string, age int, deptno int) Partitioned by
(datestamp string;
```

```
INSERT INTO department PARTITION (datestamp = '2015-10-23') VALUES
('Jason', 20, 10), ('Nelson', 30, 20);
```

How it works...

The first statement in the preceding section shows us how to insert a row inside the table named `sales`. Once the command is run, we can verify the data by running the following command:

```
SELECT * FROM sales WHERE id = 1;
```

The output of the preceding SELECT statement is shown in the following figure:

```
hive> select * from sales where id = 1;
OK

1       John    Terry   H-43 Sector-23  Delhi   India   10.10.10.10     P_1     15-11-1985
Time taken: 0.268 seconds, Fetched: 2 row(s)
```

The second statement inserts the values into the table named `sales`, but only seven out of nine columns consists of values. The last two columns are inserted as null values. Once the command is run, we can verify the data by running the following command:

```
SELECT * FROM sales WHERE id = 2;
```

The output of the preceding SELECT statement is shown in the following figure:

```
hive> select * from sales where id = 2;
OK
2       Terry   John    H-43 Sector-23  Delhi   India   10.10.10.10
Time taken: 0.155 seconds, Fetched: 1 row(s)
```

The third query fails as it tries to insert only seven columns out of nine. The error is shown next:

```
FAILED: SemanticException [Error 10044]: Line 1:12 Cannot insert into
target table because column number/types are different 'sales': Table
insclause-0 has 9 columns, but query has 7 columns.
```

The fourth statement inserts rows into `employee` tables that are clustered by age and bucketed into two buckets. First, we will create an `employee` table, the output of which is shown next:

```
hive> Create table employees (name string, age int, job string) clustered by (age) into 2 buckets stored as orc;
OK
Time taken: 0.308 seconds
```

Once the table is created, we will insert the data as mentioned in the fourth statement. Once the command is run, we can verify the data by running the following command:

`SELECT * FROM employees;`

The output of the preceding `SELECT` statement is shown in the following figure:

```
hive> SELECT * FROM employees;
OK
John      30        IT
Jerry     35        Sales
Time taken: 0.11 seconds, Fetched: 2 row(s)
```

The fifth row inserts data into partitions. First, we will create a partitioned table named DEPARTMENT, the output of which is shown next:

```
hive> Create table department (name string, age int, deptno int) Partitioned by (datestamp string);
OK
Time taken: 0.108 seconds
```

Once the table is created, we will insert the data as mentioned in the fourth statement. Once the command is run, we can verify the data by running the following command:

`SELECT * FROM department;`

The output of the preceding `SELECT` statement is shown in the following screenshot:

```
hive> select * from department;
OK
Jason     20        10        2015-10-23
Nelson    30        20        2015-10-23
Time taken: 0.152 seconds, Fetched: 2 row(s)
```

There's more...

In Hive, the value for each column must be provided in the `INSERT` clause, unlike traditional RDEMS where the user can specify values for specific columns. However, if the user does not wish to specify all the columns, he/she can specify `NULL` else an error is thrown as specified in the preceding example.

Insertion is not possible on tables that are created using the SORTED BY clause.

Hive does not support complex datatypes.

Dynamic partitioning is supported in the same way as INSERT SELECT.

Updating data

In this recipe, you will learn how to update data in a table in Hive.

Updating data in a Hive table is the traditional way of updating data in a table in any RDBMS. Updating data in a table can only be performed if the table supports **Atomicity**, **Consistency**, **Isolation**, **Durability** (**ACID**) properties. The general format of updating data in a table is as follows:

```
UPDATE tablename SET column = value [, column = value ...] [WHERE
expression]
```

Where:

- ► `tablename`: This is the name of the table
- ► `values_row`: This is the value that is to be inserted into the table.
- ► `WHERE` expression: This is an optional clause. Only rows that match the WHERE clause will be updated

Getting ready

This recipe requires having Hive installed as described in the *Installing Hive* recipe of *Chapter 1, Developing Hive*. You will also need the Hive CLI or Beeline client to run the commands.

This recipe requires transactions enabled, so refer to *Enabling transactions in Hive* in Hive for that.

How to do it...

Follow these steps to update data in a table in Hive:

```
UPDATE sales SET lname = 'Thomas' WHERE id = 1;
UPDATE sales SET ip = '20.20.20.20' WHERE id = 2;
```

How it works...

The first statement will update the `lname` column to `Thomas` in the `Sales` table.

If the preceding table does not support ACID properties, the following error is thrown:

```
FAILED: SemanticException [Error 10297]: Attempt to do update or delete
on table default.sales that does not use an AcidOutputFormat or is not
bucketed.
```

The second statement updates the IP from `10.10.10.10` to `20.20.20.20` in the `Sales` table.

There's more...

> ▸ Rows that match the `WHERE` clause/criteria will be updated
>
> ▸ Partitioning columns cannot be updated
>
> ▸ Bucketing columns cannot be updated
>
> ▸ Update is not possible on tables that are created using the `SORTED BY` clause

Deleting data

In this recipe, you will learn how to delete data from a table in Hive.

Deleting data from a Hive table is the traditional way of deleting data in a table in any RDBMS. Deleting data in a table can only be performed if the table supports ACID properties.

 Deletion is not possible on tables that are created using the `SORTED BY` clause.

The general format of deleting data in a table is as follows:

```
DELETE FROM tablename [WHERE expression]
```

Where:

> ▸ `tablename`: This is the name of the table
>
> ▸ `WHERE` expression: This is an optional clause. Only rows that match the `WHERE` clause will be deleted

Getting ready

This recipe requires having Hive installed as described in the *Installing Hive* recipe of *Chapter 1, Developing Hive*. You will also need the Hive CLI or Beeline client to run the commands.

This recipe requires transactions enabled, so refer to *Enabling transactions in Hive* for that.

How to do it...

Follow the next step to delete data in a table in Hive:

```
DELETE FROM sales WHERE id = 1;
```

How it works...

The preceding statement DELETE FROM sales WHERE id = 1;, will delete the rows where id equals 1.

If the preceding table does not support ACID properties, the following error is thrown:

```
FAILED: SemanticException [Error 10297]: Attempt to do update or delete
on table default.sales that does not use an AcidOutputFormat or is not
bucketed.
```

Upon successful completion of this operation, the changes will be auto-committed.

6
Hive Extensibility Features

In previous chapters, we learned about different ways to load data in Hive along with recently added updates and deletes in Hive.

In this chapter, we will cover the following recipes in detail:

- Serialization and deserialization formats and data types
- Exploring views
- Exploring indexes
- Hive partitioning
- Creating buckets in Hive
- Analytics functions in Hive
- Windowing in Hive
- File formats

Introduction

In this chapter, we are going to cover some of the key features of Hive including partitions, bucketing, windowing, and analytics functions. In the practical demonstration, we have used the following sales data set:

```
Schema : id, fname, state, zip, ip, pid
```

```
0        Zena      Tennessee      21550    192.168.56.101    PI_09
1        Elaine    Alaska   06429 192.168.56.101   PI_03
2        Sage      Nevada   08899 192.168.56.102   PI_03
3        Cade      Missouri       11233    192.168.56.103    PI_06
4        Abra      New Jersey     21550    192.168.56.101    PI_09
5        Stone     Nebraska       03560    192.168.56.104    PI_08
6        Regina    Tennessee      21550    192.168.56.105    PI_10
7        Donovan   New York       95234    192.168.56.106    PI_05
8        Aileen    Illinois       68284    192.168.56.106    PI_02
9        Mariam    Hawaii   95234 192.168.56.107   PI_07
```

Serialization and deserialization formats and data types

Serialization and deserialization formats are popularly known as **SerDes**. Hive allows the framework to read or write data in a particular format. These formats parse the structured or unstructured data bytes stored in HDFS in accordance with the schema definition of Hive tables. Hive provides a set of in-built `SerDes` and also allows the user to create custom `SerDes` based on their data definition. These are as follows:

- `LazySimpleSerDe`
- `RegexSerDe`
- `AvroSerDe`
- `OrcSerde`
- `ParquetHiveSerDe`
- `JSONSerDe`
- `CSVSerDe`

How to do it...

You can use different types of `SerDes` for reading or writing the data in a particular format.

LazySimpleSerDe

This is the default `SerDes` format of Hive. When a user creates a table in Hive without any explicit `SerDes` definition, `LazySimpleSerDe` gets associated with the table. `LazySimpleSerDe` takes line feed (`\n`) as the record separator and tab (`'\t'`) as the attribute (column) delimiter. It parse the data bytes it receives from HDFS and generates the record and columns from it. The columns are then mapped to the schema definition of the table to which the data is associated.

For example, let's create a table without specifying any `SerDes` definition:

```
hive> CREATE TABLE sales ( id INT, fname STRING, lname STRING, address
STRING, city STRING, state STRING, zip STRING, ip STRING, pid STRING, dop
STRING) ROW FORMAT DELIMITED FIELDS TERMINATED BY '\t';
```

When you create a `sales` table, by default it is set with `LazySimpleSerDe`, which takes a new line as the record delimiter and the `'\t'` tab as the column separator. You can specify the columns delimiter other than tab in the same way; for example `ROW FORMAT DELIMITED FIELDS TERMINATED BY ','` would consider a comma as the column delimiter while parsing HDFS bytes. It is important to note that only 1 byte delimiters are allowed in this `SerDes` format.

If we check in the metastore, we would find the following `SerDes` entry for the `sales` table:

```
mysql> select * from TBLS;
+--------+-------------+-------+------------------+-------+-----------+-------+----------+----------+--------------+--------------+-----------------+
| TBL_ID | CREATE_TIME | DB_ID | LAST_ACCESS_TIME | OWNER | RETENTION | SD_ID | TBL_NAME | TBL_TYPE | VIEW_EXPANDED_TEXT |
|        |             |       |                  |       |           |       | VIEW_ORIGINAL_TEXT |
+--------+-------------+-------+------------------+-------+-----------+-------+----------+----------+--------------+--------------+-----------------+
|     11 |  1455771821 |     1 |                0 | root  |         0 |    11 | sales    | MANAGED_TABLE | NULL |
|        |             |       |             NULL |       |           |       |          |          |              |
```

In the preceding screenshot, the `SD_ID` (in this example, the value is 43) column specifies the ID of `SerDes` that is used for this table. Now, let's check the corresponding `SerDes` information in the metastore table `SERDES`.

```
mysql> select * from SERDES;
+----------+------+----------------------------------------------+
| SERDE_ID | NAME | SLIB                                         |
+----------+------+----------------------------------------------+
|       11 | NULL | org.apache.hadoop.hive.serde2.lazy.LazySimpleSerDe |
```

The preceding image is showing the corresponding `SerDes` name for id=43, which is `LazySimpleSerde`. So this means when no `SerDes` is defined in the table create statement, then by default `LazySimpleSerde` is used.

RegexSerDe

`RegexSerDe` is included as part of the Hive package distribution. It allows Hive to query data based on a particular `Regex` pattern. The records in HDFS data are mapped to the table schema. For example, let's take some sample `log` data:

```
66.249.68.6 - - [14/Jan/2016:06:25:03 -0800] "GET /protechskills.com
HTTP/1.1" 200
23.145.12.1 - - [14/Jan/2016:06:26:05 -0600] "POST /protechskills.com
HTTP/1.1" 200
```

We would create a table that corresponds to the `log` data in HDFS files and create a table for it as follows:

```
hive>CREATE TABLE web_logs(remote_ip STRING,dt STRING,httpmethod
STRING,request STRING,protocol STRING)
ROW FORMAT SERDE 'org.apache.hadoop.hive.contrib.serde2.RegexSerDe'
WITH SERDEPROPERTIES("input.regex" = "([^ ]*) ([^ ]*) ([^ ]*) (?:-|\
[([^\]]*)\]) ([^ \"]*|\"[^\"]*\") (-|[0-9]*)",
"output.format.string" = "%1$s %2$s %3$s %4$s %5$s"
);
```

Once we defined a `Regex` for the data, we can query the data as simple Hive SQL queries.

```
hive> SELECT remote_ip, protocol FROM web_logs ORDER BY httpmethod;
```

JSONSerDe

If the underlying data in HDFS is in JSON format, it could be queried using Hive by associating `JSONSerDe` with the table. For example, if the data in HDFS is in the following form:

```
{"id":1,"created_at":2016-02-22,"text":"hi","user_id":12, "user_
name":"shrey"}
{"id":2,"created_at":2016-02-23,"text":"hi","user_id":13, "user_
name":"hanish"}
{"id":3,"created_at":2016-02-24,"text":"hi","user_id":14, "user_
name":"saurabh"}
```

 Download `hive-json-serde-02.jar` from `https://storage.googleapis.com/google-code-archive-downloads/v2/code.google.com/hive-json-serde/hive-json-serde-0.2.jar`.

```
hive> add jar /opt/hive-json-serde-0.2.jar
```

We can create a Hive table for this data format and use `JSONSerDe` to map JSON keys to the Hive table schema as follows:

```
CREATE EXTERNAL TABLE messages (
msg_id BIGINT,
tstamp STRING,
text STRING,
user_id BIGINT,
user_name STRING
)
ROW FORMAT SERDE "org.apache.hadoop.hive.contrib.serde2.JsonSerde"
WITH SERDEPROPERTIES (
"msg_id"="$.id",
"tstamp"="$.created_at",
"text"="$.text",
"user_id"="$.user.id",
"user_name"="$.user.name"
)
LOCATION '/data/messages';
```

In the preceding example, the `SerDes` properties are used to map JSON fields in the document to columns in the Hive table. The `$.user.id` field searches for the `id` key in the user map and associates the key to `user_id` in the Hive table.

CSVSerDe

`CSVSerDe` is used to parse the `CSV` data stored in HDFS. Before Hive 0.14, it was not a part of the Hive distribution, thus it needed to be added as an external dependency; but from Hive 0.14 and later, this `SerDes` is included in the Hive distribution. The following is an example of `CSVSerDe` usage with sample data:

```
CREATE TABLE my_table(a string, b string, ...)
ROW FORMAT SERDE 'org.apache.hadoop.hive.serde2.OpenCSVSerde'
WITH SERDEPROPERTIES (
    "separatorChar" = "\t",
    "quoteChar"     = "'",
    "escapeChar"    = "\\"
)
STORED AS TEXTFILE;
```

There's more...

Apart from predefined SerDes, Hive also provisions the user to create their own SerDes based on how data should be deserialized on reads.

 More on Hive SerDes and creating a custom SerDes is available at https://cwiki.apache.org/confluence/display/Hive/SerDe.

See also

You can read more about this CSVSerDe mode at https://github.com/ogrodnek/csv-serde.

Exploring views

Views in SQL provide abstraction from querying a table directly. A view could be a combination of multiple tables joined or grouped on a set of columns. In RDBMS, views could be broadly categorized into two types:

- ► Materialized views
- ► Non-materialized views

Hive supports only non-materialized views and as it does not support materialized data, the view is strictly bound to the tables it is based on. In other words, it also means if the columns of the tables are altered or dropped, it would affect the view or even fail the view.

How to do it...

These views are the logical constructs that do not store data with them. When a view is created in Hive, the underlying query is stored in the metastore. When the view is queried, the view's clauses or conditions are evaluated before the underlying query clause. For example, if the query has a limit of 200 and the view has a limit of 100 then the query would return 100 results.

An example of a view definition is as follows:

```
CREATE VIEW sales_view AS SELECT * FROM SALES WHERE ip = '192.168.56.101'
or ip='192.168.56.106';
```

The view can then be used in the same way as any other table in Hive. An example of this is as follows:

```
SELECT * FROM sales_view WHERE pid = 'PI_02' or pid = 'PI_03';
```

This command will return the data as shown in the following screenshot:

```
hive> SELECT * FROM sales_view WHERE pid = 'PI_02' or pid = 'PI_03';
OK
1       Elaine  Alaska  06429   192.168.56.101  PI_03
8       Aileen  Illinois        68284   192.168.56.106  PI_02
Time taken: 0.986 seconds, Fetched: 2 row(s)
```

How it works...

A view is treated as a table in Hive. You can check the views in the Hive database by running show tables.

Now, let's see how the metadata for views is stored in the Hive metastore.

In the metastore, the query of a view is stored in a table. When the query on a view is executed, the query in it is executed first and then the view filter is applied:

```
mysql> select * from TBLS;
+--------+-------------+-------+-----------------+-------+-----------+-------+-----------------+---------------+----------------+
| TBL_ID | CREATE_TIME | DB_ID | LAST_ACCESS_TIME | OWNER | RETENTION | SD_ID | TBL_NAME | TBL_TYPE | VIEW_EXPANDED_TEXT | VIEW_ORIGINAL_TEXT |
+--------+-------------+-------+-----------------+-------+-----------+-------+-----------------+---------------+----------------+
|     19 | 1455870935  |   1 |               0 | root  |         0 |    43 | sales_part       | MANAGED TABLE | NULL | NULL |
|     23 | 1455917422  |   1 |               0 | root  |         0 |    59 | sales_part_state | MANAGED TABLE | NULL | NULL |
|     36 | 1456027593  |   1 |               0 | root  |         0 |    86 | sales_buck       | MANAGED TABLE | NULL | NULL |
|     41 | 1456039175  |   1 |               0 | root  |         0 |    91 | web_logs         | MANAGED TABLE | NULL | NULL |
|     47 | 1456041934  |   1 |               0 | root  |         0 |    97 | messages         | EXTERNAL TABLE | NULL | NULL |
|     52 | 1456276770  |   1 |               0 | root  |         0 |   102 | sales            | MANAGED TABLE | NULL | NULL |
|     56 | 1456277369  |   1 |               0 | root  |         0 |   106 | sales_view       | VIRTUAL VIEW  | SELECT `sales`.`id`, `sales`.`fname`, `sales`.`state`, `sales`.`zip`, `sales`.`ip`, `sales`.`pid` FROM `default`.`SALES` WHERE `sales`.`ip` = '192.168.56.101' or `sales`.`ip`='192.168.56.106' | SELECT * FROM SALES WHERE ip = '192.168.56.101' or ip='192.168.56.106' |
```

The following is the snippet of the explain plan for a view:

```
EXPLAIN SELECT * FROM sales_view
WHERE pid = 'PI_02' OR pid = 'PI_03' ;
```

```
hive> EXPLAIN SELECT * FROM sales_view WHERE pid = 'PI_02' OR pid = 'PI_03' ;
OK
STAGE DEPENDENCIES:
  Stage-0 is a root stage

STAGE PLANS:
  Stage: Stage-0
    Fetch Operator
      limit: -1
      Processor Tree:
        TableScan
          alias: sales
          Statistics: Num rows: 10 Data size: 430 Basic stats: COMPLETE Column stats: NONE
          Filter Operator
            predicate: (((ip = '192.168.56.101') or (ip = '192.168.56.106')) and ((pid = 'PI_02') or (pid = 'PI_03'))) (type: boolean)
            Statistics: Num rows: 10 Data size: 430 Basic stats: COMPLETE Column stats: NONE
            Select Operator
              expressions: id (type: int), fname (type: string), state (type: string), zip (type: string), ip (type: string), pid (type: string)
              outputColumnNames: col0, col1, col2, col3, col4, col5
              Statistics: Num rows: 10 Data size: 430 Basic stats: COMPLETE Column stats: NONE
              ListSink
```

Exploring indexes

Indexes are useful for increasing the performance of frequent queries based on certain columns. But Hive has limited a capability to index data as indexing large datasets requires sufficient additional storage space and processing overheads. Hive can index the columns to speed up some operations. It stores the indexed data in another table.

How to do it...

Indexes could be created on the tables in Hive. Let us create a `sales` table in Hive on which we are going to create indexes:

```
Create table sales(id int, fname string, state string, zip string, ip string, pid string) Row format delimited fields terminated by '\t';
```

Let us create an index on the `state` column of this table:

```
CREATE INDEX index_ip ON TABLE sales(ip) AS 'org.apache.hadoop.hive.ql.index.compact.CompactIndexHandler' WITH DEFERRED REBUILD;
```

In the metastore, it is stored in the `IDXS` table as shown in the following screenshot:

```
mysql> select * from IDXS;
+----------+-------------+------------------+-----------------------------------------------------------+------------+--------------+------------------+-------------+
| INDEX_ID | CREATE_TIME | DEFERRED_REBUILD | INDEX_HANDLER_CLASS                                       | INDEX_NAME | INDEX_TBL_ID | LAST_ACCESS_TIME | ORIG_TBL_ID |
| SD_ID    |             |                  |                                                           |            |              |                  |             |
+----------+-------------+------------------+-----------------------------------------------------------+------------+--------------+------------------+-------------+
|        6 |  1456277672 |                  | org.apache.hadoop.hive.ql.index.compact.CompactIndexHandler | index_ip  |           57 |       1456277672 |          52 |
|      108 |             |                  |                                                           |            |              |                  |             |
+----------+-------------+------------------+-----------------------------------------------------------+------------+--------------+------------------+-------------+
1 row in set (0.00 sec)
```

Hive partitioning

Partitioning in Hive can be best explained with an example. Suppose a telecom organization generates 1 TB of data every day and different regional managers query this data based on their own state. For each query by a regional manager, Hive scans the complete data in HDFS and files the results for a particular state.

The manager runs the same query daily for his own state analysis and the query gives the result in four hours on a 1 TB dataset. For analytics, the same query could be executed daily on a one-month or six-month dataset. The query would take ten hours on a month's data.

If the data is somehow partitioned based on state, then when a regional manager runs the same query for his state, only the data of that state is scanned and the execution time could be reduced significantly.

How to do it...

Partitioning can be done in one of the following two ways:

- Static partitioning
- Dynamic partitioning

Static partitioning

In static partitioning, you need to manually insert data in different partitions of a table. Let's use a table partitioned on the states of India. For each state, you need to manually insert the data from the data source to a state partition in the partitioned table. So for 29 states, you need to write the equivalent number of Hive queries to insert data in each partition. Let's understand this using the following example.

First, we create a nonpartitioned table, `sales`, which is the source of data for our partitioned table, and load data into it:

```
CREATE TABLE sales (id int, fname string, state string, zip string, ip
string, pid string) row format delimited fields terminated by '\t';
LOAD DATA LOCAL INPATH '/opt/data/sample_10' INTO TABLE sales;
```

If we query the table `sales` for a particular state, it would scan the entire data in `sales`.

Now, let's create a partition table and insert data from `sales` in to different partitions:

```
CREATE TABLE sales_part(id int, fname string, state string, zip string,
ip string) partitioned by (pid string) row format delimited fields
terminated by '\t';
```

In static partitioning, you need to insert data into different partitions of the partitioned table as follows:

```
Insert into sales_part partition (pid= 'PI_03') select
id,fname,state,zip,ip from sales where pid= 'PI_03';

Insert into sales_part partition (pid= 'PI_02') select
id,fname,state,zip,ip from sales where pid= 'PI_02';

Insert into sales_part partition (pid= 'PI_05') select
id,fname,state,zip,ip from sales where pid= 'PI_05';
```

If we check for the partitions in HDFS, we would find the directory structure as follows:

Dynamic partitioning

Let us look at a scenario where we have 50 product IDs and we need to partition data for all the unique product IDs available in the dataset. If we go for static partitioning, we need to run the INSERT INTO command for all 50 distinct product IDs. That is where it is better to go with dynamic partitioning. In this type, partitions would be created for all the unique values in the dataset for a given partition column.

By default, Hive does not allow dynamic partitioning. We need to enable it by setting the following properties on the CLI or in hive-site.xml:

```
hive> set hive.exec.dynamic.partition = true;

hive> set hive.exec.dynamic.partition.mode = nonstrict;
```

Once dynamic partitioning is enabled, we can create partitions for all unique values for any columns, say state of the state table, as follows:

```
hive> create table sales_part_state (id int, fname string, zip string, ip
string, pid string) partitioned by (state string) row format delimited
fields terminated by '\t';

hive> Insert into sales_part_state partition(state) select
id,fname,zip,ip,pid,state from sales;
```

It will create partitions for all unique values of state in the `sales` table. The HDFS structure for different partitions is as follows:

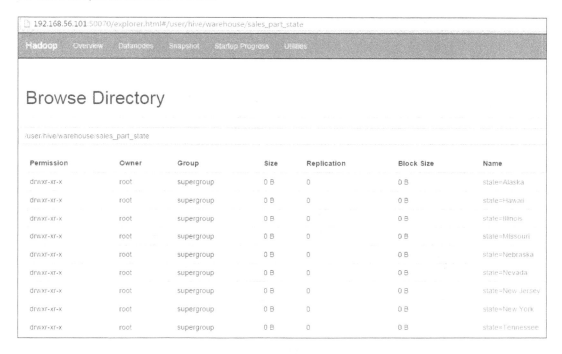

Now, let's see how things are stored in the metastore:

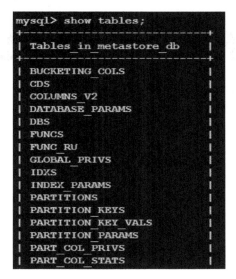

Every partition created for static and dynamic partitioning is stored in the PARTITIONS table in the metastore as follows:

```
mysql> select * from PARTITIONS;
+---------+-------------+------------------+------------------+-------+--------+
| PART_ID | CREATE_TIME | LAST_ACCESS_TIME | PART_NAME        | SD_ID | TBL_ID |
+---------+-------------+------------------+------------------+-------+--------+
|      25 |  1455870997 |                0 | pid=PI_03        |    44 |     19 |
|      26 |  1455870997 |                0 | pid=PI_06        |    45 |     19 |
|      27 |  1455870997 |                0 | pid=PI_08        |    46 |     19 |
|      28 |  1455870998 |                0 | pid=PI_07        |    47 |     19 |
|      29 |  1455870998 |                0 | pid=PI_02        |    48 |     19 |
|      30 |  1455870998 |                0 | pid=PI_10        |    49 |     19 |
|      31 |  1455870998 |                0 | pid=PI_09        |    50 |     19 |
|      32 |  1455870998 |                0 | pid=PI_05        |    51 |     19 |
|      37 |  1455917531 |                0 | state=Nevada     |    60 |     23 |
|      38 |  1455917532 |                0 | state=New York   |    61 |     23 |
|      39 |  1455917532 |                0 | state=New Jersey |    62 |     23 |
|      40 |  1455917532 |                0 | state=Alaska     |    63 |     23 |
|      41 |  1455917533 |                0 | state=Tennessee  |    64 |     23 |
|      42 |  1455917533 |                0 | state=Missouri   |    65 |     23 |
|      43 |  1455917533 |                0 | state=Hawaii     |    66 |     23 |
|      44 |  1455917533 |                0 | state=Illinois   |    67 |     23 |
|      45 |  1455917534 |                0 | state=Nebraska   |    68 |     23 |
+---------+-------------+------------------+------------------+-------+--------+
```

The partition keys are stored separately and linked to the PARTITIONS table with the TBL_ID field as follows:

```
mysql> select * from PARTITION_KEYS;
+--------+---------------+-----------+-----------+-------------+
| TBL_ID | PKEY_COMMENT  | PKEY_NAME | PKEY_TYPE | INTEGER_IDX |
+--------+---------------+-----------+-----------+-------------+
|     19 | NULL          | pid       | string    |           0 |
|     23 | NULL          | state     | string    |           0 |
+--------+---------------+-----------+-----------+-------------+
```

The partition values are stored in a separate table, PARTITION_KEY_VALS, and linked to the PARTITIONS table with the PART_ID field as follows:

```
mysql> select * from PARTITION_KEY_VALS;
+---------+--------------+-------------+
| PART_ID | PART_KEY_VAL | INTEGER_IDX |
+---------+--------------+-------------+
|      25 | PI_03        |           0 |
|      26 | PI_06        |           0 |
|      27 | PI_08        |           0 |
|      28 | PI_07        |           0 |
|      29 | PI_02        |           0 |
|      30 | PI_10        |           0 |
|      31 | PI_09        |           0 |
|      32 | PI_05        |           0 |
|      37 | Nevada       |           0 |
|      38 | New York     |           0 |
|      39 | New Jersey   |           0 |
|      40 | Alaska       |           0 |
|      41 | Tennessee    |           0 |
|      42 | Missouri     |           0 |
|      43 | Hawaii       |           0 |
|      44 | Illinois     |           0 |
|      45 | Nebraska     |           0 |
+---------+--------------+-------------+
```

Creating buckets in Hive

In the scenario where we query on a unique values column of a dataset, partitioning is not a good fit. If we go with a partition on a column with high unique values like ID, it would create a large number of small datasets in HDFS and partition entries in the metastore, thus increasing the load on `NameNode` and the metastore service.

To optimize queries on such a dataset, we group the data into a particular number of buckets and the data is divided into the maximum number of buckets.

How to do it...

Using the same `sales` dataset, if we need to optimize queries on a column with high unique column values such as ID, we create buckets on that column as follows:

```
create table sales_buck (id int, fname string, state string, zip string,
ip string, pid string) clustered by (id) into 50 buckets row format
delimited fields terminated by '\t';
```

Here, we have defined 50 buckets for this table, which means that the complete dataset is divided and stored in 50 buckets based on the `ID` column value.

By default, bucketing is disabled in Hive. You need to enable bucketing before loading data in a bucketed table by setting the following property:

```
set hive.enforce.bucketing=true;
```

Assuming you already have the `sales` table that we created in the *Hive partitioning* recipe, we would now load the data in `sales_buck` from the table `sales` as follows:

```
insert into table sales_buck select * from sales;
```

If you closely monitor the execution of MapReduce jobs running for this `insert` statement, you would see that 50 reducers produce 50 output files as buckets for this table, partitioned on `ID`:

```
hive> create table sales_buck (id int, fname string, state string, zip string, ip string, pid string) clustered by (id) into 50 buckets row format de
limited fields terminated by '\t';
OK
Time taken: 0.238 seconds
hive> set hive.enforce.bucketing=true;
hive> insert into table sales_buck select * from sales;
Query ID = root_20160224073617_42330cfc-4cd8-42f1-b69b-7a6cdc4565f1
Total jobs = 1
Launching Job 1 out of 1
Number of reduce tasks determined at compile time: 50
In order to change the average load for a reducer (in bytes):
  set hive.exec.reducers.bytes.per.reducer=<number>
In order to limit the maximum number of reducers:
  set hive.exec.reducers.max=<number>
In order to set a constant number of reducers:
  set mapreduce.job.reducers=<number>
Starting Job = job_1456273553806_0004, Tracking URL = http://localhost:8088/proxy/application_1456273553806_0004/
Kill Command = /opt/hadoop-2.6.0//bin/hadoop job  -kill job_1456273553806_0004
Hadoop job information for Stage-1: number of mappers: number of reducers: 50
2016-02-24 07:36:41,958 Stage-1 map = 0%,  reduce = 0%
```

If you have access to HDFS, you can check that 50 files are created in the warehouse directory of the `sales_buck` table, which would be by default `/user/hive/warehouse/sales_buck/`. If the location of the table is not known, you can check for the location by executing the `describe formatted sales_buck;` command on the Hive CLI.

🗋 192.168.56.101:50070/explorer.html#/user/hive/warehouse/sales_buck

| Hadoop | Overview | Datanodes | Snapshot | Startup Progress | Utilities |

Browse Directory

/user/hive/warehouse/sales_buck

Permission	Owner	Group	Size	Replication	Block Size	Name
-rwxr-xr-x	root	supergroup	87 B	3	256 MB	000000_1
-rwxr-xr-x	root	supergroup	106 B	3	256 MB	000001_1
-rwxr-xr-x	root	supergroup	90 B	3	256 MB	000002_1
-rwxr-xr-x	root	supergroup	95 B	3	256 MB	000003_2
-rwxr-xr-x	root	supergroup	99 B	3	256 MB	000004_1
-rwxr-xr-x	root	supergroup	93 B	3	256 MB	000005_1
-rwxr-xr-x	root	supergroup	94 B	3	256 MB	000006_0
-rwxr-xr-x	root	supergroup	105 B	3	256 MB	000007_0
-rwxr-xr-x	root	supergroup	109 B	3	256 MB	000008_0
-rwxr-xr-x	root	supergroup	88 B	3	256 MB	000009_0

Now, when the user queries the `sales_buck` table for an ID or a range of IDs, Hive knows which bucket to look in for a particular ID. The query engine would only scan that bucket and return the resultset.

Metastore view of bucketing

In the following screenshot after executing the `select * from BUCKETING_COLS;` we will be presented with the following result:

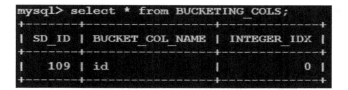

Analytics functions in Hive

Hive provides the following set of analytical functions:

- RANK
- DENSE_RANK
- ROW_NUMBER
- PERCENT_RANK
- CUME_DIST
- NTILE

Common and useful sets of analytical functions are ranking functions where rows from resultset are ranked according to a scheme.

How to do it...

Let's analyze each function in detail. We will be using the same `sales` dataset and applying analytical functions to it:

- ▸ ROW_NUMBER: This function will provide a unique number to each row in resultset based on the ORDER BY clause within the PARTITION. For example, if we want to assign row_number to each fname, which is also partitioned by IP address in the sales dataset, the query would be:

hive> select fname,ip,ROW_NUMBER() OVER (ORDER BY ip) as rownum from sales;

```
fname     ip            rownum
Abra      192.168.56.101  1
Elaine    192.168.56.101  2
Zena      192.168.56.101  3
Sage      192.168.56.102  4
Cade      192.168.56.103  5
Stone     192.168.56.104  6
Regina    192.168.56.105  7
Aileen    192.168.56.106  8
Donovan   192.168.56.106  9
Mariam    192.168.56.107  10
```

- ▸ RANK: It is similar to ROW_NUMBER, but the equal rows are ranked with the same number. For example, if we use RANK in the previous query instead of ROW_NUM:

hive> select fname,ip,RANK() OVER (ORDER BY ip) as ranknum, RANK() OVER (PARTITION BY ip order by fname) from sales ;

```
fname     ip            ranknum  rank_window_1
Abra      192.168.56.101  1          1
Elaine    192.168.56.101  1          2
Zena      192.168.56.101  1          3
Sage      192.168.56.102  4          1
Cade      192.168.56.103  5          1
Stone     192.168.56.104  6          1
Regina    192.168.56.105  7          1
Aileen    192.168.56.106  8          1
Donovan   192.168.56.106  8          2
Mariam    192.168.56.107  10         1
```

▶ DENSE_RANK: In a normal RANK function, we see a gap between the numbers in rows. DENSE_RANK is a function with no gap. For example, the output of the preceding query with DENSE_RANK is as follows:

```
select fname,ip,DENSE_RANK() OVER (ORDER BY ip) as densenum,
DENSE_RANK() OVER (PARTITION BY ip order by fname) from sales ;
```

fname	ip	densenum	dense_rank_window_1
Abra	192.168.56.101	1	1
Elaine	192.168.56.101	1	2
Zena	192.168.56.101	1	3
Sage	192.168.56.102	2	1
Cade	192.168.56.103	3	1
Stone	192.168.56.104	4	1
Regina	192.168.56.105	5	1
Aileen	192.168.56.106	6	1
Donovan	192.168.56.106	6	2
Mariam	192.168.56.107	7	1

For comparison, if we put all three together then the output would be:

```
select fname,ip,ROW_NUMBER() OVER (ORDER BY ip), RANK() OVER
(ORDER BY ip), DENSE_RANK() OVER (ORDER BY ip) from sales;
```

fname	ip	row_number_window_0	rank_window_1	dense_rank_window_2
Abra	192.168.56.101	1	1	1
Elaine	192.168.56.101	2	1	1
Zena	192.168.56.101	3	1	1
Sage	192.168.56.102	4	4	2
Cade	192.168.56.103	5	5	3
Stone	192.168.56.104	6	6	4
Regina	192.168.56.105	7	7	5
Aileen	192.168.56.106	8	8	6
Donovan	192.168.56.106	9	8	6
Mariam	192.168.56.107	10	10	7

Use cases: Analytical ranking functions are useful for solving complex problems in datasets including removing duplicates in data, splitting a string, and so on.

▶ CUME_DIST: CUME_DIST is shorthand for cumulative distribution. It is also a less well-known analytical function in Hive. It computes the relative position of a column value in a group. For a row, r, the cumulative distribution of r is calculated as:

```
Cum_dist(r) = Num of rows with value lower than or equals to r /
total rows in resultset or partition
```

For example, the output of the query with `CUME_DIST` is:

```
SELECT fname, ip, CUME_DIST() OVER (PARTITION BY ip ORDER BY
fname) AS cume_dist FROM sales;
```

```
fname     ip           cume_dist
Abra      192.168.56.101   0.3333333333333333
Elaine    192.168.56.101   0.6666666666666666
Zena      192.168.56.101   1.0
Sage      192.168.56.102   1.0
Cade      192.168.56.103   1.0
Stone     192.168.56.104   1.0
Regina    192.168.56.105   1.0
Aileen    192.168.56.106   0.5
Donovan   192.168.56.106   1.0
Mariam    192.168.56.107   1.0
```

► NTILE: NTILE distributes the number of rows in a partition into a certain number of groups. When the row is fetched, NTILE returns the group number associated with it. The groups are numerically tagged, starting with one. Here is an example:

```
SELECT fname, id, NTILE(4) OVER (ORDER BY id DESC) AS quartile
FROM sales WHERE ip = '192.168.56.101';
```

The output of the preceding statement is shown in the following screenshot:

```
fname     id      quartile
Abra      4       1
Elaine    1       2
Zena      0       3
```

Here, if there are n rows with the `ip='192.168.56.101'` quartile in four buckets, then IDs are equally divided into buckets and the `n%4` bucket has more rows than other buckets:

```
SELECT fname, id, NTILE(2) OVER (ORDER BY id DESC) AS quartile
FROM sales WHERE ip = '192.168.56.101';
```

The output of the preceding statement is shown in the following screenshot:

```
fname     id      quartile
Abra      4       1
Elaine    1       1
Zena      0       2
```

> ▶ PERCENT_RANK: It is very similar to the CUME_DIST function. It returns a value from 0 to 1 inclusive. The first row in any dataset has percent_rank 0 and the return value is of the double type.

```
SELECT ip, fname, PERCENT_RANK() OVER (PARTITION BY ip ORDER BY
fname) AS percent_rank FROM sales;
```

```
ip              fname      percent_rank
192.168.56.101  Abra       0.0
192.168.56.101  Elaine     0.5
192.168.56.101  Zena       1.0
192.168.56.102  Sage       0.0
192.168.56.103  Cade       0.0
192.168.56.104  Stone      0.0
192.168.56.105  Regina     0.0
192.168.56.106  Aileen     0.0
192.168.56.106  Donovan    1.0
192.168.56.107  Mariam     0.0
```

See also

You can learn more about analytics functions in Hive here: http://docs.hortonworks.com/HDPDocuments/HDP2/HDP-2.0.0.2/ds_Hive/language_manual/ptf-window.html#WindowingandAnalytics-EnhancementstoHiveQL.

Windowing in Hive

Windowing in Hive allows an analyst to create a window of data to operate aggregation and other analytical functions, such as LEAD and LAG.

The windowing specification in HiveQL comprises:

- ▶ Partition
- ▶ Order by
- ▶ Window frame
- ▶ Source name for window definition

Let's look into each of these specifications in detail:

- **Partition specification**: It includes a column reference from the table. It could not be any aggregation or other window specification.
- **Order specification**: It comprises a combination of one or more columns. The ordering could be `ASC` or `DESC`, which by default is `ASC`.

  Handling NULLs: There is no support for `Nulls` first or last specification. In Hive, Nulls are returned first.
- **Window frame**: A frame has a start boundary and an optional end boundary:
  - **Frame type**: Window frames could be any of the following types:

    - **ROW**
    - **RANGE**
- **Frame boundary**: A frame is associated with a direction or an amount. A direction value could be `PRECEDING` or `FOLLOWING` and the amount could be an integer value or keyword `UNBOUNDED`.
- **Effective window frames**:
  - `BETWEEN <start boundary> AND CURRENT ROW`: When only the start boundary of a frame is specified.
  - `RANGE BETWEEN UNBOUNDED PRECEDING AND CURRENT ROW`: When only the order is specified but no window frame is specified.
  - `ROW BETWEEN UNBOUNDED PRECEDING AND UNBOUNDED FOLLOWING`: When no order and no window frame are specified.
- **Source name for window definition**: A row `R` in the input table belongs to a partition as defined in the partition specification. If no partition is specified, all rows belong to a single partition. The order of a row `R` in a partition is based on the order specification. Hive supports windowing functions explained in the following section.

How to do it...

Let's look into the implementation and working of different windowing functions as follows:

- `LEAD`
- `LAG`
- `FIRST_VALUE`
- `LAST_VALUE`

- OVER clause

  - OVER with Aggregates

  - COUNT

  - MIN

  - MAX

  - AVG

  - OVER with PARTITION BY

  - OVER with PARTITION BY and ORDER BY

The following are some examples for the preceding functions:

- PARTITION BY with one partitioning column, no ORDER BY, and no window specification:

  ```
  SELECT fname,ip, COUNT(pid) OVER (PARTITION BY ip) FROM sales;
  ```

fname	ip	count_window_0
Abra	192.168.56.101	3
Elaine	192.168.56.101	3
Zena	192.168.56.101	3
Sage	192.168.56.102	1
Cade	192.168.56.103	1
Stone	192.168.56.104	1
Regina	192.168.56.105	1
Aileen	192.168.56.106	2
Donovan	192.168.56.106	2
Mariam	192.168.56.107	1

- PARTITION BY with two partitioning columns, no ORDER BY, and no window specification:

  ```
  SELECT fname,ip,zip,pid, COUNT(pid) OVER (PARTITION BY ip, zip)
  FROM sales;
  ```

fname	ip	zip	pid	count_window_0
Elaine	192.168.56.101	06429	PI_03	1
Abra	192.168.56.101	21550	PI_09	2
Zena	192.168.56.101	21550	PI_09	2
Sage	192.168.56.102	08899	PI_03	1
Cade	192.168.56.103	11233	PI_06	1
Stone	192.168.56.104	03560	PI_08	1
Regina	192.168.56.105	21550	PI_10	1
Aileen	192.168.56.106	68284	PI_02	1
Donovan	192.168.56.106	95234	PI_05	1
Mariam	192.168.56.107	95234	PI_07	1

▶ PARTITION BY with one partitioning column, one ORDER BY column, and no window specification:

```
SELECT fname,pid, COUNT(pid) OVER (PARTITION BY ip ORDER BY fname)
FROM sales;
```

```
fname    pid     count_window_0
Abra     PI_09   1
Elaine   PI_03   2
Zena     PI_09   3
Sage     PI_03   1
Cade     PI_06   1
Stone    PI_08   1
Regina   PI_10   1
Aileen   PI_02   1
Donovan  PI_05   2
Mariam   PI_07   1
```

▶ PARTITION BY with two partitioning columns, one ORDER BY column, and no window specification:

```
SELECT fname,ip,pid, COUNT(pid) OVER (PARTITION BY ip, pid ORDER
BY fname) FROM sales;
```

```
fname    ip              pid     count_window_0
Elaine   192.168.56.101  PI_03   1
Abra     192.168.56.101  PI_09   1
Zena     192.168.56.101  PI_09   2
Sage     192.168.56.102  PI_03   1
Cade     192.168.56.103  PI_06   1
Stone    192.168.56.104  PI_08   1
Regina   192.168.56.105  PI_10   1
Aileen   192.168.56.106  PI_02   1
Donovan  192.168.56.106  PI_05   1
Mariam   192.168.56.107  PI_07   1
```

▶ PARTITION BY with partitioning, ORDER BY, and a window specification:

```
SELECT fname, ip, COUNT(pid) OVER (PARTITION BY ip ORDER BY fname
ROWS BETWEEN UNBOUNDED PRECEDING AND CURRENT ROW) FROM sales;
```

```
fname    ip              count_window_0
Abra     192.168.56.101  1
Elaine   192.168.56.101  2
Zena     192.168.56.101  3
Sage     192.168.56.102  1
Cade     192.168.56.103  1
Stone    192.168.56.104  1
Regina   192.168.56.105  1
Aileen   192.168.56.106  1
Donovan  192.168.56.106  2
Mariam   192.168.56.107  1
```

```
SELECT fname, ip, COUNT(pid) OVER (PARTITION BY ip ORDER BY fname
ROWS BETWEEN 2 PRECEDING AND CURRENT ROW) FROM sales;
```

```
fname    ip           count_window_0
Abra     192.168.56.101  1
Elaine   192.168.56.101  2
Zena     192.168.56.101  3
Sage     192.168.56.102  1
Cade     192.168.56.103  1
Stone    192.168.56.104  1
Regina   192.168.56.105  1
Aileen   192.168.56.106  1
Donovan  192.168.56.106  2
Mariam   192.168.56.107  1
```

```
SELECT fname, ip ,COUNT(pid) OVER (PARTITION BY ip ORDER BY fname
ROWS BETWEEN 2 PRECEDING AND 2 FOLLOWING) FROM sales;
```

```
fname    ip           count_window_0
Abra     192.168.56.101  3
Elaine   192.168.56.101  3
Zena     192.168.56.101  3
Sage     192.168.56.102  1
Cade     192.168.56.103  1
Stone    192.168.56.104  1
Regina   192.168.56.105  1
Aileen   192.168.56.106  2
Donovan  192.168.56.106  2
Mariam   192.168.56.107  1
```

```
SELECT fname, ip, COUNT(pid) OVER (PARTITION BY ip ORDER BY fname
ROWS BETWEEN CURRENT ROW AND UNBOUNDED FOLLOWING) FROM sales;
```

```
fname    ip           count_window_0
Abra     192.168.56.101  3
Elaine   192.168.56.101  2
Zena     192.168.56.101  1
Sage     192.168.56.102  1
Cade     192.168.56.103  1
Stone    192.168.56.104  1
Regina   192.168.56.105  1
Aileen   192.168.56.106  2
Donovan  192.168.56.106  1
Mariam   192.168.56.107  1
```

There can be multiple OVER clauses in a single query. A single OVER clause only applies to the immediately preceding function call for example:

```
SELECT fname,ip,zip, COUNT(pid) OVER (PARTITION BY ip), COUNT(ip)
OVER (PARTITION BY zip) FROM sales;
```

```
fname     ip            zip      _c3    count_window_1
Stone     192.168.56.104  03560    1      1
Elaine    192.168.56.101  06429    3      1
Sage      192.168.56.102  08899    1      1
Cade      192.168.56.103  11233    1      1
Regina    192.168.56.105  21550    1      3
Zena      192.168.56.101  21550    3      3
Abra      192.168.56.101  21550    3      3
Aileen    192.168.56.106  68284    2      1
Mariam    192.168.56.107  95234    1      2
Donovan   192.168.56.106  95234    2      2
```

LEAD

The LEAD function is used to return the data from the next set of rows. If the number of rows is not specified, the default lead is of one row. Hive would return NULL if the lead exceeds the current window:

```
SELECT fname,pid, LEAD(pid) OVER (PARTITION BY ip ORDER BY ip)
FROM sales;
```

```
fname     pid      lead_window_0
Abra      PI_09    PI_03
Elaine    PI_03    PI_09
Zena      PI_09    NULL
Sage      PI_03    NULL
Cade      PI_06    NULL
Stone     PI_08    NULL
Regina    PI_10    NULL
Aileen    PI_02    PI_05
Donovan   PI_05    NULL
Mariam    PI_07    NULL
```

LAG

The LAG function is used to return the data from the previous set of rows. If the number of rows is not specified, the default lag is of one row. Hive would return NULL if the lag for the current row is exceeds before the beginning of the window:

```
SELECT fname,pid, LAG(pid) OVER (PARTITION BY ip ORDER BY ip)
FROM sales;
```

```
fname    pid       lag_window_0
Abra     PI_09     NULL
Elaine   PI_03     PI_09
Zena     PI_09     PI_03
Sage     PI_03     NULL
Cade     PI_06     NULL
Stone    PI_08     NULL
Regina   PI_10     NULL
Aileen   PI_02     NULL
Donovan  PI_05     PI_02
Mariam   PI_07     NULL
```

 Contrary to the definition of LEAD and LAG provided in the Hive wiki, LEAD and LAG do not work with the windowing clause.

FIRST_VALUE

This function returns the value from the first row in the window:

```
select fname, ip, first_value(pid) over (partition by ip order by fname)
as pid from sales;
```

```
fname     ip              pid
Abra      192.168.56.101  PI_09
Elaine    192.168.56.101  PI_09
Zena      192.168.56.101  PI_09
Sage      192.168.56.102  PI_03
Cade      192.168.56.103  PI_06
Stone     192.168.56.104  PI_08
Regina    192.168.56.105  PI_10
Aileen    192.168.56.106  PI_02
Donovan   192.168.56.106  PI_02
Mariam    192.168.56.107  PI_07
```

LAST_VALUE

This function returns the value from the last row in the window. The value is then applied to every row in that group. It would return NULL if the input expression is NULL:

```
select fname, ip, last_value(pid) over (partition by ip order by fname)
as pid from sales;
```

```
fname      ip           pid
Abra       192.168.56.101    PI_09
Elaine     192.168.56.101    PI_03
Zena       192.168.56.101    PI_09
Sage       192.168.56.102    PI_03
Cade       192.168.56.103    PI_06
Stone      192.168.56.104    PI_08
Regina     192.168.56.105    PI_10
Aileen     192.168.56.106    PI_02
Donovan    192.168.56.106    PI_05
Mariam     192.168.56.107    PI_07
```

See also

You can read more about this at http://www.cloudera.com/documentation/archive/impala/2-x/2-0-x/topics/impala_analytic_functions.html#last_value_unique_1.

File formats

In most of our examples, we have used files in plain text format, but Hive provides a set of file formats that provides optimization at the storage or processing level, or both in some cases. Different types of file format supported by Hive are as follows:

- ▶ TEXTFILE
- ▶ SEQUENCEFILE
- ▶ RCFILE
- ▶ ORC
- ▶ PARQUET
- ▶ AVRO

Each of these formats have a specified structure to store data on the disk. You can also define your own file format and get the data stored in that format by using the INPUTFORMAT class specification provided by Hadoop/Hive.

How to do it...

In all file formats other than text, the table only accepts data in that particular format, such as **Row Columnar** or **Optimized Row Columnar** (**RC** or **ORC**). If the source data is in that format, it could be easily loaded to the Hive table using the LOAD command. But if the source data is in some other format, say TEXT stored in another table in Hive, then the data could be inserted using the INSERT INTO command as follows:

```
INSERT INTO sales_orc select * from sales;
```

- ▶ TEXTFILE: This is the default format specification in Hive. When you create a table and do not specify any other value for STORED AS in DDL, it would assume that you are going to associate a file in the TEXT format to this table. The following are the two examples of reading and storing the data in plain text:

  - ❑ First example without using STORED AS:

    ```
    create table sales ( id int, fname string, lname string,
    address string, city string, state string, zip string, ip
    string, pid string, dop string) row format delimited fields
    terminated by '\t';
    ```

  - ❑ Second example using STORED AS:

    ```
    create table sales ( id int, fname string, lname string,
    address string, city string, state string, zip string, ip
    string, pid string, dop string) row format delimited fields
    terminated by '\t STORED AS TEXTFILE';
    ```

> You can also specify the default file format for your Hive client by specifying hive.default.fileformat in hive-site.xml.

- ▶ SEQUENCEFILE: When you want to save disk storage while keeping large datasets, it's better to store the file in the SEQUENCEFILE format. The details of compression are available at https://cwiki.apache.org/confluence/display/Hive/CompressedStorage. Use the following command to create a table with the SEQUENCEFILE format:

```
create table sales ( id int, fname string, lname string, address
string, city string, state string, zip string, ip string, pid
string, dop string) row format delimited fields terminated by '\t'
STORED AS SEQUENCEFILE;
```

▶ RCFILE: RCFILE, also known as **Record Columnar File**, stores data in a compressed format on the disk. It provides the following features of storage and processing optimization:

  ❑ Fast storage of data

  ❑ Optimized storage utilization

  ❑ Better query processing

The RCFILE format flattens the data in terms of both rows and columns. Thus, if you need a certain column for analytics, it would not scan the complete data; instead, it would return the required columns.

Use the following command to create a table with the RCFILE format:

```
create table sales ( id int, fname string, lname string, address
string, city string, state string, zip string, ip string, pid
string, dop string) row format delimited fields terminated by '\t'
STORED AS RCFILE;
```

Benchmarking statistics show that it could reduce the data size up to 14 percent of the original text size as shown in this link http://datametica.com/rcorc-file-format/.

▶ **Optimized Row Columnar** (**ORC**): This is a highly efficient way of storing and processing data in Hive. Data stored in the ORC format improves performance in reading, writing, and processing data with Hive.

▶ **File structure**: The ORC file contains stripes, which is a set of rows, along with other information in the file footer. At the end of the file, there is a postscript that holds compression parameters and the size of the compressed footer. The default size of a stripe is 250 MB.

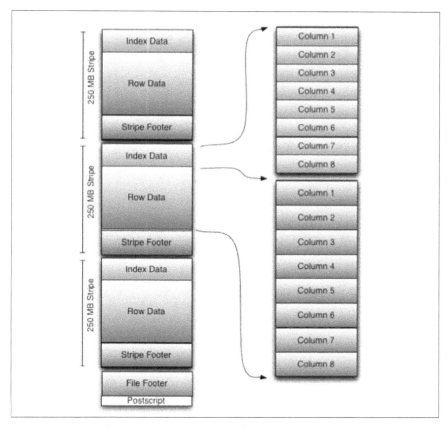

Source: https://cwiki.apache.org/confluence/display/Hive/
LanguageManual+ORC.

Use the following command to create a table with the ORC format:

```
create table sales ( id int, fname string, lname string, address
string, city string, state string, zip string, ip string, pid
string, dop string) row format delimited fields terminated by '\t'
STORED AS ORC;
```

▶ PARQUET: This is a column-oriented storage format that is efficient at querying particular columns in the table. Use the following command to create a table with the ORC format:

```
create table sales ( id int, fname string, lname string, address
string, city string, state string, zip string, ip string, pid
string, dop string) row format delimited fields terminated by '\t'
STORED AS PARQUETFILE;
```

7
Joins and Join Optimization

In this chapter, you will learn:

- ▸ Understanding the joins concept
- ▸ Using a left/right/full outer join
- ▸ Using a left semi join
- ▸ Using a cross join
- ▸ Using a map-side join
- ▸ Using a bucket map join
- ▸ Using a bucket sort merge map join
- ▸ Using a skew join

Understanding the joins concept

A join in Hive is used for the same purpose as in a traditional RDBMS. A join is used to fetch meaningful data from two or more tables based on a common value or field. In other words, a join is used to combine data from multiple tables. A join is performed whenever multiple tables are specified inside the FROM clause.

As of now, joins based on equality conditions only are supported in Hive. It does not support any join condition that is based on non-equality conditions.

The general syntax of defining a join is as follows:

```
join_table:
    table_reference JOIN table_factor [join_condition]
  | table_reference {LEFT|RIGHT|FULL} [OUTER] JOIN table_reference
    join_condition
  | table_reference LEFT SEMI JOIN table_reference join_condition
  | table_reference CROSS JOIN table_reference [join_condition]

table_reference:
    table_factor
  | join_table

  table_factor:
    tbl_name [alias]
  | table_subquery alias
  | ( table_references )

join_condition:
    ON equality_expression
```

In the following list a few functions of joins are illustrated:

- ▶ `table_reference`: Is the table name or the joining table that is used in the join query. `table_reference` can also be a query alias.
- ▶ `table_factor`: It is the same as `table_reference`. It is a table name used in a join query. It can also be a sub-query alias.
- ▶ `join_condition`: `join_condition`: Is the `join` clause that will join two or more tables based on an equality condition. The `AND` keyword is used in case a join is required on more than two tables.

Getting ready

This recipe requires having Hive installed as described in the *Installing Hive* recipe of *Chapter 1, Developing Hive*. You will also need the Hive CLI or Beeline client to run the commands.

How to do it...

Follow these steps to create a join in Hive:

```
SELECT a.* FROM Sales a JOIN Sales_orc b ON a.id = b.id;
SELECT a.* FROM Sales a JOIN Sales_orc b ON a.id <> b.id;
SELECT a.* FROM Sales a, Sales_orc b where a.id = b.id;
SELECT a.*, b.* FROM Sales a JOIN Sales_orc b ON a.id = b.id;
```

```
SELECT a.fname, b.lname FROM Sales a JOIN Sales_orc b ON a.id = b.id;
SELECT a.* FROM Sales a JOIN Sales_orc b ON a.id = b.id and a.fname =
b.fname;
SELECT a.fname, b.lname, c.address FROM Sales a JOIN Sales_orc b ON
a.id = b.id join Sales_info c ON c.id = b.id;
SELECT a.fname, b.lname, c.address FROM Sales a JOIN Sales_orc b ON
a.id = b.id join Sales_info c ON c.address = b.address;
```

How it works...

First, let us see the count of records in all the three tables: `Sales`, `Sales_orc`, and `Sales_info` used in the preceding examples as shown in the following screenshots:

```
hive> SELECT COUNT(*) FROM Sales;
OK
10000
Time taken: 24.154 seconds, Fetched: 1 row(s)
```

```
SELECT COUNT(*) FROM Sales_orc;
OK
51
Time taken: 19.793 seconds, Fetched: 1 row(s)
```

```
hive> SELECT COUNT(*) FROM Sales_info;
OK
101
Time taken: 19.925 seconds, Fetched: 1 row(s)
```

The first statement is a simple join statement that joins two tables: `Sales` and `Sales_orc`. This works in the same manner as in a traditional RDBMS. The output is shown in the following screenshot:

```
hive> SELECT a.* FROM Sales a JOIN Sales_orc b ON a.id = b.id;
OK
0    Zena    Ross    41228 West India Ln.        Powell    Tennessee      21550  192.168.56.127  PI_09
50   Dorothy Duke    47365 West Corona Blvd. Jeffersonville  Colorado      50217  192.168.56.206  PI_01
48   Jocelyn Warner  44429 Ogdensburg St.      Chester Washington      80832  192.168.56.201  PI_01
46   Bradley Mcgowan 65530 South Hackensack Ct.        Fullerton    Illinois          73467  192.168.56.141  PI_02
```

The second statement throws an error as Hive supports only *equality join* conditions and not non-equality conditions. The output is as shown next:

```
hive> SELECT a.* FROM Sales a JOIN Sales_orc b ON a.id <> b.id;
FAILED: SemanticException [Error 10017]: Line 1:44 Both left and right aliases encountered in JOIN 'id'
hive>
```

The third statement works in the same manner as the first statement. This is the SQL-89 way of writing a JOIN statement just like in a traditional RDBMS as compared to the first statement, which is SQL-92, and used most commonly now. The output is as shown next:

```
hive> SELECT a.* FROM Sales a, Sales_orc b where a.id = b.id;
OK
0       Zena    Ross    41228 West India Ln.     Powell  Tennessee       21550   192.168.56.127  PI_09
50      Dorothy Duke    47365 West Corona Blvd. Jeffersonville  Colorado         50217   192.168.56.206  PI_01
48      Jocelyn Warner  44429 Ogdensburg St.     Chester Washington       80832   192.168.56.201  PI_01
46      Bradley Mcgowan 65530 South Hackensack Ct.      Fullerton       Illinois         73467   192.168.56.141  PI_02
44      Hoyt    Howard  27401 North Qatar Ave.   Chicopee        New York        21279   192.168.56.80   PI_02
```

The fourth statement displays all the columns from both the tables Sales and Sales_orc. The output is as shown next:

```
hive> SELECT a.*, b.* FROM Sales a JOIN Sales_orc b ON a.id = b.id;
OK
0       Zena    Ross    41228 West India Ln.     Powell  Tennessee       21550   192.168.56.127  PI_09   0       Zena
e       21550   192.168.56.127  PI_09
50      Dorothy Duke    47365 West Corona Blvd. Jeffersonville  Colorado         50217   192.168.56.206  PI_01   50
nville  Colorado        50217   192.168.56.206  PI_01
```

The fifth statement displays the first name from the Sales table and the last name from the Sales_orc table. This is in comparison to the earlier statement, which displays all the columns from both the tables. The output is as shown next:

```
hive> SELECT a.fname, b.lname FROM Sales a JOIN Sales_orc b ON a.id = b.id;
OK
Zena    Ross
Dorothy Duke
Jocelyn Warner
Bradley Mcgowan
Hoyt    Howard
Wynter  Galloway
Fiona   Patton
Marvin  Gamble
```

The sixth statement shows that we can have multiple join conditions in a single join statement separated by an AND clause just like in a traditional RDBMS. The output is as shown next:

```
hive> SELECT a.* FROM Sales a JOIN Sales_orc b ON a.id = b.id and a.fname = b.fname;
OK
0       Zena    Ross    41228 West India Ln.     Powell  Tennessee       21550   192.168.56.127  PI_09
50      Dorothy Duke    47365 West Corona Blvd. Jeffersonville  Colorado         50217   192.168.56.206  PI_01
48      Jocelyn Warner  44429 Ogdensburg St.     Chester Washington       80832   192.168.56.201  PI_01
46      Bradley Mcgowan 65530 South Hackensack Ct.      Fullerton       Illinois         73467   192.168.56.141  PI_02
44      Hoyt    Howard  27401 North Qatar Ave.   Chicopee        New York        21279   192.168.56.80   PI_02
42      Wynter  Galloway        68748 West Nicaragua Ave.       Aguadilla       Utah    61982   192.168.56.157  PI_04
40      Fiona   Patton  53793 North Norfolk Island Ln.  Hornell South Carolina  03962   192.168.56.70   PI_05
```

The seventh statement joins three tables: `Sales`, `Sales_orc`, and `Sales_info`. For this statement, only a single map/reduce job is run because as per Hive if joining clauses contain the same columns from tables, then only one map/reduce job is run. As per this example, `Sales_orc` uses the `id` column in both the joining clauses so only one map/reduce job is created. The output is as shown next:

```
hive> SELECT a.fname, b.lname, c.address FROM Sales a JOIN Sales_orc b ON a.id = b.id join Sales_info c ON c.id = b.id;
OK
Zena     Ross    41228 West India Ln.
Dorothy Duke     47365 West Corona Blvd.
Jocelyn Warner  44429  Ogdensburg St.
Bradley Mcgowan 65530 South Hackensack Ct.
Hoyt     Howard  27401 North Qatar Ave.
Wynter  Galloway        68748 West Nicaragua Ave.
```

The last statement joins three multiple tables, but this time the map/reduce jobs are two in place on one. The result of the `Sales` and `Sales_orc` tables is the first of the two map/reduce jobs, which is joined to the `Sales_info` table, the second map/reduce job. The output is as shown next:

```
hive> SELECT a.fname, b.lname, c.address FROM Sales a JOIN Sales_orc b ON a.id = b.id join Sales_info c ON c.address = b.address;
OK
Zena     Ross    41228 West India Ln.
Dorothy Duke     47365 West Corona Blvd.
Jocelyn Warner  44429  Ogdensburg St.
Bradley Mcgowan 65530 South Hackensack Ct.
Hoyt     Howard  27401 North Qatar Ave.
```

Using a left/right/full outer join

In this recipe, you will learn how to use left, right and full outer joins in Hive.

In Hive, left/right/full outer joins behave in the same manner as in relation to RDBMS. For a left outer join, all the rows from the table on the left are displayed and the matching rows from the right. All the unmatched rows from the table on the right will be dropped and `Null` will be displayed. A right outer join is just the reverse of a left outer join.

The left outer join is as follows:

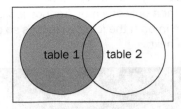

Left join in Hive

A right outer join behaves the opposite to a left outer join. In this join, all the rows from the right table and the matching rows from the left table are displayed. All the unmatched rows from the table on the left will be dropped and `Null` will be displayed.

A right outer join is as follows:

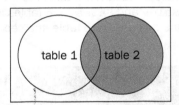

Right join in Hive

In a full outer join, all the rows will be displayed from both the tables. A full outer join combines the result of the left outer join and the right outer join.

A full outer join is as follows:

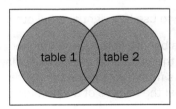

Full join in Hive

The general syntax for the left/right/full outer join is as follows:

```
SELECT [alias1].column_name(s), [alias2].column_name(s)
FROM table_name [alias1]
LEFT/RIGHT/FULL OUTER JOIN table_name2 [alias2]
ON [alias1].column_name = [alias2].column_name;
```

Following are some functions explained, that are used in the full outer join syntax:

▶ [alias1]: Is an optional clause. The table name can also be used instead of the alias name

▶ [alias2]: Is an optional clause. The table name can also be used instead of the alias name

How to do it...

Follow these steps to create a left/right/full outer join in Hive:

```
SELECT * FROM Sales a LEFT OUTER JOIN Sales_orc b ON a.id = b.id;

SELECT * FROM Sales a RIGHT OUTER JOIN Sales_orc b ON a.id = b.id;

SELECT * FROM Sales a FULL OUTER JOIN Sales_orc b ON a.id = b.id;

SELECT * FROM Sales a LEFT OUTER JOIN Sales_orc b ON a.id = b.id WHERE
a.fname = 'John';

SELECT * FROM Sales a RIGHT OUTER JOIN Sales_orc b ON a.id = b.id
WHERE a.fname = 'John';
```

How it works...

The first statement is an example of a left outer join. In this example, all the rows from the Sales table and the matching rows from the Sales_orc table are displayed. The non-matching rows will be dropped and NULL will be displayed. The output is as shown next:

The second statement is an example of a right outer join. In this example, all the rows from the `Sales_orc` table and the matching rows from the `Sales` table are displayed. The non-matching rows will be dropped and `NULL` will be displayed. The output is as shown next:

```
hive> SELECT * FROM Sales a RIGHT OUTER JOIN Sales_orc b ON a.id = b.id;
OK
0       Zena    Ross    41228 West India Ln.    Powell  Tennessee       21550   192.168.56.127  PI_09   0       Zena    Ross
e       21550   192.168.56.127  PI_09
1       Elaine  Bishop  15903 North North Adams Blvd.   Hawaiian Gardens        Alaska  06429   192.168.56.105  PI_03   1
Blvd.   Hawaiian Gardens        Alaska  06429   192.168.56.105  PI_03
2       Sage    Carroll 6880 Greenland Ct.      Guayanilla      Nevada  08899   192.168.56.40   PI_03   2       Sage    Carroll
evada   08899   192.168.56.40   PI_03
3       Cade    Singleton       64021 South Bulgaria Ave.       Derby   Missouri        11233   192.168.56.171  PI_06   3
aria Ave.       Derby   Missouri        11233   192.168.56.171  PI_06
4       Abra    Wright  50155 South Mongolia Ln.        Port Jervis     New Jersey      17751   192.168.56.52   PI_09   4
Port Jervis     New Jersey      17751   192.168.56.52   PI_09
```

The third statement is an example of a full outer join. In this example, all the rows from the `Sales_orc` table and the `Sales` table are displayed. `Null` is displayed where the joining condition is not met. The output is as shown next:

```
hive> SELECT * FROM Sales a FULL OUTER JOIN Sales_orc b ON a.id = b.id;
9979    Amaya   Madden  89534 West Tokelau Blvd.        Moorhead        New York        10087   192.168.56.0    PI_04   NULL
ULL     NULL    NULL
9980    Mira    Phelps  74956 North Turkmenistan Ct.    Carolina        North Carolina  62789   192.168.56.6    PI_04   NULL
ULL     NULL    NULL
9981    Cain    Shepherd        65814 West Christmas Island Blvd.       Oneonta North Carolina  17014   192.168.56.140  PI_06
ULL     NULL    NULL    NULL
9982    Ria     Hansen  23700 West Bradford Blvd.       Missoula        West Virginia   99380   192.168.56.121  PI_06   NULL
ULL     NULL    NULL
9983    Tate    Roach   18461 North Japan Way   Wheeling        California      16368   192.168.56.38   PI_05   NULL    NULL
ULL     NULL
9984    Dolan   Briggs  46722 East Congo Blvd.  Ansonia Missouri        58463   192.168.56.247  PI_06   NULL    NULL    NULL
ULL
9985    MacKenzie       Swanson 56966 South Chad Ln.    Hialeah Washington      82211   192.168.56.221  PI_02   NULL    NULL
```

The fourth statement first joins the two tables based on the left outer join and then filters out the rows based on the `WHERE` clause. The output is as shown next:

```
hive> SELECT * FROM Sales a LEFT OUTER JOIN Sales_orc b ON a.id = b.id WHERE a.fname = 'John';
OK
9898    John    Norman  88176 South Cambodia Ave.       Laguna Woods    Delaware        87857   192.168.56.123  PI_06   NULL    NULL
ULL     NULL    NULL
5552    John    Leonard 92838 Cameroon Ave.     Brookfield      Massachusetts   82157   192.168.56.183  PI_06   NULL    NULL    NULL
ULL     NULL
5438    John    Case    45250 North Micronesia Blvd.    La Puente       Idaho   27577   192.168.56.172  PI_10   NULL    NULL    NULL
ULL     NULL
9587    John    Rivers  49544 South Norton Ln.  Scarborough     Missouri        71896   192.168.56.91   PI_05   NULL    NULL    NULL
ULL     NULL
7759    John    Conley  72203 South Areceibo Ln.        Chattanooga     South Carolina  91570   192.168.56.37   PI_04   NULL    NULL
ULL     NULL    NULL
5109    John    Hancock 75125 India Way Methuen North Dakota     39688   192.168.56.121  PI_02   NULL    NULL    NULL
ULL
3841    John    Flowers 98976 North Bolivia St. San Luis Obispo Texas   86173   192.168.56.71   PI_06   NULL    NULL    NULL
ULL
3411    John    Russo   41922 South Sierra Leone Ave.   Chesapeake      Wyoming 43952   192.168.56.98   PI_06   NULL    NULL    NULL
ULL     NULL
971     John    Merritt 55106 South Armenia Way Ypsilanti       California      13701   192.168.56.7    PI_09   NULL    NULL    NULL
ULL     NULL
Time taken: 27.702 seconds. Fetched: 9 row(s)
```

The sixth statement first joins the two tables based on the right outer join and then filters out the rows based on the WHERE clause. The output is as shown next:

```
hive> SELECT * FROM Sales a RIGHT OUTER JOIN Sales_orc b ON a.id = b.id WHERE a.fname = 'John';
OK
971     John    Merritt 55106 South Armenia Way Ypsilanti        California       13701   192.168.56.7    PI_09   971     John
1       California      13701   192.168.56.7    PI_09
Time taken: 20.568 seconds, Fetched: 1 row(s)
```

Using a left semi join

In this recipe, you will learn how to use a left semi join in Hive.

The left semi join is used in place of the IN/EXISTS sub-query in Hive. In a traditional RDBMS, the IN and EXISTS clauses are widely used whereas in Hive, the left semi join is used as a replacement of the same.

In the left semi join, the right-hand side table can only be used in the join clause but not in the WHERE or the SELECT clause.

The general syntax of the left semi join is as follows:

```
join_condition
   | table_reference LEFT SEMI JOIN table_reference join_condition
```

Where:

▸ table_reference: Is the table name or the joining table that is used in the join query. table_reference can also be a query alias.

▸ join_condition: join_condition: Is the join clause that will join two or more tables based on an equality condition. The AND keyword is used in case a join is required on more than two tables.

How to do it...

Run the following commands to create a left semi join in Hive:

```
SELECT a.* FROM Sales a LEFT SEMI JOIN Sales_orc b ON a.id = b.id;


SELECT a.*, b.* FROM Sales a LEFT SEMI JOIN Sales_orc b ON a.id = b.id;


SELECT a.* FROM Sales a LEFT SEMI JOIN Sales_orc b ON a.id = b.id WHERE
b.id = 1;
```

How it works...

The first statement returns all the rows from the `Sales` tables. This statement works exactly the same as mentioned next:

```
SELECT a.* FROM Sales a WHERE a.id IN (SELECT b.id FROM Sales_orc b);
```

The output of both the queries is shown next:

```
hive> SELECT a.* FROM Sales a LEFT SEMI JOIN Sales_orc b ON a.id = b.id;
OK
0      Zena    Ross    41228 West India Ln.       Powell  Tennessee       21550   192.168.56.127  PI_09
50     Dorothy Duke    47365 West Corona Blvd. Jeffersonville  Colorado       50217   192.168.56.206  PI_01
48     Jocelyn Warner  44429 Ogdensburg St.    Chester Washington      80832   192.168.56.201  PI_01
46     Bradley Mcgowan 65530 South Hackensack Ct.      Fullerton       Illinois        73467   192.168.56.141  PI_02
44     Hoyt    Howard  27401 North Qatar Ave.  Chicopee        New York        21279   192.168.56.80   PI_02
42     Wynter  Galloway        68748 West Nicaragua Ave.       Aguadilla       Utah    61982   192.168.56.157  PI_04
40     Fiona   Patton  53793 North Norfolk Island Ln.  Hornell South Carolina  03962   192.168.56.70   PI_05
38     Marvin  Gamble  98294 South Liberia St. Manitowoc       Missouri        41805   192.168.56.136  PI_03
36     Merritt Waters  73679 North Norfolk Island St.  San Juan Capistrano     Louisiana       45934   192.168.56.157  PI_02
```

```
hive> SELECT a.* FROM Sales a WHERE a.id IN (SELECT b.id FROM Sales_orc b);
OK
0      Zena    Ross    41228 West India Ln.       Powell  Tennessee       21550   192.168.56.127  PI_09
50     Dorothy Duke    47365 West Corona Blvd. Jeffersonville  Colorado       50217   192.168.56.206  PI_01
48     Jocelyn Warner  44429 Ogdensburg St.    Chester Washington      80832   192.168.56.201  PI_01
46     Bradley Mcgowan 65530 South Hackensack Ct.      Fullerton       Illinois        73467   192.168.56.141  PI_02
44     Hoyt    Howard  27401 North Qatar Ave.  Chicopee        New York        21279   192.168.56.80   PI_02
42     Wynter  Galloway        68748 West Nicaragua Ave.       Aguadilla       Utah    61982   192.168.56.157  PI_04
40     Fiona   Patton  53793 North Norfolk Island Ln.  Hornell South Carolina  03962   192.168.56.70   PI_05
38     Marvin  Gamble  98294 South Liberia St. Manitowoc       Missouri        41805   192.168.56.136  PI_03
36     Merritt Waters  73679 North Norfolk Island St.  San Juan Capistrano     Louisiana       45934   192.168.56.157  PI_02
```

The second statement throws an error as `FAILED: SemanticException [Error 10009]: Line 1:12 Invalid table alias 'b'`. As mentioned earlier, in a left semi join, the right-hand side table cannot be used in a `SELECT` clause. The output of the query is shown next:

```
hive> SELECT a.*, b.* FROM Sales a LEFT SEMI JOIN Sales_orc b ON a.id = b.id;
FAILED: SemanticException [Error 10009]: Line 1:12 Invalid table alias 'b'
```

The third statement will also throw an error as `FAILED: SemanticException [Error 10009]: Line 1:12 Invalid table alias 'b'`. As mentioned earlier, in a left semi join, the right-hand side table cannot be used in a `WHERE` clause. The output of the query is shown next:

```
hive> SELECT a.* FROM Sales a LEFT SEMI JOIN Sales_orc b ON a.id = b.id WHERE b.id = 1;
FAILED: SemanticException [Error 10004]: Line 1:72 Invalid table alias or column reference 'b':
p_id, dop)
```

Using a cross join

In this recipe, you will learn how to use a cross join in Hive.

Cross join, also known as **Cartesian** product, is a way of joining multiple tables in which all the rows or tuples from one table are paired with the rows and tuples from another table. For example, if the left-hand side table has 10 rows and the right-hand side table has 13 rows then the result set after joining the two tables will be 130 rows. That means all the rows from the left-hand side table (having 10 rows) are paired with all the tables from the right-hand side table (having 13 rows).

If there is a `WHERE` clause in the SQL statement that includes a cross join, then first the cross join takes place and then the result set is filtered out with the help of the `WHERE` clause. This means cross joins are not an efficient and optimized way of joining the tables.

The general syntax of a cross join is as follows:

```
join_condition
  | table_reference [CROSS] JOIN table_reference join_condition
```

Where:

- `table_reference`: Is the table name or the joining table that is used in the join query. `table_reference` can also be a query alias.

- `join_condition`: `join_condition`: Is the `join` clause that will join two or more tables based on an equality condition. The `AND` keyword is used in case a join is required on more than two tables.

How to do it...

Cross joins can be implemented using the `JOIN` keyword or `CROSS JOIN` keyword. If the `CROSS` keyword is not specified then by default a cross join is applied.

The following are examples to use cross joins in tables:

- `SELECT * FROM Sales JOIN Sales_orc;`
- `SELECT * FROM Sales JOIN Sales_orc WHERE Sales.id = 1;`
- `SELECT * FROM Sales CROSS JOIN Sales_orc;`
- `SELECT * FROM Sales a CROSS JOIN Sales_orc b JOIN Location c on a.id = c.id;`

How it works...

The first statement pairs all rows from one table with the rows of another table. The output of the query is shown next:

```
hive> SELECT * FROM Sales JOIN Sales_orc;
4999    Jamal    Howell  26029  Pitcairn Ln.       Stafford          South Carolina  26305
asthampton        California          53026   192.168.56.152  PI_01
4999    Jamal    Howell  26029  Pitcairn Ln.       Stafford          South Carolina  26305
ullerton          Illinois            73467   192.168.56.141  PI_02
4999    Jamal    Howell  26029  Pitcairn Ln.       Stafford          South Carolina  26305
rth      Virginia            57375   192.168.56.10   PI_05
4999    Jamal    Howell  26029  Pitcairn Ln.       Stafford          South Carolina  26305
ashington         80832   192.168.56.201  PI_01
4999    Jamal    Howell  26029  Pitcairn Ln.       Stafford          South Carolina  26305
ichigan 69621     192.168.56.191  PI_01
4999    Jamal    Howell  26029  Pitcairn Ln.       Stafford          South Carolina  26305
nville  Colorado          50217   192.168.56.206  PI_01
4999    Jamal    Howell  26029  Pitcairn Ln.       Stafford          South Carolina  26305
i        California          13701   192.168.56.7    PI_09
Time taken: 32.72 seconds, Fetched: 520000 row(s)
```

The second statement takes as much time in execution as the one in the first example, even though the result set is filtered out with the help of the WHERE clause. This means that the cross join is processed first, then the WHERE clause. The output of the query is shown next:

```
hive> SELECT * FROM Sales JOIN Sales_orc WHERE Sales.id = 1;
1        Elaine  Bishop  15903  North North Adams Blvd.    Hawaiian Gardens      Alaska  06429
t.      Fullerton         Illinois          73467   192.168.56.141  PI_02
1        Elaine  Bishop  15903  North North Adams Blvd.    Hawaiian Gardens      Alaska  06429
omersworth        Virginia          57375   192.168.56.10   PI_05
1        Elaine  Bishop  15903  North North Adams Blvd.    Hawaiian Gardens      Alaska  06429
hester  Washington        80832   192.168.56.201  PI_01
1        Elaine  Bishop  15903  North North Adams Blvd.    Hawaiian Gardens      Alaska  06429
ilford  Michigan          69621   192.168.56.191  PI_01
1        Elaine  Bishop  15903  North North Adams Blvd.    Hawaiian Gardens      Alaska  06429
effersonville    Colorado          50217   192.168.56.206  PI_01
1        Elaine  Bishop  15903  North North Adams Blvd.    Hawaiian Gardens      Alaska  06429
psilanti          California          13701   192.168.56.7    PI_09
Time taken: 30.331 seconds, Fetched: 52 row(s)
```

We can also use the CROSS keyword for CROSS joins. The third statement gives the same result as the one in the first example. The output of the query is shown next:

```
hive> SELECT * FROM Sales CROSS JOIN Sales_orc;
4999    Jamal    Howell  26029  Pitcairn Ln.       Stafford          South Carolina  26305
ashington         80832   192.168.56.201  PI_01
4999    Jamal    Howell  26029  Pitcairn Ln.       Stafford          South Carolina  26305
ichigan 69621     192.168.56.191  PI_01
4999    Jamal    Howell  26029  Pitcairn Ln.       Stafford          South Carolina  26305
nville  Colorado          50217   192.168.56.206  PI_01
4999    Jamal    Howell  26029  Pitcairn Ln.       Stafford          South Carolina  26305
i        California          13701   192.168.56.7    PI_09
Time taken: 35.41 seconds, Fetched: 520000 row(s)
```

We can also club multiple join clauses into a single statement as shown in the fourth statement. In this example, first the cross join is performed between the `Sales` and `Sales_orc` table and the result set is then joined with the `Location` table. The output of the query is shown next:

```
hive> SELECT * FROM Sales a CROSS JOIN Sales_orc b JOIN Location c on a.id = c.id;
1       Elaine  Bishop  15903 North North Adams Blvd.   Hawaiian Gardens        Alaska  06429   192.168.56.105
omersworth      Virginia        57375   192.168.56.10   PI_05   1       Elaine  Bishop  15903 North North Adams
56.105  PI_03
1       Elaine  Bishop  15903 North North Adams Blvd.   Hawaiian Gardens        Alaska  06429   192.168.56.105
hester  Washington      80832   192.168.56.201  PI_01   1       Elaine  Bishop  15903 North North Adams Blvd.
I_03
1       Elaine  Bishop  15903 North North Adams Blvd.   Hawaiian Gardens        Alaska  06429   192.168.56.105
ilford  Michigan        69621   192.168.56.191  PI_01   1       Elaine  Bishop  15903 North North Adams Blvd.
I_03
1       Elaine  Bishop  15903 North North Adams Blvd.   Hawaiian Gardens        Alaska  06429   192.168.56.105
effersonville   Colorado        50217   192.168.56.206  PI_01   1       Elaine  Bishop  15903 North North Adams
56.105  PI_03
1       Elaine  Bishop  15903 North North Adams Blvd.   Hawaiian Gardens        Alaska  06429   192.168.56.105
psilanti        California       13701   192.168.56.7    PI_09   1       Elaine  Bishop  15903 North North Adams
56.105  PI_03
Time taken: 31.478 seconds, Fetched: 572 row(s)
```

Using a map-side join

In this recipe, you will learn how to use a map-side joins in Hive.

While joining multiple tables in Hive, there comes a scenario where one of the tables is small in terms of rows while another is large. In order to produce the result in an efficient manner, Hive uses map-side joins. In map-side joins, the smaller table is cached in the memory while the large table is streamed through mappers. By doing so, Hive completes the joining at the mapper side only, thereby removing the reducer job. By doing so, performance is improved tremendously.

How to do it...

There are two ways of using map-side joins in Hive.

One is to use the `/*+ MAPJOIN(<table_name>)*/` hint just after the select keyword. `table_name` has to be the table that is smaller in size. This is the old way of using map-side joins.

The other way of using a map-side join is to set the following property to `true` and then run a `join` query:

set hive.auto.convert.join=true;

Follow these steps to use a `map-side` join in Hive:

```
SELECT /*+ MAPJOIN(Sales_orc)*/ a.fname, b.lname FROM Sales a JOIN Sales_
orc b ON a.id = b.id;
```

```
SELECT a.* FROM Sales a JOIN Sales_orc b ON a.id = b.id and a.fname =
b.fname;
```

How it works...

Let us first run the set `hive.auto.convert.join=true;` command on the Hive shell.
The output of this command is shown next:

```
hive> set hive.auto.convert.join=true;
```

The first statement uses the `MAPJOIN` hint to optimize the execution time of the query. In this
example, the `Sales_orc` table is smaller compared to the `Sales` table. The output of the
first statement is shown in the following screenshot. The highlighted statement shows that
there are no reducers used while processing this query. The total time taken by this query is
40 seconds:

```
hive> SELECT /*+ MAPJOIN(Sales_orc)*/ a.fname, b.lname FROM Sales a JOIN Sales_orc b ON a.id = b.id;
Query ID = hadoop_20160211234040_f59e1ffc-7908-4ca3-b086-d0e6d0ace54c
Total jobs = 1
Execution log at: /tmp/hadoop/hadoop_20160211234040_f59e1ffc-7908-4ca3-b086-d0e6d0ace54c.log
2016-02-11 11:41:02     Starting to launch local task to process map join;     maximum memory = 518979584
2016-02-11 11:41:03     Dump the side-table for tag: 1 with group count: 52 into file: file:/tmp/hadoop/bff
1_535059690879355711-1/-local-10003/HashTable-Stage-3/MapJoin-mapfile41--.hashtable
2016-02-11 11:41:03     Uploaded 1 File to: file:/tmp/hadoop/bff9849e-5768-4216-b002-125c786e33a5/hive_2016
le-Stage-3/MapJoin-mapfile41--.hashtable (1648 bytes)
2016-02-11 11:41:03     End of local task; Time Taken: 1.716 sec.
Execution completed successfully
MapredLocal task succeeded
Launching Job 1 out of 1
Number of reduce tasks is set to 0 since there's no reduce operator
Starting Job = job_1455043728844_0066, Tracking URL = http://node1:8088/proxy/application_1455043728844_006
Kill Command = /opt/hadoop-2.6.0//bin/hadoop job  -kill job_1455043728844_0066
Hadoop job information for Stage-3: number of mappers: 2; number of reducers: 0
2016-02-11 23:41:12,845 Stage-3 map = 0%,  reduce = 0%
2016-02-11 23:41:24,828 Stage-3 map = 100%,  reduce = 0%, Cumulative CPU 1.79 sec
MapReduce Total cumulative CPU time: 1 seconds 790 msec
Ended Job = job_1455043728844_0066
MapReduce Jobs Launched:
Stage-Stage-3: Map: 2   Cumulative CPU: 3.56 sec   HDFS Read: 297078 HDFS Write: 725 SUCCESS
Total MapReduce CPU Time Spent: 3 seconds 560 msec
OK
Zena    Ross
Dorothy Duke
Jocelyn Warner
Bradley Mcgowan
Hoyt    Howard
Wynter  Galloway
Time taken: 40.022 seconds, Fetched: 52 row(s)
```

The second statement does not use the `MAPJOIN` hint. In this case, the property `hive.auto.convert.join` is set to true. In this, all the queries will be treated as `MAPJOIN` queries whereas the hint is used for a specific query:

```
hive> SELECT a.fname, b.lname FROM Sales a JOIN Sales_orc b ON a.id = b.id;
Query ID = hadoop_20160212000505_2d585c51-690c-4d5a-b533-1865332feb7f
Total jobs = 1
Execution log at: /tmp/hadoop/hadoop_20160212000505_2d585c51-690c-4d5a-b533-1865332feb7f.log
2016-02-12 12:05:42     Starting to launch local task to process map join;     maximum memory = 518979584
2016-02-12 12:05:43     Dump the side-table for tag: 1 with group count: 52 into file: file:/tmp/hadoop/bff984
9_8850161040585641990-1/-local-10003/HashTable-Stage-3/MapJoin-mapfile51--.hashtable
2016-02-12 12:05:43     Uploaded 1 File to: file:/tmp/hadoop/bff9849e-5768-4216-b002-125c786e33a5/hive_2016-02
ble-Stage-3/MapJoin-mapfile51--.hashtable (1648 bytes)
2016-02-12 12:05:43     End of local task; Time Taken: 1.649 sec.
Execution completed successfully
MapredLocal task succeeded
Launching Job 1 out of 1
Number of reduce tasks is set to 0 since there's no reduce operator
Starting Job = job_1455043728844_0067, Tracking URL = http://node1:8088/proxy/application_1455043728844_0067/
Kill Command = /opt/hadoop-2.6.0//bin/hadoop job  -kill job_1455043728844_0067
Hadoop job information for Stage-3: number of mappers: 2; number of reducers: 0
2016-02-12 00:05:51,672 Stage-3 map = 0%,  reduce = 0%
2016-02-12 00:06:03,715 Stage-3 map = 100%,  reduce = 0%, Cumulative CPU 3.55 sec
MapReduce Total cumulative CPU time: 3 seconds 550 msec
Ended Job = job_1455043728844_0067
MapReduce Jobs Launched:
Stage-Stage-3: Map: 2   Cumulative CPU: 3.55 sec   HDFS Read: 297090 HDFS Write: 725 SUCCESS
Total MapReduce CPU Time Spent: 3 seconds 550 msec
OK
Zena     Ross
Dorothy Duke
Jocelyn Warner
Bradley Mcgowan
Hoyt     Howard
Wynter  Galloway
Time taken: 30.108 seconds, Fetched: 52 row(s)
```

Now, let us run the set `hive.auto.convert.join=false;` command on the Hive shell and run the second statement. The output of the second command is shown next:

```
hive> set hive.auto.convert.join=false;
hive> SELECT a.* FROM Sales a JOIN Sales_orc b ON a.id = b.id and a.fname = b.fname;
Query ID = hadoop_20160227013636_46cb8b3b-23fd-453f-b5fb-44399a3347fd
Total jobs = 1
Launching Job 1 out of 1
Number of reduce tasks not specified. Estimated from input data size: 1
In order to change the average load for a reducer (in bytes):
  set hive.exec.reducers.bytes.per.reducer=<number>
In order to limit the maximum number of reducers:
  set hive.exec.reducers.max=<number>
In order to set a constant number of reducers:
  set mapreduce.job.reduces=<number>
Starting Job = job_1456515901041_0001, Tracking URL = http://node1:8088/proxy/application
Kill Command = /opt/hadoop-2.6.0//bin/hadoop job  -kill job_1456515901041_0001
Hadoop job information for Stage-1: number of mappers: 3; number of reducers: 1
2016-02-27 01:36:52,350 Stage-1 map = 0%,  reduce = 0%
2016-02-27 01:37:07,556 Stage-1 map = 33%,  reduce = 0%, Cumulative CPU 1.44 sec
2016-02-27 01:37:08,706 Stage-1 map = 67%,  reduce = 0%, Cumulative CPU 3.35 sec
2016-02-27 01:37:09,782 Stage-1 map = 100%,  reduce = 0%, Cumulative CPU 5.23 sec
```

There are a few restrictions while using a `map-side` join. The following are not supported:

- ▶ Union followed by a MapJoin
- ▶ Lateral view followed by a MapJoin
- ▶ Reduce sink (group by/join/sort by/cluster by/distribute by) followed by MapJoin
- ▶ MapJoin followed by union
- ▶ MapJoin followed by join
- ▶ MapJoin followed by MapJoin

 Also, the `MAPJOIN` hint should only be used when either the data is sorted or the table is bucketed. In this case, the join is automatically converted into a bucket map join or a bucket sort merge map join, which is discussed in the later part of this chapter. So use the set `hive.auto.convert.join=true;` instead of hint in the statement.

Using a bucket map join

In this recipe, you will learn how to use a bucket map join in Hive.

A bucket map join is used when the tables are large and all the tables used in the join are bucketed on the join columns. In this type of join, one table should have buckets in multiples of the number of buckets in another table. For example, if one table has 2 buckets then the other table must have either 2 buckets or a multiple of 2 buckets (2, 4, 6, and so on). If the preceding condition is satisfied then the joining can be done at the mapper side only, otherwise a normal inner join is performed. This means that only the required buckets are fetched on the mapper side and not the complete table. That is, only the matching buckets of all small tables are replicated onto each mapper. Doing this, the efficiency of the query is improved drastically. In a bucket map join, data is not sorted.

Hive does not support a bucket map join by default. The following property needs to be set to true for the query to work as a bucket map join:

```
set hive.optimize.bucketmapjoin = true
```

In this type of join, not only tables need to be bucketed but also data needs to be bucketed while inserting. For this, the following property needs to be set before inserting the data:

```
set hive.enforce.bucketing = true
```

The general syntax for a bucket map join is as follows:

```
SELECT /*+ MAPJOIN(table2) */ column1, column2, column3
FROM table1 [alias_name1] JOIN table2 [alias_name2]
ON table1 [alias_name1].key = table2 [alias_name2].key
```

Where:

- `table1`: Is the bigger or larger table
- `table2`: Is the smaller table
- `[alias_name1]`: Is the alias name for `table1`
- `[alias_name2]`: Is the alias name for `table2`

Getting ready

This recipe requires having Hive installed as described in the *Installing Hive* recipe of *Chapter 1, Developing Hive*. You will also need the Hive CLI or Beeline client to run the commands.

How to do it...

Follow these steps to use a bucket map join in Hive:

- `SELECT /*+ MAPJOIN(Sales_orc) */ a.*, b.* FROM Sales a JOIN Sales_orc b ON a.id = b.id;`
- `SELECT /*+ MAPJOIN(Sales_orc, Location) */ a.*, b.*, c.* FROM Sales a JOIN Sales_orc b ON a.id = b.id JOIN Location ON a.id = c.id;`

How it works...

In the first statement, `Sales_orc` has less data compared to the `Sales` table. The `Sales` table is having the buckets in multiples of the buckets for `Sales_orc`. Only the matching buckets are replicated onto each mapper.

The second statement works in the same manner as the first one. The only difference is that in the preceding statement there is a join on more than two tables. The `Sales_orc` buckets and `Location` buckets are fetched or replicated onto the mapper of the `Sales` table, performing the joins at the mapper side only.

Using a bucket sort merge map join

In this recipe, you will learn how to use a bucket sort merge map join in Hive.

A bucket sort merge map join is an advanced version of a bucket map join. If the data in the tables is sorted and bucketed on the join columns at the same time then a bucket sort merge map join comes into the picture. In this type of join, all the tables must have an equal number of buckets as each mapper will read a bucket from each table and will perform a bucket sort merge map join.

It is mandatory for the data to be sorted in this join condition. The following parameter needs to be set to true for sorting the data or data can be sorted manually:

`Set hive.enforce.sorting = true;`

 If data in the buckets is not sorted then there is a possibility that a wrong result or output is generated as Hive does not check whether the buckets are sorted or not.

The following parameters need to be set for:

```
set hive.input.format = org.apache.hadoop.hive.ql.io.
BucketizedHiveInputFormat;

set hive.optimize.bucketmapjoin = true;

set hive.optimize.bucketmapjoin.sortedmerge = true;
```

The general syntax for a bucket map join is as follows:

```
SELECT /*+ MAPJOIN(table2) */ column1, column2, column3…
FROM table1 [alias_name1] JOIN table2 [alias_name2]
ON table1 [alias_name1].key = table2 [alias_name2].key
```

Where:

- `table1`: Is the bigger or larger table
- `table2`: Is the smaller table
- `[alias_name1]`: Is the alias name for `table1`
- `[alias_name2]`: Is the alias name for `table2`

Getting ready

This recipe requires having Hive installed as described in the *Installing Hive* recipe of *Chapter 1, Developing Hive*. You will also need the Hive CLI or Beeline client to run the commands.

How to do it...

Follow these steps to use a bucket sort merge map join in Hive:

- ▶ SELECT /*+ MAPJOIN(Sales_orc) */ a.*, b.* FROM Sales a JOIN Sales_orc b ON a.id = b.id;
- ▶ SELECT /*+ MAPJOIN(Sales_orc, Location) */ a.*, b.*, c.* FROM Sales a JOIN Sales_orc b ON a.id = b.id JOIN Location ON a.id = c.id;

How it works...

In the first statement, Sales_orc is having the same number of buckets as in the Sales table. The Sales table is having the buckets in multiples of the buckets for Sales_orc. Each mapper will read a bucket from the Sales table and the corresponding bucket from the Sales_orc table and will perform a bucket sort merge map join.

The second statement works in the same manner as the first one. The only difference is that in the preceding statement there is a join on more than two tables.

Using a skew join

In this recipe, you will learn how to use a skew join in Hive.

A skew join is used when there is a table with skew data in the joining column. A skew table is a table that is having values that are present in large numbers in the table compared to other data. Skew data is stored in a separate file while the rest of the data is stored in a separate file.

If there is a need to perform a join on a column of a table that is appearing quite often in the table, the data for that particular column will go to a single reducer, which will become a bottleneck while performing the join. To reduce this, a skew join is used.

The following parameter needs to be set for a skew join:

```
set hive.optimize.skewjoin=true;
set hive.skewjoin.key=100000;
```

How to do it...

Run the following command to use a bucket sort merge map join in Hive:

```
SELECT a.* FROM Sales a JOIN Sales_orc b ON a.id = b.id;
```

How it works...

Let us suppose that there are two tables, Sales and Sales_orc, as shown next:

```
hive> desc Sales;
OK
id                      int
fname                   string
lname                   string
address                 string
city                    string
state                   string
ip                      string
p_id                    string
dop                     string
Time taken: 0.172 seconds, Fetched: 9 row(s)
```

The Sales table

```
hive> desc Sales_orc;
OK
id                      int
fname                   string
lname                   string
address                 string
city                    string
state                   string
ip                      string
p_id                    string
dop                     string
Time taken: 0.161 seconds, Fetched: 9 row(s)
```

The Sales_orc table

There is a join that needs to be performed on the ID column that is present in both tables. The Sales table is having a column ID, which is highly skewed on 10. That is, the value 10 for the ID column is appearing in large numbers compared to other values for the same column. The Sales_orc table also having the value 10 for the ID column but not as much compared to the Sales table. Now, considering this, first the Sales_orc table is read and the rows with ID=10 are stored in the in-memory hash table. Once it is done, the set of mappers read the Sales table having ID=10 and the value from the Sales_orc table is compared and the partial output is computed at the mapper itself and no data needs to go to the reducer, improving performance drastically.

This way, we end up reading only Sales_orc twice. The skewed keys in Sales are only read and processed by the Mapper, and not sent to the reducer. The rest of the keys in Sales go through only a single Map/Reduce. The assumption is that Sales_orc has few rows with keys that are skewed in A. So these rows can be loaded into the memory.

8

Statistics in Hive

In previous chapters, you learned different types of joins in Hive and optimizations available in Hive joins.

In this chapter, we will cover the following recipes in detail:

- ▶ Bringing statistics in to Hive
- ▶ Table and partition statistics in Hive
- ▶ Column statistics in Hive
- ▶ Top K statistics in Hive

Bringing statistics in to Hive

Statistics in terms of the number of records in a table or partitions or histograms of a column is important. Also, it could help in query optimization. Statistical data is required as an input to many functions so that it can compare different plans. Statistics also help users by storing answers to some of the most frequently queried data and prevent long-running execution plans each time a query is executed. Common examples include unique visitors to the site, top 10 stories read by the visitors, and so on.

How to do it...

There are the following different levels at which statistics can be derived:

- ▶ Statistics at table level—These statistics can be used to derive the number of rows and files, size, and so on in a table.
- ▶ Statistics at partition level—These statistics can be used to derive the number of rows and files, size, and so on in all partitions or specified partitions of a table.

► Statistics at column level—These statistics can be used to derive the number of distinct values and NULL values, average size, and other parameters of all columns or specified columns of a table or partition.

Table and partition statistics in Hive

The first development in statistical computation is to support tables and partition-level statistics. With other metadata, the table and partition statistics are also stored in a configured metastore. The statistics are supported for both existing and new tables. The following are the statistics currently supported for tables and partitions:

► The number of rows

► The number of files

► Size in bytes

► Max, min, and average row sizes

► Max, min, and average file sizes

► The number of partitions (in the case of tables)

Getting ready

This recipe requires Hive installed as described in the *Installing Hive* recipe of *Chapter 1, Developing Hive*. You will also need Hive CLI or the beeline client to run the commands.

How to do it...

For newly created table or partitions using the INSERT OVERWRITE command, statistics are computed automatically at table level. If you want to disable statistics calculations for a table, you need to set hive.stats.autogather to false either for the session or permanently in hive-site.xml.

For tables already present in Hive, you can use the ANALYZE command to gather statistics and store them in the Hive metastore. The commands could be used as follows:

```
ANALYZE TABLE [db_name.]tablename [PARTITION(partcol1[=val1],
partcol2[=val2], ...)] COMPUTE STATISTICS [FOR COLUMNS] [NOSCAN];
```

For example, let's create a table named sales with a sample dataset as mentioned in the following screenshot:

The following SQL code will create a table named `sales`:

```
CREATE TABLE sales ( id INT, fname STRING, lname STRING, address STRING,
city STRING, state STRING, ip STRING, pid STRING) ROW FORMAT DELIMITED
FIELDS TERMINATED BY '\t';
```

Now load some sample data into the table mentioned earlier:

```
LOAD DATA LOCAL inpath '/opt/products_sales_data.txt' into table product_
sales;
```

When you execute the command `desc formatted` on this table, it will list all the details about the table as follows:

For gathering the statistics about this table, let's analyze this table with the following command:

```
ANALYZE TABLE sales COMPUTE STATISTICS;
```

This command would run `map-reduce` on the table to compute the statistics, and after successful completion of this `map-reduce` job, if we again describe the table, we find the following statistics:

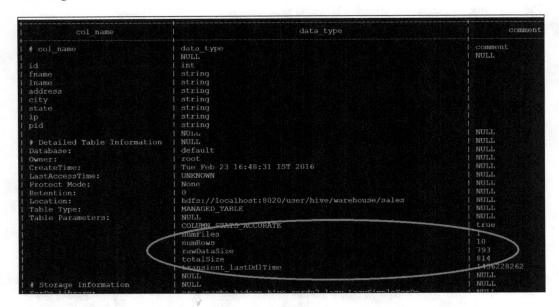

Statistics for a partitioned table

Let's create a partitioned table with product ID (field named `pid`) as a partition column for the same `sales` dataset:

```
CREATE TABLE sales_part (id INT, fname STRING, lname STRING, address
STRING, city STRING, state STRING, ip STRING) PARTITIONED BY (pid STRING)
ROW FORMAT DELIMITED FIELDS TERMINATED BY '\t';
```

For dynamic partitioning, let's first enable dynamic partitioning using the following commands:

```
set hive.exec.dynamic.partition=true;
```

```
set hive.exec.dynamic.partition.mode=nonstrict;
```

Now let's put the data in a partitioned table as follows:

INSERT INTO sales_part PARTITION(pid) SELECT id, fname, lname, address, city, state, ip, pid FROM sales;

We would then analyze all partitions or a set of partitions for the table `sales_part`.

To derive the statistics of a particular partition, you can specify the partition name in the `ANALYZE` command, as shown here:

ANALYZE TABLE sales_part PARTITION(pid= 'PI_09') COMPUTE STATISTICS;

The previously mentioned command will run a `map-reduce` job to derive statistics of a specified partition with a product ID equal to `PI_09`. Here, the specified partition name is `pid= 'PI_09'`.

Run the `DESCRIBE FORMATTED` command to check the statistics:

DESCRIBE FORMATTED sales_part PARTITION(pid='PI_09');

```
0: jdbc:hive2://localhost:10000> DESCRIBE FORMATTED sales_part PARTITION(pid='PI_09');
+--------------------------------+-------------------------------------------------------------+-----------+
|            col_name            |                         data_type                           |  comment  |
+--------------------------------+-------------------------------------------------------------+-----------+
| # col_name                     | data_type                                                   | comment   |
|                                | NULL                                                        | NULL      |
| id                             | int                                                         |           |
| fname                          | string                                                      |           |
| lname                          | string                                                      |           |
| address                        | string                                                      |           |
| city                           | string                                                      |           |
| state                          | string                                                      |           |
| ip                             | string                                                      |           |
|                                | NULL                                                        | NULL      |
| # Partition Information        | NULL                                                        | NULL      |
| # col_name                     | data_type                                                   | comment   |
|                                | NULL                                                        | NULL      |
| pid                            | string                                                      |           |
|                                | NULL                                                        | NULL      |
| # Detailed Partition Information | NULL                                                      | NULL      |
| Partition Value:               | [PI_09]                                                     | NULL      |
| Database:                      | default                                                     | NULL      |
| Table:                         | sales_part                                                  | NULL      |
| CreateTime:                    | Tue Feb 23 17:33:30 IST 2016                                | NULL      |
| LastAccessTime:                | UNKNOWN                                                     | NULL      |
| Protect Mode:                  | None                                                        | NULL      |
| Location:                      | hdfs://localhost:8020/user/hive/warehouse/sales_part/pid=PI_09 | NULL   |
| Partition Parameters:          | NULL                                                        | NULL      |
|                                | COLUMN_STATS_ACCURATE                                       | true      |
|                                | numFiles                                                    | 1         |
|                                | numRows                                                     | 2         |
|                                | rawDataSize                                                 | 139       |
|                                | totalSize                                                   | 141       |
|                                | transient_lastDdlTime                                       | 1456229093|
|                                | NULL                                                        | NULL      |
```

To derive the statistics of all partitions, you can specify only the partitioned column name without specifying any value in the `ANALYZE` command, as shown here:

ANALYZE TABLE sales_part PARTITION(pid) COMPUTE STATISTICS;

The previously mentioned command will derive statistics of all partitions of the table. The following is a snippet of the MapReduce job for analyzing all partitions of the `sales_part` table:

```
0: jdbc:hive2://localhost:10000> ANALYZE TABLE sales_part PARTITION(pid) COMPUTE STATISTICS;
INFO  : Number of reduce tasks is set to 0 since there's no reduce operator
WARN  : Hadoop command-line option parsing not performed. Implement the Tool interface and execute your applicat
INFO  : number of splits:1
INFO  : Submitting tokens for job: job_1456225438486_0004
INFO  : The url to track the job: http://localhost:8088/proxy/application_1456225438486_0004/
INFO  : Starting Job = job_1456225438486_0004, Tracking URL = http://localhost:8088/proxy/application_1456225438
INFO  : Kill Command = /opt/hadoop-2.6.0/bin/hadoop job  -kill job_1456225438486_0004
INFO  : Hadoop job information for Stage-0: number of mappers: 1; number of reducers: 0
INFO  : 2016-02-23 17:43:47,088 Stage-0 map = 0%,  reduce = 0%
INFO  : 2016-02-23 17:44:07,339 Stage-0 map = 100%,  reduce = 0%, Cumulative CPU 1.93 sec
INFO  : MapReduce Total cumulative CPU time: 1 seconds 930 msec
INFO  : Ended Job = job_1456225438486_0004
INFO  : Partition default.sales_part{pid=PI_02} stats: [numFiles=1, numRows=1, totalSize=86, rawDataSize=85]
INFO  : Partition default.sales_part{pid=PI_03} stats: [numFiles=1, numRows=1, totalSize=152, rawDataSize=150]
INFO  : Partition default.sales_part{pid=PI_05} stats: [numFiles=1, numRows=1, totalSize=84, rawDataSize=83]
INFO  : Partition default.sales_part{pid=PI_06} stats: [numFiles=1, numRows=1, totalSize=73, rawDataSize=72]
INFO  : Partition default.sales_part{pid=PI_07} stats: [numFiles=1, numRows=1, totalSize=66, rawDataSize=65]
INFO  : Partition default.sales_part{pid=PI_08} stats: [numFiles=1, numRows=1, totalSize=71, rawDataSize=70]
INFO  : Partition default.sales_part{pid=PI_09} stats: [numFiles=1, numRows=2, totalSize=141, rawDataSize=139]
INFO  : Partition default.sales_part{pid=PI_10} stats: [numFiles=1, numRows=1, totalSize=70, rawDataSize=69]
No rows affected (45.43 seconds)
```

To check for statistics of a partition, use the following command:

```
DESCRIBE FORMATTED sales_part PARTITION(pid='PI_09');
```

The following are some of the important properties of table and partition statistics that could be configured at the session level in the CLI or beeline client and permanently in the configuration file `hive-site.xml`:

- `hive.stats.dbclass`: The datastore to store the statistics:
  - **Default Value**: `jdbc:derby` (Hive 0.7 to 0.12) or `fs` (Hive 0.13 and later)
  - **Valid Values**: `jdbc:derby`, `jdbc:mysql`, `fs`, and `hbase`

- `hive.stats.autogather`: Whether to calculate statistics of a table or partition:
  - **Default Value**: `true`
  - Works with the `INSERT OVERWRITE` command

- `hive.stats.jdbcdriver`: The **Java Database Connectivity** (**JDBC**) driver of the database that is used as default to store temporary Hive statistics:
  - **Default Value**: `org.apache.derby.jdbc.EmbeddedDriver`

- `hive.stats.dbconnectionstring`: The connection string of the database that is used as default to store temporary Hive statistics:
  - **Default Value**: `jdbc:derby:;databaseName=TempStatsStore;create=true`

Column statistics in Hive

Similar to table and partition statistics, Hive also supports the analysis of column statistics. The following are the statistics captured by Hive when a column or set of columns are analyzed:

- ▶ The number of distinct values
- ▶ The number of NULL values
- ▶ Minimum or maximum K values where K could be given by a user
- ▶ Histogram: frequency and height balanced
- ▶ Average size of the column
- ▶ Average or sum of all values in the column if their type is numerical
- ▶ Percentiles of the value

How to do it...

As discussed in the previous recipe, Hive provides the `analyze` command to compute table or partition statistics. The same command could be used to compute statistics for one or more column of a Hive table or partition. The HiveQL in order to compute column statistics is as follows:

```
hive> ANALYZE TABLE t1 [PARTITION p1] COMPUTE STATISTICS FOR [COLUMNS c1,
c2..]
```

 An `analyze` command does not support table or column aliases.

In the following example, the use of the `analyze` command is illustrated:

1. Compute statistics for a table: Let's compute the column statistics for the `sales` table:

   ```
   ANALYZE TABLE sales COMPUTE STATISTICS FOR COLUMNS ip, pid;
   ```

2. Compute statistics for a partitioned table: Let's compute the column statistics for the `sales_part` table:

   ```
   ANALYZE TABLE sales_part PARTITION(pid='PI_09') COMPUTE STATISTICS
   FOR COLUMNS fname, ip;
   ```

How it works...

When column statistics are derived using the `ANALYZE` command, all information retrieved using this command is stored in the Hive metastore.

The following tables are created to store column-level statistics in the Hive metastore:

- ▶ `TAB_COL_STATS`: Column statistics derived from a table are stored in the metastore table `TAB_COL_STATS`.

- ▶ For example, when we run the query mentioned later to calculate `pid` and `ip` columns stats of the sales table, the stats are stored in the metastore table `TAB_COL_STATS` with all the information:

  ANALYZE TABLE sales COMPUTE STATISTICS FOR COLUMNS ip,pid;

- ▶ Now, let's check the statistics that are stored in the metastore table:

- ▶ `PART_COL_STATS`: Column statistics derived from a particular partition of a table are stored in the metastore table `PART_COL_STATS`.

- ▶ For example, when we run the query mentioned later to calculate the `fname` and `ip` columns statistics of specified partition of the sales table, the statistics are stored in the metastore table `PART_COL_STATS` with all the information:

  ANALYZE TABLE sales_part PARTITION(pid='PI_09') COMPUTE STATISTICS FOR COLUMNS fname, ip;

- ▶ Now, let's check the statistics that are stored in the metastore table:

This screenshot is showing the column statistics stored in the Hive metastore
(in our case, MySQL).

Top K statistics in Hive

It is the mechanism of collecting the top K column values of a Hive table. In this, the top
K values of the most skewed column are stored in the partition. This is applicable for both
existing and newly created tables.

How to do it...

Top K statistics computation is disabled by default. The following are some of the properties
that could be set to compute and store top K statistics:

- `hive.stats.topk.collect`

    This would enable computing top K and putting it into skewed information:

    - **Default Value**: `false`
    - **Valid Values**: `true`, `false`

- `hive.stats.topk.num`

    - Using this property, you can specify K value for your top K result

- `hive.stats.topk.minpercent`

    - It is the minimal percentage of a row value to be in top K result
    - It could be any `float` value between 0.0 and 100

Let's set the following properties for top K statistics:

```
hive> set hive.stats.topk.collect=true;
hive> set hive.stats.topk.num=4;
hive> set hive.stats.topk.minpercent=0;
hive> set hive.stats.topk.poolsize=100;
```

First, let's create a partitioned table using the following command:

```
hive> CREATE TABLE sales_topk (fname STRING, ip STRING) PARTITIONED BY
(pid STRING);
```

Now insert some data, as shown in the following command:

```
hive> INSERT OVERWRITE TABLE sales_topk PARTITION (pid='PI_09') SELECT
fname, ip FROM sales;
```

While executing the previous command, Hive will derive the top K statistics. To check the top K statistics run the following command:

```
hive> DESCRIBE FORMATTED sales_topk partition (pid='PI_09');
```

The expected output once the feature is available in Hive is:

- ▸ **Skewed Columns:** [ip]
- ▸ **Skewed Values:** [[192.168.56.101], [192.168.56.106]]

> This is currently in progress; all steps and documentation is taken from the Hive Wiki `https://cwiki.apache.org/confluence/display/Hive/Top+K+Stats`.

9
Functions in Hive

Hive provides an extensive set of functions that we will be covering in this chapter; they are as follows:

- ▶ Using built-in functions
- ▶ Using the built-in **User defined Aggregation Function** (**UDAF**)
- ▶ Using the built-in **User Defined Table Function** (**UDTF**)
- ▶ Creating custom **User-Defined Functions** (**UDF**)

Using built-in functions

There are various built-in functions available in Hive that can be used in queries for executing various operations. These functions are used to extract or manipulate data in Hive tables.

Built-in functions are divided into the following categories:

- ▶ Mathematical functions
- ▶ Collection functions
- ▶ Type conversion functions
- ▶ Date functions
- ▶ String functions
- ▶ Conditional functions
- ▶ Miscellaneous functions

How to do it...

In the following sections, a few built-in functions are explained.

Mathematical functions

Hive supports various functions to run some mathematical operations on field values. There are a large number of mathematical functions available in Hive that can be used in queries. Most of the mathematical functions are the same as supported in RDBMS:

Function Name	Return Type	Description
abs(DOUBLE x)	DOUBLE	It will return an absolute value of x.
acos(DOUBLE x), acos(DECIMAL x)	DOUBLE	It will return an arc cosine value of x if the value of x is equal to or between -1 and 1. Otherwise, it will return NULL.
asin(DOUBLE x), asin(DECIMAL x)	DOUBLE	It will return an arc sin value of x if the value of x is equal to or between -1 and 1. Otherwise it will return NULL.
atan(DOUBLE x), atan(DECIMAL x)	DOUBLE	It will return an arc tangent value of x.
bin(BIGINT x)	STRING	It will return the binary value of the number "x" in string format.
cbrt(DOUBLE x)	DOUBLE	It will return the cube root value of x.
ceil(DOUBLE x)	BIGINT	It will return the ceil value of x that is the minimum number greater than or equal to x.
ceiling(DOUBLE x)	BIGINT	It is the same as the ceil function.
conv(BIGINT x, INT from_base, INT to_base)	STRING	It is used to convert the number x from one base to another base. The value returned will be in string format.
conv(STRING x, INT from_base, INT to_base)	STRING	It is used to convert the string x from one base to another base. The value returned will be in String format.
cos(DOUBLE|DECIMAL x)	DOUBLE	It is used derive a cosine value of x, where x is in radians.
degrees(DOUBLE|DECIMAL x)	DOUBLE	It is used to convert x from radians to degree format, where the x parameter is in double or decimal format.
e()	DOUBLE	It will return the value of exponential e.
exp(DOUBLE|DECIMAL x)	DOUBLE	It will return the exponential value of x, where e is the base of the natural algorithm.

Function Name	Return Type	Description
`factorial(INT x)`	BIGINT	It will return the factorial value of the number x.
`floor(DOUBLE x)`	BIGINT	It will return the floor value of x that is the maximum number less than or equal to x.
`greatest(T v1, T v2, and T Vn)`	T	It will return the maximum value from the list of values specified. The data type can be any but must be the same for all values passed to this function. If any argument is `NULL` then it will return `NULL`.
`hex(BIGINT| STRING|BINARY x)`	STRING	It is used to get a hexadecimal value of the number x of the bigint, string, or binary data type. In the case of string, it will convert each character into its hexadecimal format and will return the resulting string.
`least(T v1, T v2, and so on)`	T	It will return the lowest value from the list of values specified. The data type can be any but must be the same for all values passed to this function. If any argument is `NULL` then it will return `NULL`.
`negative(INT x)`	INT	It will return a negative value of x.
`negative(DOUBLE x)`	DOUBLE	It will return a negative value of x.
`pi()`	DOUBLE	It will return a value of `pi`.
`pmod(INT x, INT y)`	INT	It will return a positive value of x modulus y, that is, x mod y.
`pmod(DOUBLE x, DOUBLE y)`	DOUBLE	It will return a positive value of x modulus y, that is, x mod y.
`positive(INT a)`	INT	It will return a positive value of x.
`positive(DOUBLE a)`	DOUBLE	It will return a positive value of x.
`pow(DOUBLE x, DOUBLE n)`	DOUBLE	It is used to derive the power n of the number x, that is, xn.
`power(DOUBLE x, DOUBLE n)`	DOUBLE	It is the same as the `pow` function.
`radians(DOUBLE| DECIMAL x)`	DOUBLE	It is used to convert x from degree to radian format, where the x parameter is in double or decimal format.
`rand()`	DOUBLE	It will return any random number.

Function Name	Return Type	Description
`rand(INT x)`	DOUBLE	It will return any random number with seed value x.
`round(DOUBLE x)`	DOUBLE	It will round off the value of x.
`round(DOUBLE x, INT n)`	DOUBLE	It will round off the value of x to n decimal places.
`sign(DOUBLE x)`	DOUBLE	It will return sign of the number. If x is positive then it will return '1.0' and if x is negative then it will return '-1.0', otherwise it will return '0.0'.
`sign(DECIMAL x)`	DECIMAL	It is the same as just described but for decimal numbers.
`sin(DOUBLE x)`	DOUBLE	It is used to derive the sine value of x, where x is in radians of the double data type.
`sin(DECIMAL x)`	DOUBLE	It is used to derive the sine value of x, where x is in radians of the decimal data type.
`sqrt(DOUBLE x)`	DOUBLE	It will return the square root value of x, where x is of the double data type.
`sqrt(DECIMAL x)`	DOUBLE	It will return the square root value of x, where x is of the decimal data type.
`tan(DOUBLE|DECIMAL x)`	DOUBLE	It is used derive the tangent value of x, where x is in radians of the double or decimal data type.
`unhex(STRING x)`	BINARY	It will return a byte conversion of the number x.

Collection functions

Hive also supports some functions that can be executed on Hive complex data types, such as array and map:

Function Name	Return Type	Description
`array_contains(ARRAY<T>, value)`	BOOLEAN	It is used to check whether a value exists in an array or not.
`map_keys(Map<K,V>)`	ARRAY<K>	It will return all the keys of a map in an unordered array.
`map_values(Map<K,V>)`	ARRAY<V>	It will return all the values of a map in an unordered array.

Function Name	Return Type	Description
`size(Array<T>)`	`INT`	It will return the number of elements in an array.
`size(Map<K,V>)`	`INT`	It will return the number of elements in a map.
`sort_array(Array<T>)`	`ARRAY<T>`	It will return the sorted array in ascending order.

Type conversion functions

Hive supports the following type conversion functions:

Function Name	Return Type	Description
`binary(string|binary)`	`BINARY`	It is used to cast the field value into binary format.
`cast(expr as T)`	`T`	It is used to cast the result of an expression to a specific data type.

Date functions

Hive supports the following built-in functions for date and time operations:

Function Name	Return Type	Description
`add_months(string startDate, int n)`	STRING	It is used to add n of months to a specified date.
`current_date()`	DATE	It will return the current date. Only the date part is returned as a result.
`current_timestamp()`	TIMESTAMP	It will return the current timestamp.
`date_add(string startDate, int n)`	STRING	It is used to add n number of days to a specified date.
`date_format(date/timestamp/string ts, string fmt)`	STRING	It is used to format the date to any specified format.
`date_sub(string startDate, int n)`	STRING	It is used to subtract n of days from a specified date.
`datediff(string endDate, string startDate)`	INT	It will return the number of days between a specified date range.
`day(string date)`	INT	It is used to extract the day part from a date.

Function Name	Return Type	Description
`dayofmonth(date)`	INT	It is the same as the day function.
`from_unixtime(bigint unixtime[, string format])`	STRING	It is used to convert UNIX epoch time to timestamp in the system time zone format.
`from_utc_timestamp(timestamp, string timezone)`	TIMESTAMP	It is used to convert UTC time to a specified time zone format.
`hour(string date)`	INT	It is used to extract the hour part from a timestamp.
`last_day(string date)`	STRING	It will return the timestamp of the last day of the month of which the specified date belongs to.
`minute(string date)`	INT	It is used to extract the minute part from a timestamp.
`month(string date)`	INT	It is used to extract the month part from a timestamp.
`months_between(date1, date2)`	DOUBLE	It will return number of months between a specific date range.
`next_day(string startDate, string dayOfWeek)`	STRING	It will return the date of the day that is after the start date and matches the specified `dayOfWeek`. There are three type of values supported in the second argument `dayOfWeek`: (a) 2 letters day of week; example MO, TU (b) 3 letters day of week; example MON, TUE, and (c) full name day of week; example MONDAY, TUESDAY.
`second(string date)`	INT	It is used to extract the second part from a timestamp.
`to_date(string timestamp)`	STRING	It will return the date part of a specified timestamp value.

Function Name	Return Type	Description
`to_utc_timestamp(timestamp, string timezone)`	TIMESTAMP	It is used to convert the timestamp of any time zone to UTC format.
`trunc(string date, string format)`	STRING	It will truncate the date as per the specified format. Formats supported are `YEAR/YYYY/YY`, `MONTH/MON/MM`.
`unix_timestamp()`	BIGINT	It will return the current UNIX timestamp in seconds.
`unix_timestamp(string date)`	BIGINT	It will convert the date to UNIX timestamp in seconds.
`unix_timestamp(string date, string pattern)`	BIGINT	It will convert the date of the specified pattern to UNIX timestamp in seconds.
`weekofyear(string date)`	INT	It will return the week number for a year of the specified date.
`year(string date)`	INT	It is used to extract the year part from a timestamp.

String functions

Hive supports the following built-in functions for operations on string objects:

Function Name	Return Type	Description
`ascii(STRING x)`	INT	It will return the numeric (ASCII) value of the first character of a string.
`base64(BINARY x)`	STRING	It is used to convert the binary value to `base-64` string format.
`concat(STRING x, STRING y...)`	STRING	It is used to concatenate two or more strings.
`concat(BINARY x, BINARY y...)`	BINARY	It is used to concatenate two or more binary values.

Function Name	Return Type	Description
concat_ws(STRING sep, STRING y...)	STRING	Similar to the concat function, it is used to concatenate two or more strings but with custom separator 'sep'.
concat_ws(STRING SEP, ARRAY<STRING> arr)	STRING	It is the same as the preceding function. It takes the array of a string as an argument and is used to concatenate all strings of the array with the specified separator.
decode(BINARY x, STRING charset)	STRING	It is used to decode the binary value into a string using the specified charset. Supported values for the charset are: UTF-8, UTF-16, UTF-16LE, UTF-16BE, US-ASCII, and ISO-8859-1.
encode(STRING x, STRING charset)	BINARY	It is used to encode the string value into a binary using the specified charset. Supported values for the charset are: UTF-8, UTF-16, UTF-16LE, UTF-16BE, US-ASCII, and ISO-8859-1.
find_in_set(STRING element, STRING elementList)	INT	It is used to find an element in a comma separated list of elements. This function returns the index/position of a string element in elementList, where element is a comma separated string of different elements. If the first argument contains a comma then it will return 0.

Function Name	Return Type	Description
`format_number(NUMBER x, INT d)`	STRING	It is used to format a number into the format `'#,###,###.##'` rounded to d decimal places.
`get_json_object(STRING json_string, STRING path)`	STRING	It is used to get a JSON object from the JSON path specified. In the JSON path, uppercase characters and special characters are not allowed. Also in JSON, keys should not start with any number.
`in_file(STRING str, STRING filename)`	BOOLEAN	It is used to check if a particular string exists as a line in a file.
`initcap(STRING x)`	STRING	It will return the string with the first letter of each word in uppercase and all other letters in the same case.
`instr(STRING x, STRING substr)`	INT	It will return the index/position of the first occurrence of substr in string 'X'. Index starts from 1 so the first character will return 1.
`length(STRING x)`	INT	It will return the length of string x.
`levenshtein(STRING x, STRING y)`	INT	It is used to calculate the `levenshtein` distance between two string arguments. The `levenshtein` distance between two words is the minimum number of changes of characters that are required to convert one word to another word.

Function Name	Return Type	Description
`locate(STRING substr, STRING x, INT n)`	INT	It will return the position of the first occurrence of the substring `substr` in string `x` after index n.
`lower(string A)`	STRING	It will return the string in lowercase.
`lcase(string A)`	STRING	It is the same as the `lower` function and is used to return the string in lowercase.
`lpad(STRING str, INT n, STRING pad)`	STRING	It is used to return the string `str` with left padded with the specified pad to length n.
`ltrim(STRING x)`	STRING	It trims the whitespaces from the left side of the string and returns the resulting string.
`ngrams(ARRAY<ARRAY<STRING>> x, INT n, INT k, INT pf)`	ARRAY<STRUCT<STRING,DOUBLE>>	It will return k most frequent `ngrams` from an array of different tokenized sentences.
`repeat(STRING x, int n)`	STRING	It will repeat string x n times, and will return the resulting string.
`reverse(string x)`	STRING	It will return the reverse of a string.
`rpad(STRING str, INT n, STRING pad)`	STRING	It is used to return the string `str` with right padded with the specified pad to length n.
`rtrim(string A)`	STRING	It trims the whitespaces from the right side of the string and return the resulting string.

Function Name	Return Type	Description
`sentences(STRING x [, STRING lang, STRING locale])`	ARRAY<ARRAY<STRING>>	It is used to tokenize the string into different sentences, where each sentence is an array of words. This function takes `lang` and `locale` as optional arguments.
`soundex(STRING x)`	STRING	It will return the `soundex` code of string x.
`space(INT n)`	STRING	It will return a blank string with n whitespaces.
`split(STRING x, STRING regex)`	ARRAY<STRING>	It will split the string as per the specified regular expression.
`str_to_map(STRING str)`	MAP<STRING,STRING>	It will split the string into a key-value pair using the delimiter "," between each key-value pair and the delimiter "=" between key and value.
`str_to_map(STRING str, STRING delimiter1, STRING delimiter2)`	MAP<STRING,STRING>	It will split the string into a key-value pair using specified delimiters. `delimiter1` splits the text into K-V pairs, and `delimiter2` splits each K-V pair into key and value.
`substr(STRING|BINARY x, INT start)`	STRING|BINARY	It will return the substring of the string or binary value starting from the specified position.
`substring(STRING|BINARY x, INT start)`	STRING|BINARY	It is the same as the `substr` function.

Function Name	Return Type	Description
`trim(STRING x)`	STRING	It trims the whitespaces from both sides of the string and returns the resulting string.
`unbase64(STRING x)`	BINARY	It will convert the string x from base64 to binary.
`upper(STRING x)`	STRING	It will return the string in uppercase.
`ucase(STRING x)`	STRING	It is the same as the `upper` function and is used to return the string in uppercase.

How it works...

Let's see how these functions can be used in real-time environments.

Mathematical functions

The following are a few examples of different mathematical functions.

- ABS: This function returns the absolute value of a number:

  ```
  hive> SELECT abs(-20.0);
  20.0
  ```

- ACOS: This function returns the arc cosine value of a number:

  ```
  hive> SELECT acos(0.5);
  1.0471975511965979
  hive> SELECT acos(1);
  0.0
  ```

- ASIN: This function returns the arc sine value of a number:

  ```
  hive> SELECT asin(0.5);
  0.5235987755982989
  hive> SELECT asin(1);
  1.5707963267948966
  ```

- BIN: This function returns the binary value of a number:

  ```
  hive> SELECT bin(14);
  1110
  hive> SELECT bin(15);
  1111
  ```

- ▶ CBRT: This function returns the cube-root value of a given number:

  ```
  hive> SELECT cbrt(27.0);
  3.0
  ```

- ▶ RAND: This function is used to generate any random number:

  ```
  hive> SELECT rand();
  0.5654304130197764
  hive> SELECT rand();
  0.3892359489373104
  ```

Collection functions

The following are a few examples of different collection functions.

For using array functions, let's create a table with the array data type:

```
CREATE TABLE table_with_array_datatype (city STRING, pins ARRAY<INT>) ROW
FORMAT DELIMITED FIELDS TERMINATED BY '\t' collection items terminated by
',';
```

Now, load some sample data, as shown in the following table:

City	Pins
Noida	[201301,201303,201307]
Delhi	[110001,110002,110003]

- ▶ ARRAY_CONTAINS: This function can be used to check if a particular element in an array exists or not. For example, we have to check in which cities the 110001 pin lies:

  ```
  hive> SELECT city, array_contains(pins,110001) FROM table_with_
  array_datatype;
  Noida    false
  Delhi    true
  ```

```
hive> select * from table_with_array_datatype;
OK
Noida    [201301,201303,201307]
Delhi    [110001,110002,110003]
Time taken: 0.065 seconds, Fetched: 2 row(s)
hive> select city,array_contains(pins,110001) from table_with_array_datatype;
OK
Noida    false
Delhi    true
Time taken: 0.107 seconds, Fetched: 2 row(s)
```

▶ `SIZE`: It is used to check the number of elements in a collection, that is, an array or map. Run the following command to get the count of pin codes in each city:

```
hive> SELECT city, size(pins) FROM table_with_array_datatype;
Noida   3
Delhi   3
Time taken: 0.108 seconds, Fetched: 2 row(s)
```

Type conversion functions

The following are a few examples of type conversion functions:

▶ `CAST`: The next example will cast a string object with the value `100` to the integer object:

```
hive> SELECT cast('1000' as INT);
1000
```

To cast an object from one data type to another data type, data must be appropriate. If data is invalid and cannot be cast as the specified data type, then this function will return `NULL`:

```
hive> SELECT cast('Hi John' as INT);
NULL
```

The following image is showing examples of the `cast` function:

```
hive> SELECT cast('1000' as INT);
OK
1000
Time taken: 0.429 seconds, Fetched: 1 row(s)
hive> SELECT cast('Hi John' as INT);
OK
NULL
Time taken: 0.315 seconds, Fetched: 1 row(s)
hive> SELECT cast('1000.5' as INT);
OK
1000
Time taken: 0.454 seconds, Fetched: 1 row(s)
```

Date functions

The following are a few examples of date functions.

▶ `ADD_MONTHS`: Run the following command to add three months to the date `'2016-01-30'`:

```
hive> SELECT add_months('2016-01-30',3);
2016-04-30
```

- ▶ CURRENT_DATE: This function return the current date of the system:

```
hive> SELECT current_date();
2016-01-23
```

- ▶ CURRENT_TIMESTAMP: This function return the current timestamp of the system:

```
hive> SELECT current_timestamp();
2016-01-23 15:51:04.616
```

- ▶ DATE_ADD: Run the following command to add five days to the date '2016-01-30':

```
hive> SELECT date_add('2016-01-30',5);
2016-02-04
```

- ▶ DATE_FORMAT: Using this function, you can format the date from one format to another format. Run the following command to convert the specified date into the format 'yyyy_MM_dd':

```
hive> SELECT date_format('2016-01-30','yyyy_MM_dd');
2016_01_30
```

- ❑ DATE_SUB:

```
hive> SELECT date_sub('2016-01-30',3);
2016-01-27
```

- ❑ DATEDIFF:

```
hive> SELECT datediff('2016-01-30', '2016-01-25');
```

- ▶ DAY, MONTH, YEAR: These functions are used to extract different parts of the date:

- ❑ Day:

```
hive> SELECT day('2016-01-30');
30
```

- ❑ Month:

```
hive> SELECT month('2016-01-30');
1
```

- ❑ Year:

```
hive> SELECT year('2016-01-30');
2016
```

- ▶ UNIX_TIMESTAMP: It will return the current UNIX timestamp in seconds:

```
hive> SELECT unix_timestamp();
1453548270
```

String functions

Let's see how string functions work in Hive:

- ASCII: This function returns the ASCII value of the first character of string. The following example will return the ASCII value of the character 'a'.

  ```
  hive> SELECT ascii('abcd');
  97
  ```

- CONCAT:

  ```
  hive> SELECT concat('value1','value2','value3');
  value1value2value3
  ```

- CONCAT_WS:

  ```
  hive> SELECT concat_ws('_','value1','value2','value3');
  value1_value2_value3
  ```

- FIND_IN_SET:

  ```
  hive> SELECT find_in_set('india', 'us,uk,india,pakistan');
  3
  ```

- LOWER, LCASE, UPPER, UCASE:

  - LOWER:

    ```
    hive> SELECT lower('heLLo woRlD');
    hello world
    ```

  - LCASE:

    ```
    hive> SELECT lcase('heLLo woRlD');
    hello world
    ```

  - UPPER:

    ```
    hive> SELECT upper('heLLo woRlD');
    HELLO WORLD
    ```

  - UCASE:

    ```
    hive> SELECT ucase('heLLo woRlD');
    HELLO WORLD
    ```

- INITCAP:

  ```
  hive> SELECT initcap('heLLo woRlD');
  Hello World
  ```

There's more

Apart from the various functions (of different categories, such as mathematical, collection, type conversion, date, and string) described previously, there are also some more functions that can be used in Hive.

Conditional functions

These are the functions that are used for conditional statements.

Function Name	Return Type	Description
CASE a WHEN b THEN c [WHEN d THEN e] * [ELSE f] END	T	When a = b then it will return c. When a = d then it will return e. Otherwise, it will return f.
CASE WHEN a THEN b [WHEN c THEN d] * [ELSE e] END	T	When a = true then it will return b. When c = true then it will return d. Otherwise, it will return e.
COALESCE(T v1, T v2, T vn)	T	It will return the first argument that is not NULL. If all arguments are NULL then it will return NULL.
if(BOOLEAN testCondition, T x, T y)	T	If testCondition is true then it will return x, otherwise it will return y.
isnotnull(a)	BOOLEAN	It will return TRUE if a is not NULL, otherwise it will return FALSE.
isnull(a)	BOOLEAN	It will return TRUE if a is NULL, otherwise it will return FALSE.
nvl(T x, T defaultValue)	T	It will return x if x is not NULL, otherwise it will return the specified defaultValue.

Miscellaneous functions

There are some other functions that are used for different purposes, such as encryption, decryption, hashing, and so on:

Function Name	Return Type	Description
current_user()	STRING	It will return the name of the current user who is connected to Hive in that session.
hash(a1[, a2...])	INT	It will return the hash value of specified arguments.
java_method(class, method[, arg1[, arg2..]])	varies	It is used to invoke static Java methods within Hive queries. The same functionality can be achieved using the reflect function.

Function Name	Return Type	Description

`reflect(class,`
`method[, arg1[,`
`arg2..]])`
	varies	It is used to invoke static Java methods within Hive queries.

See also

▶ You can read more about Hive mathematical functions at `https://cwiki.apache.org/confluence/display/Hive/LanguageManual+UDF#LanguageManualUDF-MathematicalFunctions`.

▶ Hive supports all the standards date formats. You can check the various date formats at `https://docs.oracle.com/javase/7/docs/api/java/text/SimpleDateFormat.html`.

▶ You can read more about Hive string functions at `https://cwiki.apache.org/confluence/display/Hive/LanguageManual+UDF#LanguageManualUDF-StringFunctions`.

Using the built-in User-defined Aggregation Function (UDAF)

Hive provides a set of functions to do aggregation on a dataset. These functions operate on a range of data (rows) and provide the cumulative or relative result.

How to do it...

The built-in functions could be used directly in the query. The following are some of the examples of aggregated functions available in Hive:

Function Name	Return Type	Description
`avg(col)`	DOUBLE	It is used to calculate the average of all values of a particular column.
`avg(DISTINCT col)`	DOUBLE	It is used to calculate the average of unique values of a particular column.
`collect_list(col)`	ARRAY	It will return a list of all values of a particular column in an array.
`collect_set(col)`	ARRAY	It will return a list of unique values of a particular column in an array. Duplicate values are eliminated.

Function Name	Return Type	Description
corr(col1, col2)	DOUBLE	It is used to calculate the Pearson coefficient of correlation between two columns.
count(*)	BIGINT	It will return the total number of rows of a table.
count(expr)	BIGINT	It will return the total number of rows where the specified expr is not NULL.
count(DISTINCT expr[, expr...])	BIGINT	It will return the total count of rows for unique values of the specified expr.
covar_pop(col1, col2)	DOUBLE	It is used to calculate population covariance between two columns.
covar_samp(col1, col2)	DOUBLE	It is used to calculate sample covariance between two columns.
max(col)	DOUBLE	It will return the maximum value of the specified column of a table.
min(col)	DOUBLE	It will return the minimum value of the specified column of a table.
stddev_pop(col)	DOUBLE	It is used to calculate the population standard deviation of all values of a column.
stddev_samp(col)	DOUBLE	It is used to calculate the sample standard deviation of all values of a column.
sum(col)	DOUBLE	It is used to calculate the sum of all values of a column.
sum(DISTINCT col)	DOUBLE	It is used to calculate the sum of the unique values of a column.
var_samp(col)	DOUBLE	It is used to calculate the unbiased sample variance of all values of a column.
variance(col)	DOUBLE	It is used to calculate the variance (population) of all values of a column.
var_pop(col)	DOUBLE	It is the same as the variance function.

How it works...

For all set of rows in a Hive dataset, these functions calculate the aggregated or cumulative output.

Let's create a sample table `item`, with four columns: `id`, `name`, `brand`, and `price`.

```
CREATE TABLE item(id int, name STRING, brand String, price DOUBLE) ROW
FORMAT DELIMITED FIELDS TERMINATED BY '\t';
```

Now load some sample data as shown next:

Id	Name	Brand	Price
1	U41-Laptop	Lenovo	38999.50
2	Vostro-1015	Dell	32000.90
3	H21-U123	Lenovo	22000.00
4	IP-213	HP	35000.00
5	Insipiron	Dell	41000.00

- `AVG`: This function is used to calculate the average of values for a particular column:
  - The following command will give the average of all values of a price field from the `item` table:

    ```
    hive> SELECT avg(price) from item;
    33800.08
    ```

  - The following command will give the average of the unique values of a price field from the `item` table:

    ```
    hive> SELECT avg(DISTINCT price) from item;
    33800.08
    ```

- `COLLECT_LIST`: The following command will give the list of all values of the brand field from the `item` table:

  ```
  hive> SELECT collect_list(brand) from item;
  ["Lenovo","Dell","Lenovo","HP","Dell"]
  ```

- `COLLECT_SET`: As described previously, the `COLLECT_LIST` function is used to give a list of all values, including duplicates of a column. To avoid duplicates and get a list of the unique values of a column, the `COLLECT_SET` function is used:
  - The following command will give a list of the unique values of the brand field from the `item` table:

    ```
    hive> SELECT collect_set(brand) from item;
    ["Lenovo","Dell","HP"]
    ```

- COUNT:
    - In the following command `count(*)` will return all the results from the `item` table:

    ```
    hive> SELECT count(*) from item;
    5
    ```

    - In the following command `count(DISTINCT brand)` will return all the distinct results from the `item` table:

    ```
    hive> SELECT count(DISTINCT brand) from item;
    3
    ```

- MAX, MIN: These functions are used to get the maximum and minimum value of a column respectively:
    - MAX:

    ```
    hive> SELECT max(price) from item;
    41000.0
    ```

    - MIN

    ```
    hive> SELECT min(price) from item;
    22000.0
    ```

- STDDEV_POP: The following command will calculate the population standard deviation of all values of a `price` field:

```
hive> SELECT stddev_pop(price) from item;
6675.201285774084
```

- STDDEV_SAMP: The following command will calculate the sample standard deviation of all values of a `price` field:

```
hive> SELECT stddev_samp(price) from item;
7463.101919242426
```

- SUM:
    - The following command will give the sum of all values of a `price` field:

    ```
    hive> SELECT sum(price) from item;
    169000.4
    ```

    - The following command will give the sum of only the unique values of a `price` field.

    ```
    hive> SELECT sum(DISTINCT price) from item;
    169000.4
    ```

> ▶ VARIANCE: The following command will give the variance of all values of a `price` field:

```
hive> SELECT variance(price) from item;
4.4558312205599986E7
```

See more

You can read more about Hive's built-in aggregate functions at `https://cwiki.apache.org/confluence/display/Hive/LanguageManual+UDF#LanguageManualUDF-Built-inAggregateFunctions%28UDAF%29`.

Using the built-in User Defined Table Function (UDTF)

Normal functions take one row as input and provide one row as transformed output. On the other side, built-in table-generating functions take one row as input and produce multiple output rows.

How to do it...

The built-in table-generating functions could be used directly in the query. The following are some examples of the table-generating functions available in Hive:

Function Name	Return Type	Description
explode(ARRAY)	N rows	It will return n of rows where n is the size of an array. This function represents each element of an array as a row.
explode(MAP)	N rows	It will return n number of rows where n is the size of a map. This function represents each key-value element of the map as a row containing two columns: one for key and another for value.
inline(ARRAY<STRUCT[,STRUCT]>)		It is used to explode an array of `struct` elements into a table.
json_tuple(jsonStr, k1, k2, ...)	tuple	It is used to extract a set of keys from a JSON string. This function is more efficient than `get_json_object` to retrieve more than one keys from a JSON string using a single function.

Function Name	Return Type	Description
`parse_url_tuple(url, p1, p2, ...)`	tuple	It is used to extract multiple parts of a URL at once. Supported values for `url` parts are AUTHORITY, FILE, HOST, PATH, PROTOCOL, QUERY, REF, and USERINFO. The value of a particular key in QUERY can be extracted by specifying QUERY:<KEY-NAME>.
`posexplode(ARRAY)`	N rows	This function is similar to the explode function but it also includes elements position in output.
`stack(INT n, v_1, v_2, ..., v_k)`	N rows	This function breaks up the specified k values into n rows, where k is the number of values passed to this function. Each row will contain k/n columns.

How it works...

The following are the UDTF functions:

- EXPLODE: This function takes an array or map as input and generates the output with n rows:

  1. To understand the behavior of the `explode` function, let's create a table with two columns: one is `city` with the data type STRING and the other is `pins` with the data type ARRAY<INT>.

     CREATE TABLE table_with_array_datatype (city STRING, pins ARRAY<INT>) ROW FORMAT DELIMITED FIELDS TERMINATED BY '\t' collection items terminated by ',';

     - Now, load some sample data into a table. The data in the table will look as follows:

City	Pins
Noida	[201301,201303,201307]
Delhi	[110001,110002,110003]

     - Now, run the following query to explode the data of array elements:

       SELECT explode(pins) AS pin_code FROM table_with_array_datatype;

❑ It will return the following response:

pin_code
201301
201303
201307
110001
110002
110003

❑ Now, let's see the behavior of the `explode` function with the `map` data type:

```
SELECT explode(map_field) AS (mapKey, mapValue) FROM
sampleTable;
```

▶ POSEXPLODE: This function is the same as the `explode` function but instead of returning just elements it will return the element as well as their position in the array:

❑ Let's use the same data used in the `explode` example, that is, `table_with_array_datatype` with two columns: `city` and `pins`:

```
SELECT posexplode(pins) AS position, pin_code FROM table_
with_array_datatype;
```

❑ The preceding command will return the following:

position	pin_code
1	201301
2	201303
3	201307
1	110001
2	110002
3	110003

See also

In Hive, you can also create your own custom UDTF. To write custom UDTF refer `https://cwiki.apache.org/confluence/display/Hive/DeveloperGuide+UDTF`.

Creating custom User-Defined Functions (UDF)

Built-in functions in Hive sometimes do not fit the requirements of a business use case or when data analytics required some custom manipulation of data based on certain conditions. For such cases, the user needs to define custom logic as a UDF and run it over the data.

How to do it...

For writing a custom function in Hive, you will have to extend a Hive class: `org.apache.hadoop.hive.ql.exec.UDF`.

Let's understand the concept of creating a custom UDF with the example of creating a function to reverse a string.

The following are the steps to create a custom UDF:

1. Create a new Java project using any IDE, such as Eclipse. Give this any name; let's say "HiveUDF".

2. When writing a custom UDF, there should be two libraries in the `classpath` of the project. To do so:

    1. Create a folder "`lib`" under the project.

    2. Add the following two JAR files to the `lib` folder:

        ❑ `hadoop-common-2.6.0`

        ❑ `hive-exec-1.2.1`

    3. Add these JAR files to the `classpath` of the project. Right-click on **Project | Build Path | Configure Build Path | Add Jars**.

3. Now, create a new class extending the Hive UDF class:

    ```
    package com.examples.hive;
    import org.apache.hadoop.hive.ql.exec.UDF;
    import org.apache.hadoop.io.Text;

    public class ReverseString extends UDF {
        public Text evaluate(final Text text) {
            // return NULL if value of input is NULL.
            if (text == null) {
                return null;
            }
    ```

```
            // Convert Hadoop Text object to StringBuilder
            StringBuilder stringBuilder = new StringBuilder(text.
    toString());
            // Derive reverse of string using inbuilt api of
    StringBuilder
            String reverse = stringBuilder.reverse().toString();
            // Convert String to Hadoop Text object and return that.
            return new Text(reverse);
        }
    }
```

4. Compile your project and export the project as a JAR file, say "myudf.jar".

5. Copy this JAR to the Linux machine where Hive is running.

6. When using a custom UDF, first you have to register your JAR with Hive:

    ```
    hive> ADD JAR /opt/myudf.jar;
    Added [/opt/myudf.jar] to class path
    ```

7. After running the preceding command, your JAR file for a custom function will be added to the `classpath` of Hive. You can register JAR files in that session using the following command:

    ```
    hive> LIST JARS;
    ```

    ```
    /opt/myudf.jar
    ```

8. The last step is to create a function with any name for your custom logic build into JAR:

    ```
    hive> CREATE FUNCTION string_reverse AS 'com.examples.hive.
    ReverseString';
    ```

9. In the preceding command `string_reverse` is the name given to the function and `'com.examples.hive.ReverseString'` is the fully qualified name of the class.

How it works...

After successful registration of your custom function in Hive, you can directly use that function in Hive queries. In the preceding section, we created a function to reverse a string:

```
hive> select string_reverse('abcde');
```

```
edcba
```

```
hive> select string_reverse(firstname) from sales;
```

The preceding command will return all values of `firstname` in reverse format from the `sales` table.

In this chapter, we learned various types of functions supported in Hive. We also learned how we can create our custom user-defined function and use that in Hive queries.

10
Hive Tuning

In this chapter, you will learn the following:

- ▶ Enabling predicate pushdown optimizations in Hive
- ▶ Optimizations to reduce the number of map
- ▶ Sampling

Enabling predicate pushdown optimizations in Hive

In this recipe, you will learn how to use predicate pushdown in Hive.

Getting ready

Predicate pushdown is a traditional RDBMS term, whereas in Hive, it works as predicate pushup. In this, the focus is on to execute all the expressions such as filters as early as possible to optimize the performance of a query. For example, let's look at the query mentioned later, which includes a join condition as well as a filter condition:

```
SELECT a.*, b.* FROM Sales a JOIN Sales_orc b ON a.id = b.id
WHERE a.id > 100 AND b.id > 300;
```

In the preceding query, a JOIN is performed at the ID column of both the tables and then the result set is filtered out with the help of the filter condition. The drawback here is that the join condition is executed first followed by the filter condition. Now suppose if most of the rows are filtered out by the filter expression, then in this case, executing the filter condition after the JOIN clause is of no use. There has to be a mechanism with the help of which these predicates are performed first filtering most of the rows followed by the JOIN clause. For such scenarios, predicate pushdown is used, which performs the expressions first resulting in a better performance of the query. Predicate pushdown is enabled by setting the following property to True:

```
hive.optimize.ppd=true;
```

How to do it...

If there are multiple predicates in the query, the predicate pushdown functionality implements a special function and breaks the WHERE clause into two parts, as shown in the following figure:

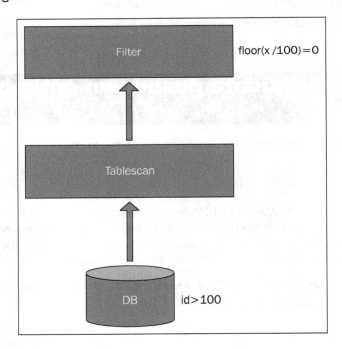

Now suppose that there is a query that contains two predicates or expressions. The first one is a filter condition (id >100), and the second one is a normal expression (x/100)=0. Now when these predicates are split into two parts, one is sent to the database where it filters out most of the rows. Another one is executed by Hive. In the preceding figure, id > 100 is evaluated at the database side, whereas floor(x/100) expression is evaluated by Hive.

How it works...

To determine the execution plan of a query, the `EXPLAIN` keyword is used. The output of the `explain` command has three outputs:

- ▸ The Abstract Syntax Tree for the query
- ▸ The dependencies between the different stages of the plan
- ▸ The description of each of the stages

Now, let's see what happens when `hive.optimize.ppd` is set to `false`. Once this property or parameter is set to `false`, we will analyze the execution plan of a query (join a query, as shown in the following screenshot):

```
hive> set hive.optimize.ppd=false;
hive> explain select a.* from sales_orc a join sales b on a.id = b.id where a.id > 100;
OK
STAGE DEPENDENCIES:
  Stage-4 is a root stage
  Stage-3 depends on stages: Stage-4
  Stage-0 depends on stages: Stage-3
```

Stage dependencies

In the preceding figure, `Stage-4` is a root stage. `Stage-3` is executed after `Stage-4` is done, and `Stage-0` is executed after `Stage-2` is done:

```
STAGE PLANS:
  Stage: Stage-4
    Map Reduce Local Work
      Alias -> Map Local Tables:
        a
          Fetch Operator
            limit: -1
      Alias -> Map Local Operator Tree:
        a
          TableScan
            alias: a
            Statistics: Num rows: 52 Data size: 4569 Basic stats: COMPLETE Column stats: NONE
            Filter Operator
              predicate: id is not null (type: boolean)
              Statistics: Num rows: 26 Data size: 2284 Basic stats: COMPLETE Column stats: NONE
              HashTable Sink Operator
                keys:
                  0 id (type: int)
                  1 id (type: int)
```

Plan for Stage-4

The preceding figure explains the plan for `Stage-4`. Because we have set the value for `hive. optimize.ppd` to `false`, the predicate in the figure does not show any expression (`id > 100`), which is there in the `JOIN` statement. In the preceding screenshot, the table having alias `b` is scanned:

```
Stage: Stage-3
  Map Reduce
    Map Operator Tree:
      TableScan
        alias: b
        Statistics: Num rows: 10000 Data size: 252858 Basic stats: COMPLETE Column stats: NONE
        Filter Operator
          predicate: id is not null (type: boolean)
          Statistics: Num rows: 5000 Data size: 126429 Basic stats: COMPLETE Column stats: NONE
          Map Join Operator
            condition map:
                Inner Join 0 to 1
            keys:
              0 id (type: int)
              1 id (type: int)
            outputColumnNames: _col0, _col1, _col2, _col3, _col4, _col5, _col6, _col7, _col8
            Statistics: Num rows: 5500 Data size: 139071 Basic stats: COMPLETE Column stats: NONE
            Filter Operator
              predicate: (_col0 > 100) (type: boolean)
              Statistics: Num rows: 1833 Data size: 46348 Basic stats: COMPLETE Column stats: NONE
              Select Operator
                expressions: _col0 (type: int), _col1 (type: string), _col2 (type: string), _col3 (type:
(type: string), _col7 (type: string), _col8 (type: string)
                outputColumnNames: _col0, _col1, _col2, _col3, _col4, _col5, _col6, _col7, _col8
                Statistics: Num rows: 1833 Data size: 46348 Basic stats: COMPLETE Column stats: NONE
                File Output Operator
                  compressed: false
                  Statistics: Num rows: 1833 Data size: 46348 Basic stats: COMPLETE Column stats: NONE
                  table:
                      input format: org.apache.hadoop.mapred.TextInputFormat
                      output format: org.apache.hadoop.hive.ql.io.HiveIgnoreKeyTextOutputFormat
                      serde: org.apache.hadoop.hive.serde2.lazy.LazySimpleSerDe
    Local Work:
      Map Reduce Local Work
```

The following screenshot explains the plan for `Stage-0`. This is the outermost stage and is executed once all the stages are completed:

```
Stage: Stage-0
  Fetch Operator
    limit: -1
    Processor Tree:
      ListSink

Time taken: 1.856 seconds, Fetched: 65 row(s)
```

Now, let's see what happens when `hive.optimize.ppd` is set to `true`. Once this property or parameter is set to `true`, we will analyze the execution plan of a query (join a query, as shown in the following screenshot):

```
hive> set hive.optimize.ppd=true;
hive> explain select a.* from sales_orc a join sales b on a.id = b.id where a.id > 100;
OK
STAGE DEPENDENCIES:
  Stage-4 is a root stage
  Stage-3 depends on stages: Stage-4
  Stage-0 depends on stages: Stage-3
```

In the preceding screenshot, `Stage-4` is a root stage. `Stage-3` is executed after `Stage-4` is done, and `Stage-0` is executed after `Stage-2` is done:

```
STAGE PLANS:
  Stage: Stage-4
    Map Reduce Local Work
      Alias -> Map Local Tables:
        a
          Fetch Operator
            limit: -1
      Alias -> Map Local Operator Tree:
        a
          TableScan
            alias: a
            Statistics: Num rows: 52 Data size: 4569 Basic stats: COMPLETE Column stats: NONE
            Filter Operator
              predicate: (id > 100) (type: boolean)
              Statistics: Num rows: 17 Data size: 1493 Basic stats: COMPLETE Column stats: NONE
              HashTable Sink Operator
                keys:
                  0 id (type: int)
                  1 id (type: int)
```

The preceding screenshot explains the plan for `Stage-4`. Because we have set the value for `hive.optimize.ppd` to `true`, the predicate in the screenshot shows an expression (`id > 100`), which is there in the `JOIN` statement. In the preceding screenshot, the table having alias as `b` is scanned and 24 rows comes out as the output:

```
  Stage: Stage-3
    Map Reduce
      Map Operator Tree:
          TableScan
            alias: b
            Statistics: Num rows: 10000 Data size: 252858 Basic stats: COMPLETE Column stats: NONE
            Filter Operator
              predicate: (id > 100) (type: boolean)
              Statistics: Num rows: 3333 Data size: 84277 Basic stats: COMPLETE Column stats: NONE
              Map Join Operator
                condition map:
                    Inner Join 0 to 1
                keys:
                  0 id (type: int)
                  1 id (type: int)
                outputColumnNames: _col0, _col1, _col2, _col3, _col4, _col5, _col6, _col7, _col8
                Statistics: Num rows: 3666 Data size: 92704 Basic stats: COMPLETE Column stats: NONE
                Select Operator
                  expressions: _col0 (type: int), _col1 (type: string), _col2 (type: string), _col3 (type
ype: string), _col7 (type: string), _col8 (type: string)
                  outputColumnNames: _col0, _col1, _col2, _col3, _col4, _col5, _col6, _col7, _col8
                  Statistics: Num rows: 3666 Data size: 92704 Basic stats: COMPLETE Column stats: NONE
                  File Output Operator
                    compressed: false
                    Statistics: Num rows: 3666 Data size: 92704 Basic stats: COMPLETE Column stats: NONE
                    table:
                        input format: org.apache.hadoop.mapred.TextInputFormat
                        output format: org.apache.hadoop.hive.ql.io.HiveIgnoreKeyTextOutputFormat
                        serde: org.apache.hadoop.hive.serde2.lazy.LazySimpleSerDe
      Local Work:
        Map Reduce Local Work
```

The preceding screenshot explains the plan for Stage-3. Because we have set the value for hive.optimize.ppd to true, the predicate in the screenshot shows an expression (id > 100), which is there in the JOIN statement. In the preceding screenshot, the table having alias as a is scanned and 10001 rows comes out as the output. After the predicate is executed, the output is 3333. This shows that WHERE clause is executed first and then the JOIN clause is executed on the result set of the WHERE condition:

```
Stage: Stage-0
  Fetch Operator
    limit: -1
    Processor Tree:
      ListSink

Time taken: 0.238 seconds, Fetched: 62 row(s)
```

The preceding screenshot explains the plan for Stage-0. This is the outermost stage and is executed once all the stages are completed.

Optimizations to reduce the number of map

In this recipe, you will learn how to reduce the number of mappers in Hive.

Getting ready

The number of mappers that is used in a map reduce job depends heavily on the input split. The number of mappers is directly proportional to the number of HDFS blocks, that is, the total number of blocks for the input files. Input split is a logical concept that is used to control the number of mappers. If there is no size defined for an input split in map reduce job, then the number of mappers will be equal to the number of HDFS blocks.

However, if you have defined a particular size for an input split, then the number of mappers will be equal to the number of input splits in the MapReduce job and not to the number of HDFS blocks for that MapReduce job.

Let's suppose that there is a file of 150 MB, and it is broken down into two parts. One part is equal to 128 MB, and the other part is equal to 22 MB. Now consider that the block configuration of HDFS block by default is 128 MB. So the number of blocks occupied by this file is going to be 2. In this case, the number of mappers is going to be equal to the number of blocks, which is 2 if there is no split size defined for the map reduce job to process this file.

Now suppose that you have specified the input split size to be 150 MB. Now the number of splits is going to be 1, whereas number of blocks will be 2. In this case, the number of mappers is going to be 1 as the number of mappers is directly proportional to the number of splits defined for the map reduce job. Split size can be defined by the user and altered according to the business requirement.

Now suppose that you have further modified the input split size to 50 MB. Now for a file of 150 MB, the number of mappers is going to be 3, which is equivalent to the number of splits for that file.

How to do it...

The number of mappers used in a query plays a very important role in the performance of the query. You can increase or decrease the number of mappers required for a particular Hive query. The following two parameters can increase or decrease the number of mappers to some extent:

```
mapreduce.input.fileinputformat.split.maxsize
mapreduce.input.fileinputformat.split.minsize
```

The preceding two parameters are for the newer version of Hive. Their equivalent names in the earlier versions are as follows:

```
mapred.max.split.size
mapred.min.split.size
```

Suppose that there is a text file of size 10,000 bytes. If you want to limit the number of mappers, then you can set the earlier-mentioned parameters, as follows:

```
hive> set mapreduce.input.fileinputformat.split.maxsize = 10000;
hive> set mapreduce.input.fileinputformat.split.minsize = 10000;
```

Limiting mappers to One

There is going to be one mapper for the MapReduce job if the parameter size is set to 10,000, as in the preceding screenshot.

However, there are going to be two mappers if the properties are set as shown in the following screenshot:

```
hive> set mapreduce.input.fileinputformat.split.maxsize = 5000;
hive> set mapreduce.input.fileinputformat.split.minsize = 5000;
```

Limiting mappers to Two

The following parameters can be set to reduce number of mappers for a MapReduce job:

```
set hive.merge.mapfiles=true;
```

The property hive.merge.mapfiles if set to true, will merge all the small files once the map job is completed:

```
set hive.input.format= org.apache.hadoop.hive.ql.io.
CombineHiveInputFormat;
set mapreduce.job.maps = XX;
```

There is one more property, `hive.input.format`, that can be used to reduce the number of mappers as well. If this property is set to `org.apache.hadoop.hive.ql.io.CombineHiveInputFormat`, which is the default value as well, then Hive will combine all files that are smaller in size than the limit specified in the parameter `mapreduce.input.fileinputformat.split.minsize` to a single file reducing the number of mappers. However, there is also one limitation in this technique. If the small-sized files are present at a different node on a different machine, Hive will not be able to combine all those files into a single file. Hence, the number of mappers will not be reduced.

In the earlier version of Hive, the `hive.input.format` was set to `org.apache.hadoop.hive.ql.io.HiveInputFormat`, which has been deprecated now. With the newer version of Hive, the following the value should be set:

```
hive.input.format = org.apache.hadoop.hive.ql.io.CombineHiveInputFormat;
```

The third parameter shows that you can manually set the number of mappers for a particular Hive query. However, this parameter is ignored if the value of `mapreduce.jobtracker.address` is set to `local`. This means that all the jobs will run in-process as a single MapReduce task.

Sampling

In this recipe, you will learn how to sample data in Hive.

Getting ready

Sampling in Hive is a way to write queries on a small chunk of data instead of the entire table. This is required when you have a large dataset and you want to work on a small piece of that dataset. Sampling queries are most efficient when they are performed on bucketed column. Sampling is required when you just need to run queries on a smaller set of data instead of accuracy of the result set of the entire data. That is, it is mostly required for testing purposes. Sampling is most efficient when it is used for auditing purposes. In auditing, sampling can be used to pick a random set of rows or data with respect to the entire data that is huge in number.

Another use case is where you need to perform some aggregation-like average on a sample of data or smaller set of data, keeping aside the accuracy of the data.

To use this sampling feature in Hive, you need to use the TABLESAMPLE clause, which helps in writing queries on a sample of data instead of the entire table that contains huge amount of data.

There are multiple ways of sampling in Hive:

- ▸ Sampling bucketed table
- ▸ Block sampling
- ▸ Length literal
- ▸ Row count

Sampling bucketed table

The sampling bucketed table method is used when we need to sample a particular out of a group of buckets or the total number of buckets. In this technique, sampling can be performed either on a column or by using a `rand()` function, indicating sampling on the entire row instead of an individual column.

The general syntax for sampling bucketed table is as follows:

```
table_sample: TABLESAMPLE (BUCKET x OUT OF y [ON colname])
```

Here, `TABLESAMPLE` is the clause that samples data instead of the entire table:

- ▸ `BUCKET`: This is the clause used to specify the exact number of buckets to be used in the query.
- ▸ `X`: This is is the number of buckets to be used in the query.
- ▸ `Y`: This is the total number of buckets or group of buckets on the table out of which `X` bucket needs to be used.
- ▸ `colname`: This is the column on which sampling has to be performed on each row of the table. It can be a nonpartitioned column in the table.

Block sampling

Block sampling is another kind of sampling that deals in percentages. In this, we provide the percentage of data that need to be sampled. The percentage here indicates the data size and not number of rows. In this sampling technique, the granularity is a single HDFS block.

The general syntax for Block Sampling is as follows:

```
block_sample: TABLESAMPLE (n PERCENT) s
```

Here, `TABLESAMPLE` is the clause that samples data instead of the entire table:

- ▸ `(n PERCENT)` is the n% data size
- ▸ `S` is the table alias

Length literal

Length literal is another way of sampling data or rows from a large set of data. In this technique, the user specifies the size of the input data or the length of the input data.

The general syntax for length literal sampling is as follows:

```
block_sample: TABLESAMPLE (ByteLengthLiteral)
ByteLengthLiteral : (Digit)+ ('b' | 'B' | 'k' | 'K' | 'm' | 'M' | 'g' | 'G')
```

Here, `ByteLengthLiteral` is the size that you need to provide for the data:

- ► (Digit) is the numeric number that you need to provide
- ► ('b'| 'B' | 'k' | 'K' | 'm' | 'M' | 'g' | 'G') is the literal indicating the size of the sample data to be read. Here, 'b' stands for bits, and 'B' stands for bytes, and so on

Row count

Row count is another type of sampling technique where you provide the number of rows instead of `ByteLengthLiteral`. In this case, sampling is done on the basis of rows or by providing the number of rows as the input. In this type of sampling, the row count provided by the user is applied to each input split.

The general syntax for block sampling is as follows:

```
block_sample: TABLESAMPLE (n ROWS)
```

Here, `(n ROWS)` is the number of rows to be provided as an input for sampling the data.

How to do it...

Follow these steps to use sampling in Hive:

```
SELECT * FROM Sales_orc TABLESAMPLE(BUCKET 1 OUT OF 10 ON id);
SELECT * FROM Sales_orc TABLESAMPLE(BUCKET 3 OUT OF 5 ON id);
SELECT * FROM Sales_orc TABLESAMPLE(BUCKET 3 OUT OF 100 ON id);
SELECT * FROM Sales_orc TABLESAMPLE(BUCKET 3 OUT OF 1000 ON id);
SELECT * FROM Sales_orc TABLESAMPLE(BUCKET 1 OUT OF 10 ON fname);
```

```
SELECT count(*) FROM Sales_orc TABLESAMPLE(BUCKET 4 OUT OF 10 ON rand());

SELECT count(*) FROM Sales_orc TABLESAMPLE(BUCKET 5 OUT OF 10 ON rand());

SELECT count(*) FROM Sales_orc TABLESAMPLE(BUCKET 4 OUT OF 10 ON rand());

SELECT count(*) FROM Sales_orc TABLESAMPLE(BUCKET 5 OUT OF 10 ON rand());

SELECT * FROM Sales_orc TABLESAMPLE(10 PERCENT);

SELECT * FROM Sales_orc TABLESAMPLE(10%);

SELECT * FROM Sales_orc TABLESAMPLE(10M);

SELECT * FROM Sales_orc TABLESAMPLE(0.1M);

SELECT * FROM Sales_orc TABLESAMPLE(10 ROWS);

SELECT * FROM Sales_orc TABLESAMPLE(100 ROWS);
```

How it works...

Let's assume that the `Sales_orc` table used in the earlier-mentioned example is having 10 buckets and 10,000 rows as total number of records in the table:

▶ The first statement is an example of a Sampling Bucketed table. In this example, all the records from the `Sales_orc` table are fetched from the first bucket of total number of 10 buckets. The `id` column is the column on which the `Sales_orc` table was created with `CLUSTERED BY id INTO 32 BUCKETS`. The total number of records for this query came out to be 1,000 rows:

```
4970    Tasha   Mcgowan 66152 South Brazil Ct.   Port Huron      Iowa
7490    Shay    Madden  1728 East Malta Ln.      Winnemucca      Iowa
4980    Peter   Harper  79440 South Bahamas Blvd.        Parker  Alaska
4990    Cleo    Bowen   86121 East Argentina Blvd.       Pembroke Pines
0       Zena    Ross    41228 West India Ln.     Powell  Tennessee
Time taken: 0.742 seconds, Fetched: 1000 row(s)
```

Limiting mappers to one

▶ In the second example, the numbers of buckets specified are 5 even though the total numbers of buckets in the `Sales_orc` table are 10. This is known as **Input Pruning**. When a table is created using a `CLUSTERED BY (column_name)` into `BUCKET` clause, Hive, with the help of `HASH` function, buckets the data into the 10 buckets (in the `Sales_orc` table as an example). In this example, Hive divides the 10 buckets into groups of 5 buckets, that is, 2 groups of 5 buckets. Once this is done, the third bucket is picked from each group thereby picking the third and eighth bucket. The total number of records for this query came out to be 2,000 rows:

```
9987    Malcolm Howard  45083 East Auburn Way    East Lansing    Nevada  33691
6497    Clio    Fitzpatrick     64429 East Clovis Ct.    Nampa   Hawaii  45515
9997    Brielle Humphrey        32559 West Solomon Islands Ct.   Providence
1997    Wanda   Hull    22547   Charlotte Amalie Blvd.   Hornell Wyoming 86484
Time taken: 0.11 seconds, Fetched: 2000 row(s)
```

> ▸ The third example is somewhat similar to the second example. The only difference is that the total number of groups in this case is 'one-tenth' of the total number of buckets. The total number of records for this query came out to be 100 rows:

```
6502    Amber    Thompson      65119 South Guadeloupe St.       New York        Kentucky
3002    Quemby   Becker  52425 West Northern Mariana Islands Way Columbus        South Dakota
7302    Cole     Robinson      82239 East Liberia Ct.   Rutland Oregon  48314   192.168.56.50
4602    Madaline        Gill   78128 North Georgia St. Moreno Valley   Michigan        28840
Time taken: 0.144 seconds, Fetched: 100 row(s)
```

> ▸ The fourth example is somewhat similar to the third example. The only difference is that the total number of groups in this case is 'one-hundredth' of the total number of buckets. The total number of records for this query came out to be 10 rows:

```
hive> SELECT * FROM Sales_orc TABLESAMPLE(BUCKET 3 OUT OF 1000 ON id);
OK
2002    Aline    Gordon   421 South Afghanistan Ln.       Hackensack      Texas
6002    Ramona   Duran    11580 East Kyrgyzstan Ct.       Port Arthur     Maine
8002    Megan    Hood     14500 North Newton Ln.  Danbury Kentucky        95235
9002    Clinton Harvey    48466 North Central African Republic Ln.        Abilene
1002    Lysandra        Monroe  43220 East Belize Way   Aberdeen        District
7002    Kato     Herrera 60413 West Boulder City St.     Fayetteville    Iowa
4002    Lee      Stone    30287 South Bosnia and Herzegovina Way  Anchorage
5002    Rhiannon        Fields  18530 West Reunion Ct.  Elizabeth City  Delaware
2       Sage     Carroll 6880  Greenland Ct.    Guayanilla      Nevada  08899
3002    Quemby   Becker   52425 West Northern Mariana Islands Way Columbus
Time taken: 0.172 seconds, Fetched: 10 row(s)
```

> ▸ The fifth example uses the column named `fname` from the `Sales_orc` table. The `fname` column is the `nonclustered` column, but still Hive uses it to sample the data. Take a look at the following screenshot:

```
9319    Clementine      Mendez  17945 West Nigeria Ave. Orem     Illinois        67450
9389    Troy     Shields 26994 South Botswana Way       Reading New Hampshire   81450
9519    Rae      Frederick      74992 West Latvia Ln.   Grand Rapids    Wyoming 99677
9529    Channing        Hansen  9886 West Australia Ln. Beaver Falls    Alaska  74070
9789    Hoyt     Rice    17080 East Congo Ln.    Brown Deer      West Virginia   83715
Time taken: 0.161 seconds, Fetched: 916 row(s)
```

> ▸ The sixth example shows the use of the `rand()` function in sampling. Until now, we were using the `id` column in the query that always gives the same result set, which cannot be used if you require random data for your business purposes such as auditing. For this purpose, you require the `rand ()` function, which gives different results every time you run the query. The output of the sixth query comes out to be `968` rows, as follows:

```
Total MapReduce CPU Time Spent: 26 seconds 870 msec
OK
968
```

- The seventh query is the same as the sixth query. The only difference is that in this query, the count for the fifth bucket is determined, whereas in the sixth query, the count for the fourth bucket was determined. The output of the seventh query comes out to be 983 rows, as follows:

```
Total MapReduce CPU Time Spent: 26 seconds 800 msec
OK
983
```

- The eighth query is exactly the same as the sixth query. It shows a different count than that of the sixth query. The output of the eighth query comes out to be 988 rows, as follows:

```
Total MapReduce CPU Time Spent: 26 seconds 870 msec
OK
988
```

- The ninth query is exactly same as the seventh query. It shows a different count than that of the seventh query. The output of the ninth query comes out to be 1015 rows, as follows:

```
Total MapReduce CPU Time Spent: 28 seconds 190 msec
OK
1015
```

- The tenth example is all about the block sampling. In this example, 10 percent means that Hive will read approximately 10 percent of the blocks. We have the following screenshot:

```
7490    Shay    Madden   1728 East Malta Ln.      Winnemucca      Iowa    02739
4980    Peter   Harper   79440 South Bahamas Blvd.        Parker  Alaska  43854
4990    Cleo    Bowen    86121 East Argentina Blvd.       Pembroke Pines  South
0       Zena    Ross     41228 West India Ln.    Powell  Tennessee       21550
Time taken: 0.203 seconds, Fetched: 1000 row(s)
```

- The eleventh example is similar to the tenth one, except the difference of the percent keyword. The '%' symbol is used, which throws an error as shown in the following screenshot:

```
hive> SELECT * FROM Sales_orc TABLESAMPLE(10%);
NoViableAltException(289@[])
        at org.apache.hadoop.hive.ql.parse.HiveParser_FromClauseParser.splitSample(HiveParse
        at org.apache.hadoop.hive.ql.parse.HiveParser_FromClauseParser.tableSample(HiveParse
        at org.apache.hadoop.hive.ql.parse.HiveParser_FromClauseParser.tableSource(HiveParse
        at org.apache.hadoop.hive.ql.parse.HiveParser_FromClauseParser.fromSource(HiveParser
        at org.apache.hadoop.hive.ql.parse.HiveParser_FromClauseParser.joinSource(HiveParser
        at org.apache.hadoop.hive.ql.parse.HiveParser_FromClauseParser.fromClause(HiveParser
        at org.apache.hadoop.hive.ql.parse.HiveParser.fromClause(HiveParser.java:44428)
```

▶ In the twelfth example, the third sampling technique, `Length` literal is shown. In this example, a value of 10 M or more is used in the query. See the following screenshot:

```
9959    Plato    Vazquez  48213 South Chico Way    Decatur Arizona 14411    192.168.56.149
9969    Micah    Talley   71206 North Swaziland St.         Christiansted   Texas    14789
9979    Amaya    Madden   89534 West Tokelau Blvd.          Moorhead        New York
9989    Plato    Gamble   79304 North Lebanon Way Atlanta Wyoming 82746     192.168.56.92
9999    Jerome   Bentley  18289 South Bulgaria Ave.         Bellingham      Tennessee
Time taken: 0.14 seconds. Fetched: 10000 row(s)
```

▶ The thirteenth example throws an error as you cannot pass a floating point number as the input. The following error is encountered if a floating point number passes as a parameter:

```
hive> SELECT * FROM Sales_orc TABLESAMPLE(0.1M);
NoViableAltException(26@[])
        at org.apache.hadoop.hive.ql.parse.HiveParser_FromClauseParser.splitSample(Hive
        at org.apache.hadoop.hive.ql.parse.HiveParser_FromClauseParser.tableSample(Hive
        at org.apache.hadoop.hive.ql.parse.HiveParser_FromClauseParser.tableSource(Hive
        at org.apache.hadoop.hive.ql.parse.HiveParser_FromClauseParser.fromSource(HiveP
        at org.apache.hadoop.hive.ql.parse.HiveParser_FromClauseParser.joinSource(HiveP
        at org.apache.hadoop.hive.ql.parse.HiveParser_FromClauseParser.fromClause(HiveP
        at org.apache.hadoop.hive.ql.parse.HiveParser.fromClause(HiveParser.java:44428)
```

▶ The fourteenth example samples the number of rows on the basis of rows provided as input. In this type of sampling, the row count provided by the user is applied to each input split:

```
hive> SELECT * FROM Sales_orc TABLESAMPLE(10 ROWS);
OK
5000    Tanner   Dotson   29583 Martinsburg Ct.  Galesburg        California
7500    Gabriel  Pace     32093 Montebello St.   Half Moon Bay    Oregon   49755
8750    Isaac    Romero   91922 West Armenia Ct. Opelousas        Alaska   91427
10      Silas    Hughes   86635 North Ghana St.  Beverly Virginia          08642
9960    Burke    Myers    45437 Cypress St.      Cary     West Virginia  25715
5010    Shea     Strickland     18243 East Burkina Faso Ln.     Palm Springs
20      Grant    Thompson       62331 North Great Falls Ln.    South El Monte
30      Germaine          Stafford       1889 East Russian Federation Ct.
5020    Michelle          Gibbs    59445 Cocos (Keeling) Islands Ln.   Jackson
40      Fiona    Patton   53793 North Norfolk Island Ln.  Hornell South Carolina
Time taken: 0.116 seconds, Fetched: 10 row(s)
```

▶ The fifteenth example samples the number of rows on the basis of the rows provided as the input. In this type of sampling, the row count provided by the user is applied to each input split. This example is similar to the previous example, but the only difference is that the input in this example is 100 rows as compared with 10 rows in the previous example:

```
9850    Morgan   West     97008  Clarksville Way  Salt Lake City  Kentucky
470     Amber    Gallegos        87729 West Fallon St.    Enfield Texas    60808
5240    Lucian   House    3166 West Belgium Way  Aguadilla        Alabama 47550
480     Ira      Walton   31380 West Macao Ln.   Portsmouth       Utah     41593
7620    Lani     Velez    24832 Mauritania Way   Dickinson        New Jersey
Time taken: 0.155 seconds, Fetched: 100 row(s)
```

11
Hive Security

In this chapter, we will cover the following recipes:

- ▶ Securing Hadoop
- ▶ Authorizing Hive
- ▶ Configuring the SQL standards-based authorization
- ▶ Authenticating Hive

Security is a major concern in all big data frameworks. It is little complex to implement security in distributed systems because components of different machines need to communicate with each other. It is very important to enable security on the data.

Securing Hadoop

In today's era of big data, most of the organizations are concentrating to use Hadoop as a centralized data store. Data size is growing day by day, and organizations want to derive some insights and make decisions using the important information. While everyone is focusing on collecting the data, but having all the data at a centralized place increases the risk of data security. Securing the data access of **Hadoop Distributed File System** (**HDFS**) is very important. Hadoop security means restricting the access of data to only authorized users and groups. Furthermore, when we talk about security, there are two major things—**Authentication** and **Authorization**.

HDFS supports a permission model for files and directories that is much equivalent to the standard **POSIX** model. Similar to **UNIX** permissions, each file and directory in HDFS is associated with an owner, group, and another users. There are three types of permissions in HDFS—read, write, and execute.

In contrast to the UNIX permission model, there is no concept of executable files. Therefore, in case of files, the read (**r**) permission is required to read a file and the write (**w**) permission is required to write or append to a file. In case of directories, the read (**r**) permission is required to list the contents of directory, the write (**w**) permission is required to create or delete the files or subdirectories, and the execute (**x**) permission is required to access the child objects (files/subdirectories) of that directory.

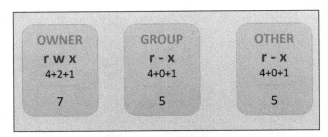

The default HDFS permission model

As shown in the previous image, by default, the permission set for owner of files or directories is **rwx** (**7**), which means that the owner of a file or directory is having full permissions—read, write, and execute. For the members of a group, the permission set is **r-x**. This means that group members can only read and execute the files/directories, and they cannot write or update anything in the files/directories. For other members, a permission set is the same as a group, that is, other members can only read and execute the files/directories, and they cannot write or update anything in the files/directories.

Although this basic permission model is sufficient to handle a large number of security requirements at a block level, but using this model, you cannot define finer level security to specific named users or groups. HDFS also has a feature to configure an **Access Control List** (**ACL**), which can be used to define fine-grained permissions at the file level as well as the directory level for specific named users or groups. For example, you want to give read access to users—John, Mike, and Kate. Then, HDFS ACLs can be used to define such kind of permissions.

HDFS ACLs are designed on the base concept of POSIX ACLs of UNIX systems.

How to do it...

First of all, you will need to enable ACLs in Hadoop. To enable ACL permissions, configure the following property in the Hadoop configure file `hdfs-site.xml` located at `<HADOOP_HOME>/etc/hadoop/hdfs-site.xml`:

```
<property>
<name>dfs.namenode.acls.enabled</name>
<value>true</value>
</property>
```

There are two main commands that are used to configure ACLs: `setfacl` and `getfacl`. The command `setfacl` is used to set **Finer Access Control Lists** (**FACL**) for files or directories, and `getfacl` is used to retrieve FACL for files or directories.

Let's see how to use these commands:

```
hdfs dfs -setfacl [-R] [-b |-k -m |-x <acl_specification> <path>] |[--set
<acl_specification> <path>]
```

Same command can be run using `hadoop fs` also. For example:

```
hadoop fs -setfacl [-R] [-b |-k -m |-x <acl_specification> <path>] |[--
set <acl_specification> <path>]
```

Here:

- ▶ `-R`: This is used to apply operation recursively for all files and subdirectories under a directory
- ▶ `-b`: This is used to remove all ACLs except the base ACLs
- ▶ `-k`: This is used to remove the default ACLs
- ▶ `-m`: This is used to modify ACLs. Using this option, new entries are added to the existing set of ACLs
- ▶ `-x`: This is used to remove specific ACLs
- ▶ `acl_specification`: It is comma-separated list of ACLs
- ▶ `path`: This is the path of file or directory for which ACL has to be applied
- ▶ `--set`: This is used to set new ACLs. It removes all existing ACLs and set the new ACLs only

Now, let's see other command that is used to retrieve the ACLs:

```
hdfs dfs -getfacl [-R] <path>
```

This command can also be run using `hadoop fs`. For example:

```
hadoop fs -getfacl [-R] <path>
```

Here:

- ▶ `-R`: This is used to retrieve ACLs recursively for all files and subdirectories under a directory
- ▶ `path`: This is the path of file/directory of which ACL is to be retrieved

The command `getfacl` will list all default ACLs as well as new ACLs defined for specified files/directories.

How it works...

If ACLs are defined for a file or directory, then while accessing that file/directory, access is validated as the following algorithm:

- ▶ If the user name is the same as the owner name of a file, then owner permissions are enforced

- ▶ If the user name matches with one of the named user ACL entry, then those permissions are enforced

- ▶ If a user's group name matches with one of the named group ACL entry, then those permissions are enforced

- ▶ In case, multiple ACLs entries are found for a user, then union of all those permissions are enforced

- ▶ If no ACL entry is found for a user, then other permissions are enforced

Let's assume that we have a file named `stock-data` containing stock market data.

To retrieve all ACLs of this file, run the following command:

```
$ hadoop fs -getfacl /stock-data
```

```
[centos@ip-172-31-22-157 hadoop-2.6.0]$ hadoop fs -getfacl /stock-data
# file: /stock-data
# owner: centos
# group: supergroup
user::rw-
group::r--
other::r--

[centos@ip-172-31-22-157 hadoop-2.6.0]$ hadoop fs -ls /stock-data
-rw-r--r--   1 centos supergroup          0 2015-12-30 08:32 /stock-data
```

Because we have not defined any custom ACL for this file as shown in the previous image, the command will return ACLs for this file.

You can check the permissions of a file or a directory using the `ls` command also. As shown in the previous image, the permission set for the stock-data file is -rw-r-r, which means read and write access for an owner as well as read access for group members and others.

Giving read and write access to user mike

In the following command we are giving read and write access to user `mike`:

```
$ hadoop fs -setfacl -m user:mike:rw- /stock-data
```

```
[centos@ip-172-31-22-157 hadoop-2.6.0]$ hadoop fs -setfacl -m user:mike:rw- /stock-data
[centos@ip-172-31-22-157 hadoop-2.6.0]$
[centos@ip-172-31-22-157 hadoop-2.6.0]$ hadoop fs -getfacl /stock-data
# file: /stock-data
# owner: centos
# group: supergroup
user::rw-
user:mike:rw-
group::r--
mask::rw-
other::r--

[centos@ip-172-31-22-157 hadoop-2.6.0]$ hadoop fs -ls /stock-data
-rw-rw-r--+   1 centos supergroup          0 2015-12-30 08:32 /stock-data
```

As shown in the previous image, first, we defined the ACLs for the user mike mike using the `setfacl` command, then we retrieved the ACLs using the `getfacl` command.

The output of the `getfacl` command will list out all default permissions as well as all ACLs. Because we defined ACLs for the user mike, so in output, there is an extra row `user:mike:rw-`.

There is an extra row in the output `mask::rw-`, which defines the special mask ACLs entry. Mask is a special type of ACLs, which filter out the access for all named users, all named groups as well as all unnamed groups. If you have not defined mask ACL, then its value is calculated using the union of all permissions.

In addition to this, the output of the `ls` command is also changed after defining ACLs. There is an extra plus (+) sign in the permissions list that indicates that there are additional ACLs defined for this file or directory.

Revoking the access of the user mike

To remove a specific ACL `-x` option is used with the `setfacl` command.

```
$ hadoop fs -setfacl -x user:mike /stock-data
```

```
[centos@ip-172-31-22-157 ~]$ hadoop fs -setfacl -x user:mike /stock-data
[centos@ip-172-31-22-157 ~]$ hadoop fs -getfacl /stock-data
# file: /stock-data
# owner: centos
# group: supergroup
user::rw-
group::r--
mask::r--
other::r--
```

In the previous screenshot after revoking the access of the user `mike`, ACLs are updated and there is no entry for the `mike` user now.

See also

You can read more about the permission model in Hadoop at `https://hadoop.apache.org/docs/current/hadoop-project-dist/hadoop-hdfs/HdfsPermissionsGuide.html`.

Authorizing Hive

Hive authorization is about verifying that a user is authorized to perform a particular action. Authentication is about verifying the identity of a user, which is different from the authorization concept.

Hive can be used in the following different ways:

- **HCatalog API**: Hive's HCatalog API is used to access Hive by many other frameworks, such as Apache Pig, MapReduce, Facebook Presto, Spark SQL, and Cloudera Impala. Using Hcatalog API, the users have direct access to HDFS data and Hive metadata. Hive metadata is directly accessible using the metastore server API.

- **Hive Command Line Interface** (**CLI**): Using Hive CLI also, users have direct access to HDFS data and Hive metadata. Hive CLI directly interacts with the Hive metastore server. Currently, Hive CLI don't support rich authorization. In next versions of Hive, Hive CLI's implementation will be changed to provide better security, and also Hive CLI will interact with HiveSerer2 rather than directly interacting with the metastore server.

- **ODBC/JDBC** and other **HiveServer2** clients such as **Beeline**: These clients don't have direct access to HDFS data and metadata. All access is done through HiveServer2. For security purpose, this is the best way to access Hive.

How to do it...

There are various ways of authorization in Hive.

Default authorization–legacy mode

The legacy authorization mode was available in earlier versions of Hive. This authorization scheme prevents the users from doing some unwanted actions. This scheme doesn't prevent malicious users from doing activities.

It manages the access control using `grant` and `revoke` statements. This mode supports Hive CLI. In case of Hive CLI, users have direct access to HDFS files and directories so they can easily break the security checks. Also, in this model, to grant privileges, the permissions needed for a user are not defined, which means that any user can grant the access to themselves, so it is not secure to use this model.

Storage-based authorization

As a storage perspective, both HDFS data as well as Hive metadata must be accessed only to authorized users. If users use HCatalog API or Hive CLI, then they have direct access to data. To protect the data, HDFS ACLs are being enabled. In this mode, HDFS permissions work as a single source of truth to protect data.

Generally in Hive metastore, database credentials are configured in the Hive configuration file `hive-site.xml`. Malicious users can easily read the metastore credentials and then could cause serious damage to data as well as metadata, so the Hive metastore server also be secured.

In this authorization, you can also enable security at a metastore level. After enabling metastore security, it will restrict the access on metadata objects by verifying that the users have respective system permissions corresponding to different files and directories of metadata objects.

To configure storage-based authorization, set the following properties in the `hive-site.xml` file:

Property	Value
`hive.metastore.pre.event.listeners`	`org.apache.hadoop.hive.ql.security.authorization.AuthorizationPreEventListener`
`hive.security.metastore.authorization.manager`	`org.apache.hadoop.hive.ql.security.authorization.StorageBasedAuthorizationProvider`
`hive.security.metastore.authenticator.manager`	`org.apache.hadoop.hive.ql.security.HadoopDefaultMetastoreAuthenticator`
`hive.security.metastore.authorization.auth.reads`	`true`

After setting all these configuration, the Hive configuration file `hive-site.xml` will look as follows:

```
<configuration>
  <property>
```

```
        <name>hive.metastore.pre.event.listeners</name>
        <value>org.apache.hadoop.hive.ql.security.authorization.
AuthorizationPreEventListener</value>
    </property>
    <property>
        <name>hive.security.metastore.authorization.manager</name>
        <value>org.apache.hadoop.hive.ql.security.authorization.
StorageBasedAuthorizationProvider</value>
    </property>
    <property>
        <name>hive.security.metastore.authenticator.manager</name>
        <value>org.apache.hadoop.hive.ql.security.
HadoopDefaultMetastoreAuthenticator</value>
    </property>
    <property>
        <name>hive.security.metastore.authorization.auth.reads</name>
        <value>true</value>
    </property>
</configuration>
```

▶ `hive.metastore.pre.event.listeners`: This property is used to define pre-event listener class which is loaded on metastore side. APIs of this class are executed before occurring of any event like creating a database/table/partition, altering a database/table/partition or dropping a database/table/partition and so on. Configuring this property turns on security at metastore level.

Set the value of this property to org.apache.hadoop.hive.ql.security.authorization. AuthorizationPreEventListener.

▶ `hive.security.metastore.authorization.manager`: This property is used to define the authorization provider class for metastore security. The default value of this property is `DefaultHiveMetastoreAuthorizationProvider`, which provides default legacy authorization described earlier. To enable storage-based authorization based on Hadoop, ACLs set the value of this property to `org.apache.hadoop.hive.ql.security.authorization.StorageBasedAuthorizationProvider`.

You can also write your own custom class to manage authorization and configure this property to enable custom authorization manager. The custom authorization manager class must implement an interface `org.apache.hadoop.hive.ql.security.authorization.HiveMetastoreAuthorizationProvider`.

- ▶ `hive.security.metastore.authenticator.manager`: This property is used to define the authentication manager class. Set the value of this property to `org.apache.hadoop.hive.ql.security.HadoopDefaultMetastoreAuthenticator`.

  You can also write your custom class to manage authentication and configure to this property. A custom authentication manager class must implement an interface `org.apache.hadoop.hive.ql.security.HiveAuthenticationProvider`.

- ▶ `hive.security.metastore.authorization.auth.reads`: This property is used to define whether metastore authorization should check for `read` access or not. The default value of this property is `true`.

SQL standards-based authorization

SQL standards-based authorization is the third way of authorizing Hive. Although previous methodology storage-based authorization also provides access control at level of partitions, tables, and databases, but that methodology does not provide access control at more granular level such as columns and rows. This is because storage-based authorization depends on the access control provided by HDFS using ACL that controls the access on the level of files and directories.

SQL Standards-based authorization can be used to enforce fine-grained security. It is recommended to use as it is fully SQL-compliant in its authorization model.

There's more

There are many things that you can do with SQL-standards based authorization. Refer to the next recipe *Configuring the SQL standards based authorization* for more details.

Configuring the SQL standards-based authorization

SQL standards-based authorization is the best way of authorizing Hive. This approach is widely used to restrict the access of data to only authorized users so that no malicious user can destroy anything by accessing the data. This authorization model is fully compliant with SQL authorization model. The `grant` and `revoke` statements are used to provide or remove the access to particular resources to users.

In order to implement the security using this model, all the queries must be served through HiveServer2 only. To interact with HiveServer2, any HiveServer2 clients (described in the *Using HiveServer2 clients* recipe of *Chapter 2, Services in Hive*) can be used. Beeline is a client that is commonly used to interact with HiveServer2 in place of HiveCLI. For a highly secure environment, it is very important to restrict the direct access of users to HDFS commands, Hive CLI, and Pig commands.

There are five primary types of privileges:

Privilege Name	Description
SELECT	It is used to give read/select access on a Hive resource
INSERT	It is used to give write/insert access on the Hive resource so that the user can add the data to a Hive table
UPDATE	It is used to give update access on the Hive resource so that the user can run update queries on data
DELETE	It is used to give delete access on the Hive resource so that the user can delete the data from the Hive table
ALL	It is used to give all privileges: select, insert, update, and delete

 All the previously mentioned privileges can be granted or revoked on Hive tables and views. These privileges don't work on the database level.

There are two types of entities to which privileges can be granted or revoked—user and role:

▶ A role is logical grouping of multiple users

▶ One user could be associated with more than one roles

▶ User names are case-sensitive in Hive, but role names are not case-sensitive

In Hive, privileges can be granted to users as well as roles. Granting of privileges to roles is widely used in organization because it is very easy to manage authorization at role level rather than individual users. If you grant a privilege to a role, then the privilege is applied to all users associated with that role.

There are two special roles in Hive: one is **public**, and another is **admin**.

By default, all users belong to the public role. This role is used when you want to give or remove permission on a table or view at a global level (all users).

An admin role is used for all users who would be acting as administrators. Users of the admin role will have all type of access to all Hive objects such as tables or views. In addition to this, the new role creation or deletion of existing role can be performed only by users having the admin role. The users who belong to the admin role, need to run the set role command to get admin privileges.

Getting Started

Before *Configuring the SQL standards-based authorization*, first, you will have to configure this authorization mode in Hive.

Set the following configuration parameters in the Hive server configuration file located at `$HIVE_HOME/conf/hiveserver2-site.xml`:

Property	Value
`hive.server2.enable.doAs`	`True`
`hive.users.in.admin.role`	`<list of users to be admin>`

`hive.security.metastore.`
`authorization.manager`
	`org.apache.hadoop.hive.`
	`ql.security.authorization.`
	`MetaStoreAuthzAPIAuthorizerEmbedOnly`

`hive.security.` `authorization.enabled`	`True`

`hive.security.`
`authorization.manager`
	`org.apache.hadoop.hive.ql.security.`
	`authorization.plugin.sqlstd.`
	`SQLStdHiveAuthorizerFactory`

`hive.security.` `authenticator.manager`	`org.apache.hadoop.hive.ql.security.` `SessionStateUserAuthenticator`
`hive.metastore.uris`	

- `hive.server2.enable.doAs`: This property is used to define whether a query should be run as an end user or not. If value of this is set to `true`, then the query is run as the user who executes the query. If value of this property is set to `false`, then all queries are run as user who started the HiveServer2 process. The default value of this property is `true`.

- `hive.users.in.admin.role`: This property is used to define some of users as administrators. Value of this property is the comma-separated list of users who need to be added to the `admin` role.

  By default, the admin role is not in current roles of any user so users defined in this list will have to run the `set role` command to get the privileges of the admin role.

- `hive.security.metastore.authorization.manager`: This property is used to deny calls to authorization APIS by Hive CLI or another remote metastore user. Set the value of this property to `org.apache.hadoop.hive.ql.security.`
`authorization.MetaStoreAuthzAPIAuthorizerEmbedOnly`.

- `hive.security.authorization.enabled`: This property is used to define whether authorization is to be enabled or not.

▶ `hive.security.authorization.manager`: This property is used to define a class that will be used to manage authorization. Set the value of this property to `org.apache.hadoop.hive.ql.security.authorization.plugin.sqlstd.SQLStdHiveAuthorizerFactory`.

▶ `hive.security.authenticator.manager`: This property is used to define a class that will be used to manage authentication. Set the value of this property to `org.apache.hadoop.hive.ql.security.SessionStateUserAuthenticator`.

▶ `hive.metastore.uris`: This property is used to define a comma-separated list of metastore URIs. As described earlier in SQL standards-based authorization, it is required that all queries should be served through HiveServer2, so direct access of metastore has to be disabled. To disable the direct access of metastore from any remote client, set the value of this property to blank (`' '`).

> These configurations can also be defined in `hive-site.xml`, but it is recommended to specify the previous configuration in the `hiveserver2-site.xml` configuration file.

HiveServer2 reads both configuration files `hive-site.xml` as well as `hiveserver2-site.xml`. If there is any property defined in both configuration files, then HiveServer2 gives property defined in the `hiveserver2-site.xml` configuration file.

After configuring all the earlier-mentioned properties, the `hiveserver2-site.xml` file will look as follows:

```
<configuration>
  <property>
    <name>hive.server2.enable.doAs</name>
    <value>true</value>
  </property>
  <property>
    <name>hive.users.in.admin.role</name>
    <value>root</value>
  </property>
  <property>
    <name>hive.security.metastore.authorization.manager</name>
    <value>org.apache.hadoop.hive.ql.security.authorization.
    MetaStoreAuthzAPIAuthorizerEmbedOnly</value>
  </property>
  <property>
    <name>hive.security.authorization.enabled</name>
    <value>true</value>
```

```
    </property>
    <property>
      <name>hive.security.authorization.manager</name>
      <value>org.apache.hadoop.hive.ql.security.authorization.
      plugin.sqlstd.SQLStdHiveAuthorizerFactory</value>
    </property>
    <property>
      <name>hive.security.authenticator.manager</name>
      <value>org.apache.hadoop.hive.ql.security.
      SessionStateUserAuthenticator</value>
    </property>
    <property>
      <name>hive.metastore.uris</name>
      <value></value>
    </property>
  </configuration>
```

Now if your Hive services are already running, then restart metastore and HiveServer2 processes otherwise start metastore and HiveServer2 processes using the following commands:

```
$HIVE_HOME/ bin/hive --service metastore &
$HIVE_HOME/ bin/hive --service hiveserver2 &
```

Run the jps command to verify that both services are running:

```
$ jps
```

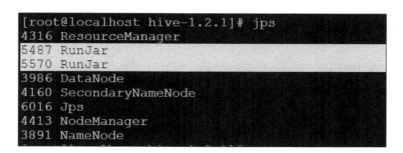

```
[root@localhost hive-1.2.1]# jps
4316 ResourceManager
5487 RunJar
5570 RunJar
3986 DataNode
4160 SecondaryNameNode
6016 Jps
4413 NodeManager
3891 NameNode
```

How to do it...

Once this authorization mode is configured properly, then you can use it to allow or restrict the access on Hive tables or views to particular users. There are different actions that can be done as a part of authorization process using the commands as mentioned in the following sections.

To list out all existing roles

This command can be run only by the users of the admin role. It will give list of all existing roles.

```
SHOW ROLES;
```

creating a role

This command can be run only by the users of the admin role. The following command can be used to create a new role:

```
CREATE ROLE rolename;
```

Deleting a role

This command also can be run only by the users of an admin role. The following command can be used to drop an existing role:

```
DROP ROLE rolename;
```

Showing list of current roles

This command can be run by any user to see his/her all current roles. By default, the output of this command doesn't list the admin role even if the user belongs to the admin role because the admin user will have to run the `set role` command to get admin privileges:

```
SHOW CURRENT ROLES;
```

Setting a role

If a user is having multiple roles, then using following command, the specified role will become the current role of a user:

```
SET ROLE rolename;
```

The following command will refresh the list of current roles of a user and will set a default list as current roles:

```
SET ROLE ALL;
```

The following command will remove all current roles of a user.

```
DROP ROLE ALL;
```

Granting a role

```
GRANT rolename1 [, rolename2, ...] TO principal_spec1 [,principal_spec2,
. . .][ WITH ADMIN OPTION ];
```

Here, `principal_spec` is either a username or a rolename.

This command can be used to assign one or more roles to specified list of users or roles. If you specify the `WITH ADMIN OPTION` in command, then a user or a role will get admin privileges so they can further grant the roles to others.

Revoking a role

```
REVOKE [ADMIN OPTION FOR] rolename1 [, rolename2, ...] FROM principal_
spec1 [,principal_spec2, . . .];
```

Here, `principal_spec` is either a username or a rolename.

This command can be used to remove one or more roles from the specified list of users or roles. If you specify the `ADMIN OPTION FOR` in command, then admin rights of user or role will also be removed.

Checking roles of a user/role

```
SHOW ROLE GRANT USER|ROLE name;
```

This command can be used to list out the roles that have been granted to a specified user or a role.

Checking principles of a role

```
SHOW PRINCIPALS rolename;
```

This command can be run only by the users of an admin role. This command is used to list all roles or users who are associated with the specified role.

Granting privileges

```
GRANT privilege_type [, privilege_type, ...] ON table_or_view_name TO
principal_spec [, principal_spec, ...][WITH GRANT OPTION];
```

Here, `principal_spec` is either a username or a rolename.

This command is used to give privileges to users or roles. If you specify the `WITH GRANT OPTION` in command, then specified users or roles can further `grant` or `revoke` the privileges to other users or roles.

Revoking privileges

```
REVOKE [GRANT OPTION FOR] privilege_type [, privilege_type, ...] ON
table_or_view_name FROM principal_spec [, principal_spec, ...];
```

Here, `principal_spec` is either a username or a rolename.

This command is used to remove privileges from users or roles.

Checking privileges of a user or role

```
SHOW GRANT USER|ROLE name ON ALL|table_or_view_name
```

This command can be used to see all privileges of a user or role on the specified table or view.

See also

You can read more about this authorization mode at `https://cwiki.apache.org/confluence/display/Hive/SQL+Standard+Based+Hive+Authorization`.

Authenticating Hive

Authentication is a process of verifying the identity of a user. There are different ways of authentication for different Hive clients. Hive CLI is currently not recommended to use as it is not safer for data security purposes, but still you can enable Kerberos authentication in Hive.

HiveServer2 is a server interface that is used to run queries against Hive and retrieve the result. It is recommended to always use HiveServer2. Most of the organizations are widely using HiveServer2 with its various security features.

How to do it...

HiveServer2 supports the following authentication options:

- Anonymous with SASL
- Anonymous without SASL
- Kerberos (GSSAPI)
- LDAP
- PAM
- Custom

Authentication can be configured using the property `hive.server2.authentication`. This property defines the authentication mode to be used for HiveServer2. The default value of this property is NONE so no authentication is enabled, and it uses plain **Simple Authentication and Security Layer** (**SASL**).

Anonymous with SASL (default no authentication)

This is the default mode of HiveServer2 in which no authentication is enabled. If you want to explicitly specify this mode, then you can configure authentication property in the Hive configuration file as:

```
<property>
  <name>hive.server2.authentication</name>
  <value>NONE</value>
</property>
```

Anonymous without SASL

Authentication without SASL can be configured by setting the following property in the Hive configuration file:

```
<property>
  <name>hive.server2.authentication</name>
  <value>NOSASL</value>
</property>
```

Kerberos

In HiveServer2, you can also configure Kerberos authentication, which works on basis of tickets to allow communication between different nodes on nonsecure network to verify the identity to one another in the secure manner.

The Kerberos authentication mode supports authentication between the thrift client and HiveServer2, and between HiveServer2 and secure Hadoop Distributed File System.

In the Kerberos authentication mode, HiveServer2 acquires a valid ticket for authentication during startup process. While configuring Kerberos authentication, you need to mention principal details of Kerberos server and a `keytab` file detail in the Hive configuration file.

Kerberos authentication can be configured by setting the following properties in the Hive configuration file `hive-site.xml`:

```
<property>
  <name>hive.server2.authentication</name>
  <value>KERBEROS</value>
</property>
```

```
<property>
  <name>hive.server2.authentication.kerberos.principal</name>
  <value> <<Kerberos principle for HiveServer2>> </value>
</property>
<property>
  <name>hive.server2.authentication.kerberos.keytab</name>
  <value> <<Keytab for server principal>> </value>
</property>
```

All client applications will need a valid Kerberos ticket to make connection with HiveServer2. If client is not having a valid ticket, then connection with HiveServer2 will be failed.

Configuring the JDBC client for Kerberos authentication

If Kerberos authentication is enabled, then the JDBC client must specify the principal name in connection string to make connection with HiveServer2. Clients will need valid Kerberos ticket to make connection with HiveServer2.

The URL format for connection string is `jdbc:hive2://<hostname>:<port>/<database>;principal=<Kerberos_Server_Principal_of_HiveServer2>`.

 If you don't specify the backslash character (/) after a port number, then JDBC driver doesn't consider the host name and run HiveServer2 in the embedded mode. It's mandatory to specify the backslash character (/) after a port number if you are specifying the host name.

Consider the following example: `jdbc:hive2://hiveserver_hostname:10000/default;principal=hive/hiveserver_hostname@YOUR-REALM.COM`.

Here, `hiveserver_hostname` is the host where HiveServer2 is running.

Access Hive using the Beeline client

```
[centos_user@host ~] $HIVE_HOME/bin/beeline

beeline> !connect jdbc:hive2://hiveserver_hostname:10000/
default;principal=hive/ hiveserver_hostname@YOUR-REALM.
COM org.apache.hive.jdbc.HiveDriver
```

Access Hive using the Hive JDBC client in Java

```
String url = " jdbc:hive2://hiveserver_hostname:10000/
default;principal=hive/ hiveserver_hostname@YOUR-REALM.COM"

Connection con = DriverManager.getConnection(url);
```

LDAP

HiveServer2 can also be configured to provide authentication with the users and groups of the Active Directory and OpenLDAP.

Lightweight Directory Access Protocol (**LDAP**) is like an Active Directory, which is used to maintain contact information and other important details. Most of the organizations use LDAP to maintain users' details, groups' detail, and different permission set for users or groups. When HiveServer2 is configured with LDAP authentication mode, then authenticity of a user is validated using the user and password details stored in LDAP. While making connection with Hive, a client sends username and password that is validated using an external LDAP service.

Authentication with OpenLDAP or Active Directory can be configured by setting the following properties in the Hive configuration file `hive-site.xml`:

```
<property>
  <name>hive.server2.authentication</name>
  <value>LDAP</value>
</property>
<property>
  <name>hive.server2.authentication.ldap.url</name>
  <value>LDAP_URL</value>
</property>
<property>
  <name>hive.server2.authentication.ldap.baseDN</name>
  <value>LDAP_BaseDN</value>
</property>
<property>
  <name>hive.server2.authentication.ldap.Domain</name>
  <value>LDAP_Domain</value>
</property>
```

▶ `hive.server2.authentication.ldap.url`: Is the connection URL of LDAP. If multiple LDAP servers are used for High Availability purpose, then comma-separated URLs can be specified as a value of this property. In case of the comma-separated list of URLs, HiveServer2 will try to make the connection with the first LDAP server. If the first server is not available, then it will try to make connection with the second server, and so on.

▶ `hive.server2.authentication.ldap.baseDN`: is the value of the base **Distinguished Name** (**DN**) of LDAP server. In case of an Active Directory, this property is not defined.

▶ `hive.server2.authentication.ldap.Domain`: Is the value of domain details of the LDAP server.

While accessing Hive using the JDBC client, the username and password are required to mention in a connection string. URL Format for connection string is:

```
jdbc:hive2://<HOSTNAME>:<PORT>/<DATABASE>;user=<USER_
NAME>;password=<PASSWORD>
```

Pluggable Authentication Modules

Pluggable Authentication Modules (**PAM**) allow to add any existing authentication mechanism to Hive. In this mode, underlying modules take care of entire authentication process such as users or groups management, password validation, and session management.

There might be some cases where organizations don't use Kerberos authentication or LDAP authentication due to integration complexity with the third-party software. A quick solution in these cases is to use PAM authentication, which allows you to enable authentication using system operating system's user and password credentials.

PAM is also a standard mechanism on most of the UNIX/LINUX distributions.

Follow these steps to configure PAM authentication:

1. Download the **Java Pluggable Authentication Modules** (**JPAM**) native library from `http://sourceforge.net/projects/jpam/files/jpam/jpam-1.1/`.

2. Extract the `JPAM` tar file on machine where HiveServer2 is running:

   ```
   $ tar -xzvf JPam-Linux_i386-1.1.tgz
   ```

3. An extracted directory will contain a JPAM library file `libjpam.so`, which must be in library path of Hive. So, add the extracted directory to environment variable `LD_LIBRARY_PATH`:

   ```
   export LD_LIBRARY_PATH=$LD_LIBRARY_PATH:<path to libjmap-
   directory>
   ```

4. The `*NIX files '/etc/shadow'` and `'/etc/login.defs'` files should be readable by user running the HiveServer2 process:

   ```
   $ sudo chmod 555 /etc/shadow
   ```

   ```
   $ sudo chmod 555 /etc/login.defs
   ```

5. Now set the following configurations in the Hive configuration file `hive-site.xml`:

   ```
   <property>
     <name>hive.server2.authentication</name>
     <value>PAM</value>
   ```

```
</property>

<property>
  <name>hive.server2.authentication.pam.services</name>
  <value>COMMA SEPARATED LIST OF PAM SERVICES</value>
</property>
```

The property `hive.server2.authentication.pam.services` defines the comma-separated list of PAM services to be used. Files with the same name as PAM services must exist in the directory `/etc/pam.d/`.

 If you want to use system credentials (user name and password details) as authentication mechanism to make Hive connection, then you can define the value of `hive.server2.authentication.pam.services` to `login, sshd`.

Restart HiveServer2 and verify the authentication using the beeline client.

Custom

This mode is used to apply a custom authentication mechanism while making connection to HiveServer2. You can write a custom class for the own authentication mechanism that must implements the `org.apache.hive.service.auth.PasswdAuthenticationProvider` interface.

To use custom mode, set the following configurations in the Hive configuration file `hive-site.xml`:

```
<property>
  <name>hive.server2.authentication</name>
  <value>CUSTOM</value>
</property>

<property>
  <name>hive.server2.custom.authentication.class</name>
  <value>CLASS_NAME</value>
</property>
```

Here, `hive.server2.custom.authentication.class` will define the class name to be used to the authentication mechanism.

This is how you can enable different modes of authentications using these mechanisms. Authentication using Kerberos and LDAP is the preferred mechanism in most of the organizations.

12
Hive Integration with Other Frameworks

In this chapter, you will learn the following topics:

- ► Working with Apache Spark
- ► Working with Accumulo
- ► Working with HBase
- ► Working with Google Drill

Working with Apache Spark

In this recipe, you will learn how to integrate Hive with Apache Spark. Apache Spark is an open source cluster computing framework. It is used as a replacement of the MapReduce framework.

Getting ready

In this topic, we will cover the use of Hive and Apache Spark. You must have Apache Spark installed on your system before going further in the topic.

1. Once the Spark is installed, start the Spark master server by executing the following command:

    ```
    ./sbin/start-master.sh
    ```

2. Check whether the Spark master server has been started or not by issuing the URL mentioned later on the web browser:

   ```
   http://<ip_address>:<port_number>
   ```

3. The exact URL is present at the following path:

   ```
   /spark-1.6.0-bin-hadoop2.6/logs/spark-hadoop-org.apache.spark.
   deploy.master.Master-1-node1.out
   ```

4. The following screenshot shows the result of the URL:

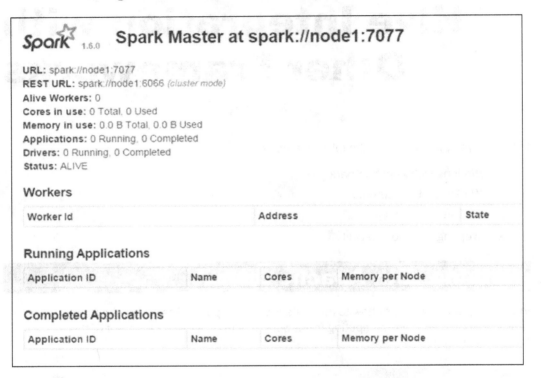

5. Once the master server is started, start the `slave` service by executing the following command:

   ```
   ./sbin/start-slave.sh <master-spark-URL>
   ```

6. Refresh the URL and find the following changes in the page:

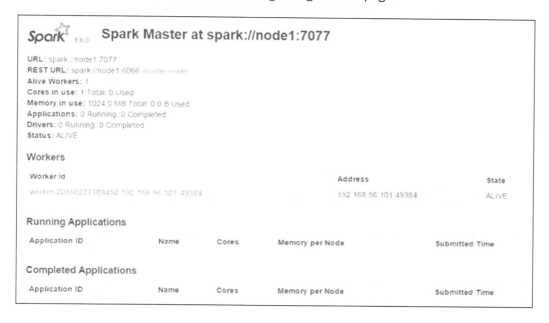

7. You will see the **Worker Id** under the worker's column with the status as **ALIVE**. Once the master and slave are started, set environment variable for Spark home:

   ```
   export SPARK_HOME=<location of Spark installation>
   ```

8. After the earlier command is executed, log in to the Hive shell. You will find Spark libraries being added to Hive path:

```
hadoop@node1:/opt/spark-1.6.0-bin-hadoop2.6/sbin$ hive
SLF4J: Class path contains multiple SLF4J bindings.
SLF4J: Found binding in [jar:file:/opt/hadoop-2.6.0/share/hadoop/common/lib/slf4j-log4j12-1.7.5
SLF4J: Found binding in [jar:file:/opt/hive-1.1.0/lib/hive-jdbc-1.1.0-standalone.jar!/org/slf4j
SLF4J: Found binding in [jar:file:/opt/hive-1.1.0/lib/slf4j-log4j12-1.7.5.jar!/org/slf4j/impl/S
SLF4J: Found binding in [jar:file:/opt/hive-1.1.0/lib/spark-assembly-1.6.0-hadoop2.6.0.jar!/org
SLF4J: Found binding in [jar:file:/opt/hive-1.1.0/lib/spark-examples-1.6.0-hadoop2.6.0.jar!/org
SLF4J: See http://www.slf4j.org/codes.html#multiple_bindings for an explanation.
SLF4J: Actual binding is of type [org.slf4j.impl.Log4jLoggerFactory]
SLF4J: Class path contains multiple SLF4J bindings.
SLF4J: Found binding in [jar:file:/opt/hadoop-2.6.0/share/hadoop/common/lib/slf4j-log4j12-1.7.5
SLF4J: Found binding in [jar:file:/opt/hive-1.1.0/lib/hive-jdbc-1.1.0-standalone.jar!/org/slf4j
SLF4J: Found binding in [jar:file:/opt/hive-1.1.0/lib/slf4j-log4j12-1.7.5.jar!/org/slf4j/impl/S
SLF4J: Found binding in [jar:file:/opt/hive-1.1.0/lib/spark-assembly-1.6.0-hadoop2.6.0.jar!/org
SLF4J: Found binding in [jar:file:/opt/hive-1.1.0/lib/spark-examples-1.6.0-hadoop2.6.0.jar!/org
SLF4J: See http://www.slf4j.org/codes.html#multiple_bindings for an explanation.
SLF4J: Actual binding is of type [org.slf4j.impl.Log4jLoggerFactory]
```

9. Set the Hive execution engine to Spark. This is achieved by issuing the following command on the Hive shell:

```
hive> set hive.execution.engine=spark;
```

10. Now configure the Spark application configuration for Hive. Execute the following commands on the Hive shell:

```
hive> set spark.master=<Spark Master URL>

hive> set spark.eventLog.enabled=true;

hive> set spark.eventLog.dir=<Spark event log folder (must exist)>

hive> set spark.executor.memory=512m;

hive> set spark.serializer=org.apache.spark.serializer.
KryoSerializer;
```

How to do it...

Follow these steps to access Hive table on the Spark engine:

```
SELECT * FROM Sales;
```

How it works...

The SELECT statement in the previous section is the same as shown in the earlier chapters of this book. The only difference this time around is that it will be executed on the Spark engine instead of the Hadoop MapReduce engine. The following screenshot shows the output:

```
hive> select a.* from sales_orc a, sales b where a.id = b.id;
Query ID = hadoop_20160227110404_63239040-aa12-4dad-8cb9-92978316550b
Total jobs = 1
SLF4J: Class path contains multiple SLF4J bindings.
SLF4J: Found binding in [jar:file:/opt/hadoop-2.6.0/share/hadoop/common/lib/slf4j-log4j12-1.7.5.j
SLF4J: Found binding in [jar:file:/opt/hive-1.1.0/lib/hive-jdbc-1.1.0-standalone.jar!/org/slf4j/i
SLF4J: Found binding in [jar:file:/opt/hive-1.1.0/lib/slf4j-log4j12-1.7.5.jar!/org/slf4j/impl/Sta
SLF4J: Found binding in [jar:file:/opt/hive-1.1.0/lib/spark-assembly-1.6.0-hadoop2.6.0.jar!]org/s
SLF4J: Found binding in [jar:file:/opt/hive-1.1.0/lib/spark-examples-1.6.0-hadoop2.6.0.jar!]org/s
SLF4J: See http://www.slf4j.org/codes.html#multiple_bindings for an explanation.
SLF4J: Actual binding is of type [org.slf4j.impl.Log4jLoggerFactory]
Java HotSpot(TM) Client VM warning: You have loaded library /opt/hadoop-2.6.0/lib/native/libhadoo
x the stack guard now.
It's highly recommended that you fix the library with 'execstack -c <libfile>', or link it with '
16/02/27 11:04:27 WARN util.NativeCodeLoader: Unable to load native-hadoop library for your platf
Execution log at: /tmp/hadoop/hadoop_20160227110404_63239040-aa12-4dad-8cb9-92978316550b.log
2016-02-27 11:04:29     Starting to launch local task to process map join;     maximum memory =
2016-02-27 11:04:30     Dump the side-table for tag: 0 with group count: 52 into file: file:/tmp/
1_2526121163082603784-1/-local-10003/HashTable-Stage-3/MapJoin-mapfile00--.hashtable
2016-02-27 11:04:30     Uploaded 1 File to: file:/tmp/hadoop/fe953321-d489-4d35-9675-4292b177dd10
ble-Stage-3/MapJoin-mapfile00--.hashtable (5752 bytes)
2016-02-27 11:04:30     End of local task; Time Taken: 1.537 sec.
Execution completed successfully
MapredLocal task succeeded
Launching Job 1 out of 1
```

Working with Accumulo

In this recipe, you will learn how to integrate Hive with Apache Accumulo.

Apache Accumulo is a sparse, distributed, sorted, and multidimensional map of key-value pairs. It is modeled after Google's Bigtable design. It's a key-value store and handles structured, semi-structured, and unstructured data. Also, it is extremely fast in accessing data to and fro tables containing large volumes of data.

Getting ready

In this topic, we will cover the use of Hive and Accumulo. You must have Apache Accumulo installed on your system before going further in the topic.

For Apache integration with Hive, there are two main components as follows:

- ► `AccumuloStorageHandler`: The main job of this class is to map the Hive table to the Accumulo tables. Also, it configures the Hive queries.

- ► `AccumuloPredicateHandler`: The main job of this class is to work on filter operations for the reduction of data. It pushes filters to Accumulo for the reduction of data. The following four properties must be provided by Hive to access the Accumulo tables:

Connection parameters
accumulo.instance.name
accumulo.zookeepers
accumulo.user.name
accumulo.user.pass

The previously mentioned four parameters or properties are actually used as connection parameters used by Hive to connect the Accumulo tables. These parameters are provided using the following command on Hive:

```
hive -hiveconf accumulo.instance.name=<instancename>
-hiveconf accumulo.zookeepers=<hostname>
-hiveconf accumulo.user.name=<username>
-hiveconf accumulo.user.pass=<password>
```

How to do it...

Follow these steps to access the Accumulo table from Hive:

```
CREATE TABLE Sales_Accumulo(
    'rowid' string,
    'id' int,
    'fname' string,
    'lname' string,
    'address' string,
    'city' string,
    'state' string,
    'ip' string,
    'p_id' string,
    'dop' string)STORED BY 'org.apache.hadoop.hive.accumulo.
AccumuloStorageHandler'
WITH SERDEPROPERTIES('accumulo.columns.mapping' = ':rowid,Sales:id,Sal
es:fname,Sales:lname,Sales:address,Sales:city,Sales:state,Sales:ip,Sal
es:p_id,Sales:dop');
SELECT * FROM Sales_ Accumulo;
```

How it works...

The first statement creates a Hive table that is tied to the Accumulo table. While creating the Hive table, the `STORED BY` clause must be provided. While creating the Hive table, if the `EXTERNAL` keyword is not provided, then on the deletion of Hive table, the Accumulo table is automatically deleted, which is the default behavior as well. If the `EXTERNAL` keyword is provided, the Accumulo table remains intact even if the Hive table is deleted.

In the first statement, apart from the normal column names, the `AccumuloStorageHandler` class name is provided to inform that this Hive table is coupled with the Accumulo table. There is also one more property named `accumulo.columns.mapping`; it is provided to map Accumulo columns with Hive columns.

Once the table is created, the table is accessed as shown in the second statement.

Working with HBase

In this recipe, you will learn how to integrate HBase with Google Drill.

HBase is a distributed database used to store large volume of data. It is written in Java and runs on top of HDFS. Therefore, it is a fast way of reading and writing large volumes of data with high throughput.

Getting ready

For integrating Hive with HBase, there are a few prerequisites that must be met. In this topic, we will cover the use of Hive and HBase. You must have HBase installed on your system before going further in the topic.

Once HBase is installed, configure the HBase as shown in the following steps:

Add the following properties to the `hbase-site.xml` file:

```
<property>
  <name>hbase.cluster.distributed</name>
  <value>true</value>
</property>
<property>
  <name>hbase.rootdir</name>
  <value>hdfs://localhost:8020/hbase</value>
</property>
```

 Change the value of the property `hbase.rootdir` if Hadoop namenode is running on different node and port.

Set or change `JAVA_HOME` in the `hbase-env.sh` file:

```
export JAVA_HOME=<java_home_path>
```

Configure an external Zookeeper: By default, HBase starts its own Zookeeper instance. If you are using an external Zookeeper, then you can configure using the following options:

HBase whether it should manage its own instance of Zookeeper or not. For doing this, configure the following property in the `$HBASE_HOME/conf/hbase-env.sh` file.

```
export HBASE_MANAGES_ZK=false
```

Add the following properties in the `hbase-site.xml` file:

```
<property>
  <name>hbase.zookeeper.property.clientPort</name>
  <value>2181</value>
  <description>Property from ZooKeeper's config zoo.cfg.The port at
which the clients will connect. </description>
</property>
<property>
```

```
<name>hbase.zookeeper.quorum</name>
<value>localhost</value>
<description>It takes comma separated list of all zookeeper
    servers. For example, "host1,host2,host3". By default value
    of his property is set to localhost for local and pseudo-
    distributed modes of operation. For a fully-distributed
    setup, this should be set to a full list of ZooKeeper quorum
    servers.
</description>
</property>
```

Run the following command in the hbase home directory to start HBase:

bin/start-hbase.sh

If your system is configured correctly, the jps command should show the HMaster and HRegionServer processes running, as shown in the following screenshot:

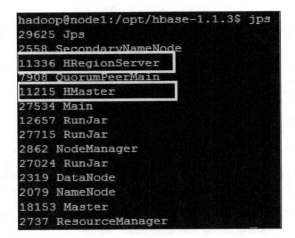

Open `HMaster` UI: By default, HBase Master runs its web interface on the `16010` port. You can open the HBase Master web interface using `http://HOST_NAME/16010`. For example:

`http://192.168.56.101:16010`

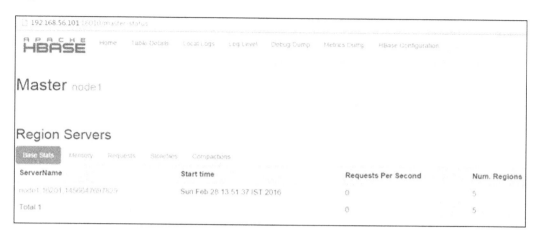

Connect to HBase: For connecting HBase using shell, run the following command in the `HBase` home directory:

`$ ./bin/hbase shell`

`hbase(main):001:0>`

How to do it...

Follow these steps to access the `HBase` table through Hive:

```
create 'users', 'cf'

put 'users', 'row1', 'cf:name', 'john'
put 'users', 'row2', 'cf:name', 'mike'
put 'users', 'row3', 'cf:name', 'honey'

scan "users"

CREATE EXTERNAL TABLE hbase_table_users(key string, name string)
STORED BY 'org.apache.hadoop.hive.hbase.HBaseStorageHandler'
WITH SERDEPROPERTIES ("hbase.columns.mapping" = "cf:name")
```

```
TBLPROPERTIES("hbase.table.name" = "users", "hbase.mapred.output.
outputtable" = "users");

SELECT * FROM hbase_table_users;
```

How it works...

The first statement in the previous section is used to create a table named users in HBase. The output of the first command is shown in the following screenshot:

```
hbase(main):031:0> create 'users', 'cf'
0 row(s) in 1.2910 seconds
```

The second statement is used to insert data in the HBase table. Here, users is the table name, and row1 row2, and row3 are the number of rows that are going to get inserted, cf specifies the column family name also called as **column name**. Here, the column name is users. The fourth string specifies the value of the column. The output of the second command is shown in the following figure:

```
=> Hbase::Table - users
hbase(main):032:0> put 'users', 'row1', 'cf:name', 'john'

0 row(s) in 0.0520 seconds

hbase(main):034:0* put 'users', 'row2', 'cf:name', 'mike'
0 row(s) in 0.0260 seconds

hbase(main):035:0> put 'users', 'row3', 'cf:name', 'honey'
0 row(s) in 0.0090 seconds
```

The third statement acts like the normal SELECT clause in Hive. In HBase, the list keyword is used for the same purpose. The output of the third command is shown in the following screenshot:

```
hbase(main):002:0> scan "users"
ROW                              COLUMN+CELL
 row1                             column=cf:name, timestamp=1456665804693, value=john
 row2                             column=cf:name, timestamp=1456665816303, value=mike
 row3                             column=cf:name, timestamp=1456665830231, value=honey
3 row(s) in 0.4830 seconds
```

- The fourth statement in the previous section is used to create a Hive table named hbase_table_users. The External keyword indicates that the reference table is already created in HBase and is going to be used in Hive.

- In this example, there are two columns key and name. These two columns nothing but correspond to the row and name column of the HBase table.

- While creating the Hive table, the STORED BY clause must be provided on the CREATE table clause. The STORED BY clause contains one class HBaseStorageHandler, which is one of the main components in integration of HBase with Hive. The main job of this class is to map the Hive table to the HBase table. Also, it configures Hive queries.

- The second important clause is the SERDEPROPERTIES clause in the Hive table creation. In this clause, the hbase.columns.mapping property maps the Hive column to that of the HBase column. The number of column mapped must be equal to the number of columns in the Hive table. There should not be any whitespaces while mapping these column names as it is taken as a string in the column name.

- TBLPROPERTIES is the clause that indicates which HBase table is going to be referenced in the Hive table. This tells that the data of the named HBase table is going to be fetched in Hive.

- The output of the fourth command in the previous section is shown in the following screenshot:

```
hive> CREATE EXTERNAL TABLE hbase_table_users(key string, name string)
    > STORED BY 'org.apache.hadoop.hive.hbase.HBaseStorageHandler'
    > WITH SERDEPROPERTIES ("hbase.columns.mapping" = "cf:name")
    > TBLPROPERTIES ("hbase.table.name" = "users", "hbase.mapred.output.outputtable" = "users");
OK
Time taken: 0.247 seconds
```

- The fifth statement shows how to access the data from Hive, as shown in the following screenshot:

```
hive> select * from hbase_table_users;
OK
hbase_table_users.key    hbase_table_users.name
row1    john
row2    mike
row3    honey
Time taken: 0.237 seconds, Fetched: 3 row(s)
```

Working with Google Drill

In this recipe, you will learn how to integrate Hive with Google Drill.

Getting ready

Google Drill is an open source SQL query engine by Apache. Google Drill is designed in such a manner that it works on semi-structured data giving quality performance on rapidly immerging data using almost same syntax used in ANSI SQL. For integrating Hive with Google Drill, there are few prerequisites that must be met. In this topic, we will cover the use of Hive and Drill. You must have Google Drill installed on your system before going further in the topic.

How to do it...

Follow these steps to access the Hive table from Google Drill:

1. Create the table `Sales_Drill` through the Hive shell:

   ```
   CREATE TABLE 'Sales_drill'(
       'id' int,
       'fname' string,
       'lname' string,
       'address' string,
       'city' string,
       'state' string,
       'ip' string,
       'p_id' string,
       'dop' string)
   row format delimited fields terminated by '\t' stored as textfile;
   ```

2. Once the table is created, load the data into the `Sales_Drill` table using the following command:

   ```
   LOAD DATA LOCAL INPATH '/opt/data/sales_drill.txt' INTO TABLE
   Sales_drill;
   ```

3. After loading the data, exit the Hive shell and start the Drill shell. For starting the Drill shell, navigate to the Drill installation directory and issue the following command:

   ```
   bin/drill-embedded
   ```

4. Once the Drill shell is started, issue the following command to query the Hive table from the Drill shell:

   ```
   SELECT id, fname, lname FROM Sales_drill WHERE id <= 10;
   ```

How it works...

The first statement mentioned previously creates a table named `Sales_drill`. This table is created on the Hive shell. The output of the first command in the previous section is shown in the following figure:

```
hive> CREATE TABLE `Sales_drill`(
    >     `id` int,
    >     `fname` string,
    >     `lname` string,
    >     `address` string,
    >     `city` string,
    >     `state` string,
    >     `ip` string,
    >     `p_id` string,
    >     `dop` string)
    > row format delimited fields terminated by '\t' stored as textfile;
OK
Time taken: 0.835 seconds
```

The second statement in the previous section loads the data from the local directory into the Hive tables `Sales_drill`. The data is loaded from a sample file, `Sales_drill.txt`, into the tables. The output of the second command in previous section is shown in the following screenshot:

```
hive> LOAD DATA LOCAL INPATH '/opt/data/sales_drill.txt' INTO TABLE Sales_drill;
Loading data to table default.sales_drill
Table default.sales_drill stats: [numFiles=4, numRows=0, totalSize=3044163, rawDataSize=0]
OK
Time taken: 0.522 seconds
```

The third statement in the previous section opens the Drill shell. The output of the third command in the previous section is underlined in red in the following screenshot:

```
hadoop@node1:/opt/Drill/apache-drill-1.4.0$ cd /opt/Drill/apache-drill-1.4.0
hadoop@node1:/opt/Drill/apache-drill-1.4.0$ bin/drill-embedded
drill-override.conf: 30: unbalanced close brace '}' with no open brace (if you ir
e quotes)
apache drill 1.4.0
"a drill is a terrible thing to waste"
0: jdbc:drill:zk=local> select id, fname, lname from sales_drill where id <= 10;
```

The fourth statement in the previous section queries the Hive table `Sales_Drill` from the Drill shell. The output of the fourth command in the previous section is shown in the following figure:

```
0: jdbc:drill:zk=local> select id, fname, lname from sales_drill where id <= 10;
OK
0       Zena    Ross
1       Elaine  Bishop
2       Sage    Carroll
3       Cade    Singleton
4       Abra    Wright
5       Stone   Palmer
6       Regina  Bryant
7       Donovan Aguirre
8       Aileen  Mendoza
9       Mariam  Henson
10      Silas   Hughes
0       Zena    Ross
1       Elaine  Bishop
2       Sage    Carroll
3       Cade    Singleton
4       Abra    Wright
5       Stone   Palmer
6       Regina  Bryant
7       Donovan Aguirre
8       Aileen  Mendoza
9       Mariam  Henson
10      Silas   Hughes
Time taken: 1.264 seconds, Fetched: 22 row(s)
```

Index

D

data
  deleting 105, 106
  inserting, into dynamic partitions 96, 97
  updating 104
  writing, into files from queries 98, 99
database schema
  altering 73
  creating 70, 71
  defining 75
  displaying 74, 75
  dropping 72, 73
  using 74
Data Definition Language (DDL) 70, 89
Data Manipulation Language (DML) 89
data sampling
  block sampling 201
  defining 200
  length literal 202
  row count 202-206
  sampling bucketed table 201
data types
  about 108
  complex data types 44
  defining 44
  primitive data types 44
date formats, Hive
  URL 184
date functions
  defining 171-173, 180, 181
Date/Time data type
  using 47
Distinguished Name (DN) 225
dynamic partitioning
  about 63, 118
  properties 64
dynamic partitions
  data, inserting into 96, 97

E

external table
  partitioning 65

F

file formats
  defining 132-135
  types 132
files
  loading, into tables 90-92
Finer Access Control Lists (FACL) 209

G

Google Drill
  working with 240-242

H

Hadoop
  read and write access, giving 211
  securing 207-210
  URL 212
  user access, revoking 211, 212
Hadoop cluster
  Hive, deploying on 2-4
Hadoop Distributed File
      System (HDFS) 1, 91, 207
HBase
  working with 234-239
HCatalog
  command-line options 11
  configuring 10
  defining 87
  HCatalog DMLs 87
high availability
  configuring, of metastore service 36
Hive
  accessing 224
  accessing, with Hue 40-42
  analytics functions 121-125
  anonymous, without SASL 223
  anonymous, with SASL 223
  authenticating 222
  authorizing 212
  buckets, creating 119-121
  compiling, from source 13, 14

V

values
  inserting into tables, from SQL 101-103
view
  altering, as select 83
  creating 81
  defining 112, 113
  dropping 82
view properties
  altering 83

W

WebHCat
  defining 88
  URL 88

windowing
  about 1
  in Hive 125-130
  in Hive, specifications 126
windowing functions
  implementing 126

Y

Yet Another Resource Negotiator (YARN) 3